Digital Mantras

Digital Mantras

The Languages of Abstract and Virtual Worlds

Steven R. Holtzman

The MIT Press
Cambridge, Massachusetts
London, England

This book was set in Stone Serif and Stone Sans by Asco Trade Typesetting Ltd., Hong Kong, and was printed and bound in the United States of America.

Library of Congress Cataloging-in-Publication Data

Holtzman, Steven R.
  Digital mantras: the languages of abstract and virtual worlds /
Steven R. Holtzman.
     p. cm.
  Includes bibliographical references and index.
  ISBN 0-262-08228-4
  1. Computers. 2. Virtual reality. I. Title.
QA76.H2786   1994
001.3′0285—dc20   94-9631
                                                                        CIP

Contents

Preface

There has been a growing interest in computers and the arts and, more recently, virtual reality. There is a growing subculture of artists, computer hackers, virtual reality enthusiasts, science fiction followers, and others ready to explore the new worlds that computer technology is making possible.

We are on the verge of a new age in creative expression: the digital age. With the development of the computer, fundamental changes are occurring in the ways we communicate, create, and express ourselves. As a result, we need to think very differently about the processes by which we communicate, create, and express ourselves.

This book aims to establish an aesthetic foundation for the use of computers for creative expression in language, music, art, and virtual reality. The use of computers in the creative process mandates that we think of communicative and creative processes in terms of abstract structures and the manipulation of such structures. A central theme of the book is that computers are the ultimate manipulators of abstract structures. Another is that computers are, ultimately, manipulators of abstract structures.

Part I, "Structures," lays a foundation for such an approach. It looks at established traditions in which language, music, and art are thought of in terms of abstract structure. The objective is to demonstrate that emerging new techniques of creativity with computers represent a continuity with traditional forms of expression; in fact, with traditions that date to the very distant past. That's why the book begins, and ends, in ancient India.

The view of language as a formal system is traced from the first concepts of a grammar in the Aryan culture of ancient India to the work of Ferdinand de Saussure and finally the generative grammars of Noam Chomsky. Certain formal aspects of traditional music theory and twentieth-century serial music are explained in terms of simple numerical relationships. Serial music theory is illustrated with examples from the works of Arnold Schoenberg, Alban Berg, and Anton Webern, and from Pierre Boulez and other postwar composers. Wassily Kandinsky, considered the first abstract artist, developed a formal and explicit language of visual harmonies and dissonances; his influential ideas regarding abstract art are also presented. All of these formal approaches to language, music, and art form a foundation for developing expressive systems with computers.

Part II, "Structure Manipulators," explores how, with the development of the computer, a formal view of expressive languages supports the application of computers for building abstract and virtual worlds in language, music, art, and new media such as virtual reality. The development of the computer is followed from Leibniz to the twentieth century. The work of a number of people in different disciplines is discussed, including artificial intelligence pioneer Terry Winograd, composers Gottfried Michael Koenig and Iannis Xenakis, and artist Harold Cohen.

In part III, "Vibration," I discuss some of the creative, aesthetic, and mystical implications of these new means of expression and new worlds. I outline an aesthetic view that proposes exploring the *idiomatic* potential of computers—that is, what can be done and conceived of only in light of the computer. I go on to discuss an unusual view of the relationship between structure and meaning. I conclude the book by placing the exploration of structure with computers in the context of mystical tradition.

A synthesis of ideas is built from a broad set of disciplines: linguistics, music, art, virtual reality, computers, and mystical and religious philosophies. Several different threads develop, weaving an intricate web from apparently unrelated themes. As the book progresses, the different disciplines and themes become more and more tightly linked to provide a perspective from which to view computers in creative processes.

In the end, the book documents a personal journey and represents a personal aesthetic. That is why it is accented with excerpts from my diary. *Digital Mantras* is meant as a stake in the ground—a reference point to initiate discussion. The journey is brief. I invite you to join me.

Acknowledgments

While the ideas presented in this book date back to the 1970s, many people have helped to develop and shape them since then. The accuracy of the material from the breadth of disciplines represented is due to the patience of a number of diligent reviewers, particularly Michael James, Oliver Muirhead, Larry Briskman, Paul Williams, Gottfried Michael Koenig, Clive Bennett, Harold Cohen, Trudy Edelson, Stephen Travis Pope, and Robert Jacobson.

Other reviewers also helped with the book, including Terry Winograd, Harriet Parcells, Rob Gemmell, Michael Richman, Lisa Cort, Stacy Styles, Ken Krich, Jeff Hudson, Marina Bosi, Harry Boadwee, Maria Gagliardi, Ray Lauzzana, Wayne Oler, Michael Siebrass, Linda Jacobson, and Robert Delaney. Every reviewer made a contribution to the final shape of this book. Bob Angus's printers (and enthusiasm) let me see it develop.

The graphic illustrations of key concepts (such as the music-clocks and the cubes) are the work of Ilene Sandler and Brad Eigen.

Randy Stickrod was instrumental. In addition to his encouragement and feedback, his help led directly to Kathleen Tibbetts, whose enthusiasm and support played a critical role, and ultimately to Bob Prior, my editor at the MIT Press.

I want to thank everyone at the MIT Press for their help. Special thanks, however, are due to Bob. He stimulated many ideas that helped refine this book to its final form. And if readers have a clearer understanding of what I have written, it is due to Matthew Abbate, who edited the book, and to his passionate attention to detail.

I want to gratefully acknowledge the support and confidence of Professor Bernard Meltzer, who provided me the opportunity to do my doctoral research—which forms the foundation for this book—at the University of Edinburgh. Jean Pollock, Jeff Tansley, and Professor Sidney Michaelson also provided essential support while I was there.

Finally, Jay Weil, my mother, and my sisters provided the encouragement that helped me see the book through to completion.

Thank you.

Steve Holtzman
November 1993

Digital Mantras

Prelude

Jispa, Northern India, 1977

It is night. The valley is surrounded by towering peaks, snow-capped silver reflections silhouetted against crisp star-studded deep deep blue sky. Every nook and cranny casts a distinct shadow and profile in this moonlit rock desert. Above, the cliff-hanging gompas (temples) are barely discernible.

This mountain desert is a terrain so tough that its 14,000-foot valleys are abandoned to those Tibetans that can find no other refuge but nonetheless would make no other landscape home. These valleys are isolated nine months of the year, cut off by snow, and are reachable only by passes that are challenging to mechanized vehicles even in the so-called months of summer.

The dirt pot-holed road ends here. Close to the Chinese border, these are the last outposts of the Indian military, an area open to visitors for the first time only the previous summer.

My chokidar, attendant to the hut that I stay in, is about to prepare tea after a dinner of rice and some greens. He squats before the fire in the familiar Asian style: feet flat on the ground, calves straight up, knee-to-butt at a sharp angle, back straight. A pot of water sits on the fire. At this altitude it will take some time to boil.

The radio is on. There is static. It hisses and sputters like only a drifting radio can. It's unclear if the radio is drifting or the signal is drifting. Out of the static and hiss some Russian is heard. The Russian speaker addresses some unknown subject briefly before returning to static and hiss. After some minutes, a Chinese speaker emerges from the noise, again unintelligible to its mountain desert audience. The signal fades and again there is hiss and static, static and hiss. The Chinese voice reemerges from the noise. And then again becomes indistinct, overcome by the static and hiss. This time the Russian speaker emerges from the rich noise. But only to eventually fade back to the noise again. Now there is an Indian voice, again, at least to me and my Tibetan companion, not understood. There is hiss and static again. The Chinese speaker. Noise. The Chinese speaker again.

Tonight's concert continues for hours, drifting from Chinese to static and hiss, Russian, Indian and noise and noise again. The performance is excellent, not unlike a rendition of John Cage's aleatoric works for radios. The sounds drift from one context to another based on some underlying aleatoric force. The direction of the wind. The heating of the radio's analog components, weary and drifting.

The chokidar squats and listens in silence. The water boils. He prepares and serves the tea. He smiles. We nod at one another, pointing to the radio, confirming our enjoyment of the rich spectrum of sounds. We pass the hours.

Noise to most ears. This chokidar, ears tuned to temple bells, gongs, chant and the mountains, listens to the richness of the textures with an openness that most ears will never share.

I   *Structures*

1   *Pāṇini*

A fertile river valley was home to an ancient civilization. The world's largest mountain range borders to the north. In the rainy season clouds drift northward burying the high peaks in snow, feeding innumerable streams flowing southward from the ever-melting snow-caps of the mountains. Not just an impenetrable frontier, these mountains are the source of two great river systems. Of the two, it is the Indus that gave its name to India.

In the early part of the third millennium B.C., civilization developed nearly simultaneously in the river valleys of the Nile, Euphrates, and Indus. Joseph Campbell said of the Indus civilization that "the cities and their civilization break into view, remain without change for a millennium, fade, and disappear like illusions in the night."[1]

The Indus civilization extended over an area some 950 miles across, from the Himalayan mountains to present-day Bombay. It was characterized by the uniformity and monotony of its culture. The artifacts of this civilization show no development or variation over a period of hundreds of years and over the entire area of its influence. For example, burnt bricks, the standard building material, were the same size and shape throughout the civilization, generation after generation.

There were two large cities 400 miles apart at opposite ends of the fertile river valley, but built to almost identical plans: Mohenjo-Daro in the south on the Indus and Harappā on the Rāvī, a tributary to the Indus. In each city there was a large citadel. Its turreted western wall, a quarter of a mile long and 50 feet high, was shielded with the burnt bricks. On top of the 200-yard-wide citadel were watchtowers, gates, and various fortifications.

Below each of these great citadels was a town a square mile in area. Wide straight streets divided the city into a grid of twelve large blocks. Only windowless brick walls faced the streets. Two major avenues 30 feet wide extended eastward from the citadel. Three broad streets 250 yards apart cut from north to south.

Within the walls, houses of the same designs were built along a maze of narrow alleys. The houses, often of two or more stories, were built, of course, from burnt bricks. Some were apparently luxurious, as indicated by the floored bathrooms, covered wells, and sophisticated sanitation systems. The houses were connected to an efficient underground plumbing system to which nothing comparable can be found until Roman cities three thousand years later. Workers' quarters were built in repetitive structures, each 20 feet by 12 feet, divided into two rooms, one twice the size of the other.

Nine strata of buildings have been found at Mohenjo-Daro. Periodic flooding of the Indus left the city covered by earth. After each flood, new houses were built almost exactly on the sites of the old. Only minor variations were made in the ground plans. For one thousand years, the street plan of the cities remained the same. All of this archaeological evidence suggests that the Indus civilization was a very sophisticated culture.

Over the centuries, the citadel's turreted wall was strengthened. Its watchtowers kept a westward guard. No defense was needed against the primitive native cultures found eastward. The mountains and sea acted as barriers to the north and south. But, approximately 2000 B.C., one gateway was entirely blocked. Danger threatened from the west.

The Indus civilization came to a very sudden demise. Toward the end, the rigid organization and laws collapsed. There was frequent flooding. The street plan was no longer maintained, and mansions became tenements as the city was inundated with refugees fleeing bands of horse-riding barbarians.

Tribes of nomadic people invaded the Indus cities. They left the cities deserted and in ruins. Groups of skeletons of men, women, and children were found on the upper level of Mohenjo-Daro. They exhibit sword and ax cuts. Cities were of no interest to these mobile invaders, and it would be a thousand years before any cities returned to the river valley. These invading tribes were the Aryans.[2]

The Aryan Migration

The Aryans are believed to have originated somewhere in the great steppeland that stretches from Poland to Central Asia. From there, sometime around the second millennium B.C., they went on the move, probably due to desiccation of their pasture lands or over-population or both. Their power as invaders came from having tamed the horse. Light chariots with two spoked wheels revolving freely on their axles were easily turned and highly maneuverable. Harnessing these chariots with two powerful horses, the Aryans had the fastest and most powerful transportation of the time. This mobility was complemented with superior weaponry developed by highly skilled bronze smiths. The result: these marauding tribesmen developed an advanced military technique and spread in bands throughout the lands of the Indus civilization.

The terrifying approach of the attacking Aryans is described in the *Ṛg Veda*:

At his deep neigh, like the thunder of heaven,
the foemen tremble in fear,
for he fights against thousands, and none can resist him,
so terrible is his charge.[3]

The Aryan Priests

The priests of these Aryan tribes possessed tremendous power. They "chanted magically potent verses to a pantheon of chariot-driving gods."[4] They perfected a very advanced poetic technique for the composition of their hymns in praise of their gods—Indra, king of the gods and wielder of the lightning bolt; Agni, the deity of fire; Soma, the liquor of the sacrifice; and Varuṇa, whose rhythm is the order of the world.

Carefully handed down by word of mouth, the hymns were collected and arranged early in the first millennium B.C. They were so sacred that even minor alterations in their text were not permitted. Though not written down for centuries, these hymns have survived to the present in a form that has not changed for three thousand years.

This great collection of hymns is the *Ṛg Veda*, still the most sacred text of the Hindus and part of living Hindu tradition. The Vedic hymns are still recited at weddings and funerals, and in the daily devotions of the modern brahman priests. In addition to its great religious significance, the *Ṛg Veda* is the earliest surviving form of the ancient Sanskrit language.

The importance of the Aryan priests rested on their understanding and control of the Vedic hymns. These hymns were part of the magical ceremonies the priests performed before and during battle to ensure the tribe's victory in war and its prosperity in peace. The priests made sacrifices to the gods and chanted spells.

The sacrifice was at the center of the Aryan cult. It was rooted in the belief that the universe itself was created from the sacrifice of a primeval man. In the Aryan sacrifice, the priests recreated this primeval sacrifice and created the world anew. Without regular sacrifices and the resulting continual renewal, all cosmic processes would cease and there would be chaos. Maintaining the order of nature, the priests were the supreme social servants.

The relationship between the world and the sacrificial horse is described by the following passage from the *Bṛhadāraṇyaka Upaniṣad*.

Dawn is the head of the sacrificial horse, the sun its eye, the wind its breath, fire its mouth; the year is the body of the sacrificial horse, heaven its back, the sky its belly, earth its chest, the four quarters its side ... the seasons its limbs, the months and fortnights its joints; days and nights are its feet, the stars its bones, the heavens its flesh ... its bowels the rivers, its liver and lungs the mountains, its hair plants and trees.[5]

Thus, it was by the accurate performance of the sacrifice that the priests maintained all things. The slightest variation of the ritual could result in serious destruction. The priests alone knew the rituals and formulas that could bring the gods to the sacrifice. In the earliest periods, they would implore the gods to come. However, later it was perceived that the gods were compelled to come by the power of the priests' magic. The priests became recognized as masters of great mystery, not only more powerful than the nobles and warriors of the Aryan tribes but more powerful than the gods themselves, able to command the gods through the potency of their spells.

At the core of the rituals was the magical power, called *brahman*, of the sacred utterances, called *mantras*. The priests, possessors of *brah-*

man, became known as *brāhmaṇa*, or in English, brahmans. The connection of the brahmans with speech became greater and greater and, ultimately, "the brahman's magic was thought to lie in the words he uttered."[6]

The Aryan Migration Traced by the Development of Their Languages

Languages tend to evolve over time. Within a linguistic community whose speakers remain in constant contact, the language will remain uniform across the population even as it slowly evolves. However, if a language is spoken by two populations that share little contact or become separated, the form and vocabulary of their language will begin to diverge. If the divergence continues, their speech will develop into separate dialects and eventually into different languages. But languages that have diverged from one another still carry traces of their common origins, from which linguistic genealogies can be constructed.

The rate at which languages diverge will depend on the circumstances of their speakers; when a population migrates *en masse*, the change will be particularly rapid. The dispersion of the tribes of the Eurasian steppelands, including the Aryans, represents exactly such a mass migration. Some invaded Europe to become the ancestors of the Greeks, Latins, Celts, and Teutons. Others appeared in Anatolia and formed the great empire of the Hittites. Others attacked the Middle Eastern civilizations and conquered Babylon. (The name of the Aryans survives today in the name Iran and in the most westerly land that these tribes reached, Eire.) The most widespread of all known language groups, called the Indo-European languages, is defined by the common origin of all of its languages: the tribes living in the Eurasian steppelands about 3000 B.C.

The migration of the Indo-European-speaking tribes can be traced through their languages. Their common origin is reflected in the similarities still found in languages spoken from Europe to India. Tables 1.1 and 1.2 illustrate such similarities between six languages with the words for the numbers one through ten and the words for *father, full,* and *skin.*

Table 1.1
The Numbers One through Ten in Six Languages[7]

Sanskrit	Greek	Latin	Gothic	Old English	English
ēka	heis	unus	ains	an	one
dvā	duo	duo	twai	twa	two
trayas	treis	tres	–	thri	three
catvāras	tettares	quattuor	fidwo	feower	four
panca	pente	quinque	fimf	fif	five
ṣaṣ	hex	sex	saihs	siex	six
sapta	hepta	septem	sibun	seofon	seven
aṣṭā	okto	octo	ahtau	eahta	eight
nava	ennea	novem	niun	nigon	nine
daśa	deka	decem	taihun	tien	ten

Table 1.2
The Words *Father, Full,* and *Skin* in Six Languages

Sanskrit	Greek	Latin	Gothic	Old English	English
pitar	pater	pater	fadar	faeder	father
purnas	pleres	plenus	fulls	full	full
–	pella	pellis	fill	fell	skin

Even after centuries of evolution, these words often sound similar. Where they sound different, there is a consistent replacement of one sound for another. Where Latin and Sanskrit begin a word with *s*, Greek begins it with *h*. Where Latin and Greek have *o*, Sanskrit has *a*. Where Gothic and Old English have *t* and *f*, Latin, Greek, and Sanskrit have *d* and *p*. This reflects their common origin in a single language.

The Grammars of the Vedic Hymns

Over time, the cultures of the invading Aryan tribesmen merged with the cultures of the indigenous inhabitants of northern India. In most of the lands in which the Aryans settled, their language gradually adapted itself to the tongues of the conquered people. Words changed and were forgotten, new words from non-Aryan sources were borrowed, grammar was simplified.

However, the Vedic hymns could not be permitted to change. It was believed that the very pronunciation of the hymns was essential to their efficacy. Unless they were recited with complete accuracy they would have no magical effectiveness. The secular language could evolve with the integration of the Aryan and indigenous cultures. But doubt could not arise as to the true pronunciation and meaning of the *Ṛg Veda.*

The priests were responsible for guarding and protecting the Vedas. And it was the belief in the potency and efficacy of the Vedas that was at the core of their power. The Aryan priests needed to counter the natural processes of linguistic evolution. Key to maintaining their power was not only the belief in the importance of the Vedas, but also the well-guarded secret systems that were devised by the priests to ensure their purity.

Out of this need to preserve the purity of the Vedas and to protect the divine truths and mystic powers that they embodied, the Aryan priests of India developed the sciences of phonetics and grammar. The oldest Indian linguistic text dates to the 5th century B.C. and followed much earlier work in the field of linguistics. By the fourth century B.C., the language of the brahman priests, which was now a very distinct language from the secular dialects, reached its classical form.

It is in this form that it was documented in the fourth century B.C. by a grammarian named Pāṇini. Pāṇini created a grammar that effectively stabilized the Sanskrit language. His grammar, the *Aṣṭādhyāyī,* is the culmination of centuries of study of the language and is one of the greatest intellectual achievements of any ancient civilization. The *Aṣṭādhyāyī* is the most detailed and scientific grammar composed before the nineteenth century in any part of the world.

By the time of Pāṇini, the sounds of Sanskrit and the words and syllables of the Vedas had been analyzed with accuracy and thoroughness. Though the Vedic texts were not written, the letters of the alphabet were recognized. India had developed a sophisticated alphabet of vowels followed by consonants, all classified very scientifically according to their mode of production.

Indian phonetics described the processes of articulation, the component sounds of Sanskrit, and the rules for combining sounds to form phonological structures. The Indians described the processes and articulatory positions by which the lips, tongue, glottis, lungs, and nasal cavity created voice and voicelessness, aspiration and non-aspiration, nasality and nonnasality. The Indians described in precise detail how phonemes interacted in words, how they changed depending on where they were articulated during a breath, and how they were affected by the tempo, tone, or number of syllables in a word. As a result, more is known about the pronunciation of Sanskrit than of any other ancient language.

Indian grammarians recognized the root as the basic element of a word. Some 2,000 monosyllabic roots were identified and classified, along with the prefixes, suffixes, and inflections that were thought to provide all the words of the language. Indian grammarians defined four classes of words: nouns, verbs, prepositions, and particles. The verb was considered the most important, the core of the sentence. In Sanskrit, only verbs can stand on their own to form complete sentences. The Sanskrit verb is of a complexity similar to the Greek, with numerous voices and moods, and is inflected for person, number, and tense. All other words were seen in relation to the verb, with nouns seen as the next most important element. The Sanskrit noun has eight cases, and both verbs and nouns have dual numbers in addition to singular and plural.

Pāṇini's grammar consists of over 4,000 grammatical rules and a manner to name the cases, moods, persons, and tenses by which linguistic phenomena are classified. The appendixes of the *Aṣṭādhyāyī* include comprehensive lists of verb and noun roots and a list of all of the sounds of Sanskrit. Pāṇini defined complex rules of euphonic combination—rules that defined how the sound of every word of a sentence was affected by its neighbors. The rules of Pāṇini's grammar could be applied to the *Ṛg Veda* to ensure its correct pronunciation, correct meter, and so on.

The core of Pāṇini's grammar is an exhaustive statement of the rules of word formation of Sanskrit. The rules are impressive in their completeness as well as their economy. Because of the oral traditions of ancient India—texts were not written but memorized—economy was a canon of scholarship. Pāṇini's rules are remarkable for the ingenuity by which he achieved his concision.

Pāṇini's grammar is not simply a descriptive grammar but a *generative grammar*. That is, it is a set of rules that can be used to generate Sanskrit words. The rules are of a general nature and, given the set of word roots, can be applied to generate large numbers of words—all the words of Sanskrit.

The rules are applied in a set order to generate proper Sanskrit words. Starting with a word root, a word is generated in stages by the application of a rule modifying the result of the previous stage. Successively applying Pāṇini's rules, a word is modified for tense, person, number, and so on.

For example, the word *ábhavat*, meaning "he was," is generated from the root *bhū*, "to be." Below is the sequence that is followed to generate *ábhavat*, the only real word in Sanskrit in the sequence.[8]

bhū	The verb root
bho	The verb root modified for past tense
bhava	Modified for masculine form
bhavat	Modified for the third person singular secondary ending
ábhavat	Modified for final form

Conclusion

A formal view of language dates back to the ancient Aryans. It was from the time of Pāṇini onward that the language of India was called *Saṃskṛta*, "perfected" or "refined." Pāṇini's comprehensive grammar was remarkable not only for its descriptive capability but also because it was a *generative* grammar. It became the definitive grammar of Sanskrit. Though some later grammarians may have had views that differed with Pāṇini, his grammar was so widely accepted that no writer or speaker of Sanskrit in the circles of the priests or of the courts dared question it. In the centuries that followed, all significant grammatical work in India centered on Pāṇini's *Aṣṭādhyāyī*, in the form of numerous commentaries on Pāṇini's grammar or in the Indian tradition of commentaries on commentaries. Sanksrit was fixed and could only develop within the framework of his rules.

Sanskrit has the most complicated and refined structure of any of the Indo-European languages. Its system of declensions is more consistent and more complex than that of classical Latin or Greek (or today's German). And it is the most *consciously* formalized of the Indo-European languages. The understanding the brahmans had of their language reflected a conscious knowledge of its workings.

Western grammarians have applied grammatical and linguistic analysis to better understand and document the workings of language. However, the brahman priests not only understood the mechanics of language, they used this understanding to modify it to accord better with their notion of perfection. Deeply rooted in the Vedic belief in the power of the spoken word when spoken properly, the brahmans' objective in their study of language was to harness this mystical power.

Among all of the chants and hymns of the ancient priests, the syllable *OM* holds a special position. *OM* is said to contain the essence of the Vedas: the utmost power and mystery.

2   *The Circle of Fifths*

Today's musical nomenclature has developed since the time of the ancient Greeks. For example, the naming of musical notes by letters of the alphabet goes back as far as the Greeks. In fact, the word *music* itself is derived from an adjectival form of the Greek muse, one of the nine sister goddesses who presided over certain arts and sciences.

After centuries of evolution, there are many peculiarities in the nomenclature commonly used by musicians. For example, although there are twelve notes in Western music, Western musicians think of the first note of the twelve as C, and the tenth and twelfth as A and B (except in German, where the eleventh note is B and the twelfth is H). To further complicate matters, all the notes have at least two names, some as many as three. The ninth note, A♭, can also be called G♯. The second note, C♯, can also be called D♭ and B♯♯. The distance between two notes that are seven semitones apart is called a fifth and twelve semitones apart an octave.

An early system of musical notation used from the seventh to fourteenth centuries consisted of grave and acute accents, called *neumes*, above and below a horizontal line. The notation gives merely approximate indications of the shape of a melody. The neumes follow the pitch of a chant as it rises and falls. (See figure 2.1.)

Over the next several centuries, this method of notation evolved into an elaborate system using five horizontal lines to precisely indicate pitch, and vertical lines and a set of small filled and unfilled circles matched with various tails and dots to precisely indicate duration. (See figure 2.2.)

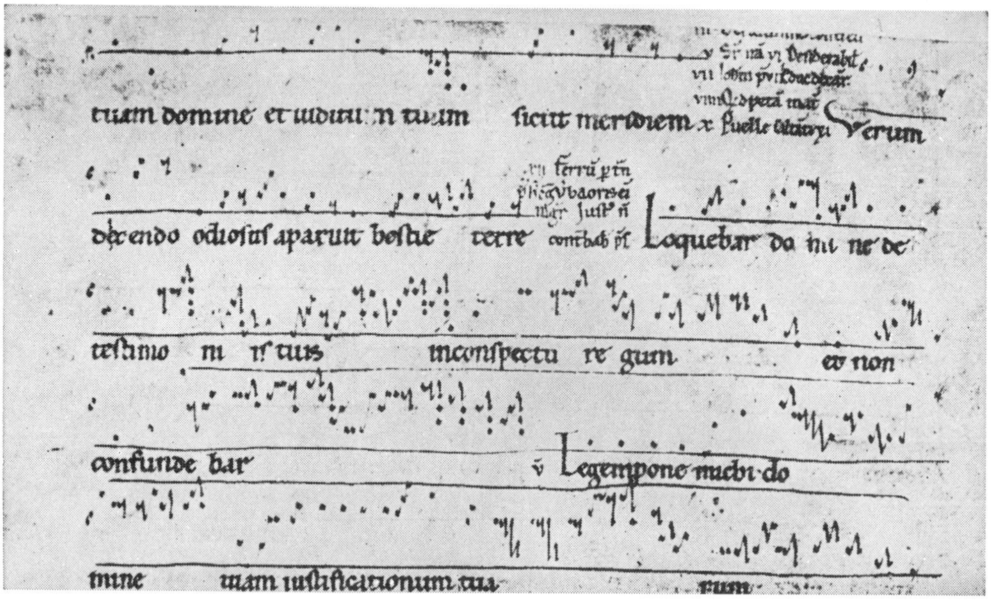

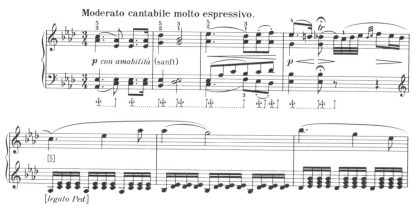

Figure 2.1
Example of notation with neumes, from a twelfth-century manuscript.

Figure 2.2
Example of nineteenth-century notation, from Beethoven's Piano Sonata in A flat, op. 110.

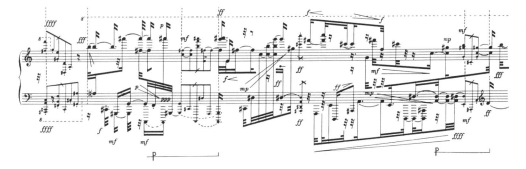

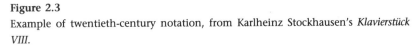

Figure 2.3
Example of twentieth-century notation, from Karlheinz Stockhausen's *Klavierstück VIII*.

The system of notation became increasingly complex as the amount of information, precision, and subtle indications composers wished to communicate grew. (See figure 2.3.)

However, when it comes to musical pitch, at least, it is possible to devise simpler notation systems. Most people don't instantly appreciate that there are seven semitones between C♯ and G♯, but everyone can immediately interpret "two" and "nine." Without a second-thought, everyone can automatically compute that the difference between two and nine is seven and that the sum of these two numbers is eleven.

Therefore, with the objective of making things a little easier to understand, we will put aside the notation of music by the traditional means of notes, bars, staves, and so on, and instead use a simpler and more easily understood representation with numbers. We will number and represent the twelve notes used in Western music as:

C, C♯, D, D♯, E, F, F♯, G, G♯, A,   A♯, and B
1, 2,   3, 4,   5, 6, 7,   8, 9,   10, 11, and 12.[1]

To look at music and musical relationships in terms of numbers and numerical relationships does not require one to conclude that there is no more to music than numbers and numerical relationships. It can be argued that the essence of music, if not the only *important* aspect of music, is what it sounds like and the effects those sounds have in evoking our emotions. For the moment, however, we will explore the formal relationships found in musical structure as they are reflected in numerical relationships.

The Pythagoreans

Approximately 500 B.C., music and arithmetic were not separate in the teachings of Pythagoras and his followers. For the Pythagoreans, the understanding of numbers was thought to be the key to understanding the physical and spiritual universe. They also believed that the harmony of music corresponded to the harmony of the cosmos. Consequently, they sought to better understand the numerical relationships that underlie music in order to better understand the harmony of the cosmos.

The Pythagoreans mathematically determined the intervals between notes through the measurement of vibrating strings. They found that different intervals could be expressed in terms of the proportions of the lengths of the strings needed to achieve a given pitch. So, for example, plucking a length of string half as long as another length produces a harmonious higher pitch; they associated the relation of these two pitches with the proportion of the string lengths, 2:1. (The pitch produced by the string half as long has a *frequency* twice as high, in modern scientific terms.)[2]

Notes and Intervals

In Western music of the last three centuries, there are twelve notes. There is no thirteenth. These twelve notes can be thought of as forming a closed loop in which the twelfth note is followed by the first note. Progressing forward from **12** we arrive at **1**, just as on a watch 12 o'clock is followed by 1 o'clock.

Imagine a clock without its minute hand and with an hour hand that takes only twelve discrete (and equal) steps to complete a circle. This hour hand measures time only in intervals of complete hours. With such a watch, the interval between any two times of the day is measured by the number of complete hours between them.

Rather than hours, in music the pitch interval between two notes is measured in *semitones*. The gap between 1 and 2, C and C♯, for instance, is one semitone, and the interval between any two notes of the twelve can be measured by the number of semitones between them.

Moving forward twelve semitones, one makes a complete circle around the clock, arriving at the same note from which one started. This interval, a complete loop, is called an octave.

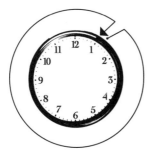

Given two notes an octave apart, the lower-pitch note vibrates at half the frequency—from a string twice the length—of the higher-pitch note, the ratio the Pythagoreans determined to be 2:1. So it isn't exactly the same note, just as one o'clock on Tuesday is not exactly the same time as one o'clock on Wednesday. However, when looking at musical relationships, it is possible to think of a complete loop around the clock, an octave, as returning you to the same note.

The Circle of Fifths

In studying the intervals between different notes, the Pythagoreans determined that some sounded harmonious while others were dissonant. They found a particular interval to be especially harmonious.

To them, it was the most beautiful. They determined that this interval was expressed as the ratio of 3:2.

This interval can also be expressed as the interval of *seven* semitones. This is a very special interval in music. It has a very fundamental role in music from the modes of Greece through Gregorian chant and the music of Palestrina, Bach, Beethoven, Wagner, Mahler, big bands, Frank Sinatra, Elvis Presley, the Beatles, and U2.

If we start with the note **1** and count seven semitones (or hours), we arrive at the note 8.

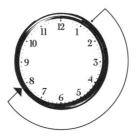

And if we count seven semitones from **8**, we arrive at 3.

Interestingly, if we continue to count forward by seven in this manner, each of the twelve notes will be arrived at once before any note is arrived at a second time: **1, 8, 3, 10, 5, 12, 7, 2, 9, 4, 11, 6.** Counting seven forward from **6**, we arrive back at **1.** This sequence of twelve notes, each seven from the previous, is called the *circle of fifths*. (Using **1** as the note C, this is equivalent to the sequence C, G, D, A, E, B, F♯, C♯, G♯, D♯, A♯, E♯.)

The History of Early Western Music

Most scholars say that Western music begins with the music of the Christian Church. The oldest surviving example of Christian church music was found in 1896 at the site of the ancient Egyptian town of Oxyrhynchos. It is a hymn of praise to the Trinity on a papyrus from the end of the third century. Only a few lines from the hymn can be reconstructed from the damaged papyrus. The hymn is represented in an ancient Greek notation that cannot be precisely interpreted. The exact pitches represented by the markings are not known.

Even so, we have an even more imprecise interpretation for any music that precedes the music of the Christian Church. Except for the writing of Greeks such as Aristoxenus, Plato, and Aristotle, this music is left almost entirely to the imagination. Unlike other arts that referred back to Greek art as a model, in music there was little to refer back to of a concrete nature. The musicologist Donald Grout explains:

All through the Middle Ages and even to the present time men have continually turned back to Greece and Rome for instruction, for correction and for inspiration in their several fields of work.... In literature as well as in some other fields (notably sculpture), medieval or Renaissance artists had the advantage of being able to study and imitate the models of antiquity. The actual poems or statues were before them. In music this was not so. The Middle Ages did not possess a single example of Greek or Roman music— nor are we today much better off. About a dozen examples—half of them mere fragments—of Greek music have been discovered, nearly all from comparatively late periods, but there is no general agreement as to just how they were meant to sound.[3]

It is difficult for us to imagine the music the Greeks wrote about, a music that was said to possess the power to influence thought and action. Likewise, we can only speculate about how and to what extent Greek, Jewish, and other Oriental music found in the eastern Mediterranean influenced the early music of the Christian Church. The only link to the music of ancient times is found between the modes of ancient Greece and the music of the Church.

The Pythagoreans, calculating various proportions and intervals, worked out several different harmonious sequences of intervals, referred to in Greek times as *modes*. A mode was defined by the order in which intervals—roughly equivalent to the number of semitones (or hours on the watch dial)—occurred between notes. A mode could start on any note so long as the intervals and their order remained the same.

During the 1,500 years that followed the Pythagoreans, modes dominated Western music, in particular the plainsong of the Church. By the fifth century there were four *authentic modes*. During the time of Pope Gregory I, 590–604, four more were added, called the *plagal modes*. Finally, nearly 1,000 years after Pope Gregory, a Swiss monk, Henry of Glarus, proposed in his book *Dodecachordon* (1547) that there should be twelve modes rather than eight.

It was also during the time of Pope Gregory that a large collection of chants was systematically compiled, revised, and assigned to various services throughout the year. This body of chants, preserved in hundreds of manuscripts dating from the ninth century and later, is commonly referred to as Gregorian chant. What changes took place in the chant between the time of Pope Gregory and the beginning of the ninth century—the earliest date to which the present form of the melodies can be traced with any certainty—again is not known.

Gregorian chant was written using only the seven notes of a given mode. Furthermore, the chant usually went from one note to the next, rarely skipping over a note. That is, the music consisted of a string of notes that were usually one or two semitones apart, depending on the appropriate next note when moving either forward or backward by one note in the mode.

The first few hundred years of Western music were mainly occupied with the development of these chants—from simple progressions in a mode to progressions with skips and jumps. These chants were *monodic*, that is, the music consisted of only a single melodic line. Western music then evolved from simple monodic chant into more complicated musical constructions with multiple melodic lines, what is called *polyphony*.

The philosopher Karl Popper has described the development of polyphonic multivoiced music as "possibly the most unprecedented, original, indeed miraculous achievement of our Western civilization, not excluding science."[4] It was a development that occurred over 500 years: the evolution from the monodic church chant of the ninth century to the great polyphonic church music of the fifteenth and sixteenth centuries.

How exactly this evolution took place is the subject of speculation. The early monodic chants were sung in church services by a congregation. It is likely that not everyone sang at the same exact pitch, but rather that they sang the same pitch at different octaves. A congregation singing would have had many voices all moving in parallel motion, but separated by octaves. Actually, it is believed that the multiple voices occurred moving in parallel at fifths apart, as well as octaves (and perhaps even other intervals such as *thirds* and *sixths*). By the tenth century, this type of doubling of voices is found in music known as *organum*. In organum, singing was accompanied with a doubling of the chant on an organ that, in effect, provided the reference bass for the congregation.

It is speculated that, at some point, doubling voices may not have doubled at a fixed interval. For example, rather than doubling consistently a fifth or an octave from the bass melody, voices might have switched between these, so that a voice was sometimes a fifth apart, other times an octave. Although still singing at permitted intervals from the bass melody, voices were no longer strictly parallel; thus doubling voices developed an independence. This evolved by the thirteenth century to completely independent voices. Over time, this was extended to multiple voices with greater and greater independence until, by the fifteenth century, music was heard with multiple voices—three, four, and even five and six voices—singing distinct and independent melodic lines. *Counterpoint* was born: music with distinct voices moving in relationship to a fixed melody. As this new expressive possibility was developed, formal techniques and conventions for composing counterpoint were established. (It is interesting that a basic rule of counterpoint is that motion between two consecutive parallel fifths or octaves is never permitted. The logic behind this ban is clear in this historical context. The result of such parallel sequences would have been a return to the parallel movements that characterized *organum*.)[5]

The rules of counterpoint primarily describe the permissible linear relationships between voices as they progress forward. For example, the rules require the avoidance of the interval known as the *diabolus in musica* (six semitones). Other rules define how voices cannot overlap, or how they may or may not move in parallel. For example, two voices cannot approach the interval of a fifth or an octave by similar motion, that is, by both moving either up or down from the previous note of each voice.

In the sixteenth century, the rules of *harmony* developed. These rules describe the permissible vertical relationships between voices, coordinating the multiple voices to ensure the avoidance of dissonance—sounds that the taste of a given time considered to be unpleasant. Although counterpoint was the dominant element of baroque music and harmony was the dominant element of nineteenth-century music, both together shape music and both are the subject of study for any student of composition.

With the development of harmony, certain intervals, sequences, and combinations of notes became more accepted than others. Over time, the modal system was abandoned. Only two of the twelve modes—those most suited to harmonic music—were still used. Today these are known to musicians as the *major* and *minor* scales. Both of these modes consist of seven notes.

These two scales, and the relationship of a *fifth*, became the foundation for Western music from the baroque period, in the music of composers such as Scarlatti, Monteverdi, Handel, and Bach, to the early twentieth century and composers such as Mahler, Strauss, and Schoenberg. This foundation has recently been reembraced by contemporary "new tonalist" composers such as Philip Glass and John Adams.

Scales

The word *scale* is derived from the Italian *scala*, meaning staircase or ladder. It is used in music to refer to a series of notes progressing upward or downward. Just like the modes that were their predecessor, a scale can start on any of the twelve notes and is characterized by the size of the intervals between notes.

The major scale is characterized by the following sequence of semitone intervals:

+2, +2, +1, +2, +2, +2.

Given **1** as the first note of the scale, moving an interval of two semitones we arrive at **3**, moving two more we arrive at **5**, then moving one we arrive at **6**, and so on until we derive the major scale beginning with **1**:

C, D, E, F, G, A, B
1, 3, 5, 6, 8, 10, 12.

With the watch's dial, this can be illustrated by:

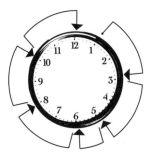

Observe that the note **8** is the fifth of the seven notes in the scale. It is because of this position in the scale that the note seven semitones from the first note of a scale is called the *fifth* note and the interval of seven semitones (8 − 1 = 7) is known as a *fifth*.[6]

The major scale beginning with the fifth of **1** (that is, the note that is seven semitones above **1**, namely **8**) can be derived in the same manner. Starting with the note **8**, we again follow the intervals of the major scale to derive:

G, A,   B, C, D, E, F♯
8, 10, 12, 1, 3, 5, 7.

Given that a scale is defined by the series of intervals it represents and that it can begin on any of the notes, we can simply rotate the start of our previous linked series of notes in order to illustrate this scale:

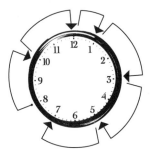

Looking at these two scales, it is important to observe that all the notes of the first scale can also be found in the second, with one exception: **6**. Similarly, all the notes of the second scale can be found in the first except one: **7**.

1, 3, 5, 6, 8, 10, 12
8, 10, 12, 1, 3, 5, <u>7</u>

This is, in fact, a general and very important property of scales and the interval of the fifth: there is only one note different between the scale of any given note and the scale beginning on the fifth of that note. It is this property that makes the relationship of a fifth so special. A note can only have this relationship (that is, a difference of only one note between its scale and the scale of another of the twelve notes) with two notes of the twelve—the note that is seven semitones from it, its fifth, and the note from which it is seven semitones, of which it is the fifth. In the case of **1**, these special notes are **8**, its fifth, and **6**, of which it is the fifth.

Scales and the Circle of Fifths

Starting with **1**, we can look at the notes of all twelve of the major scales following the circle of fifths (figure 2.4). (Recall that the sequence of the circle of fifths is **1, 8, 3, 10, 5, 12, 7, 2, 9, 4, 11, 6**.) From this we see that with each step further on the circle of fifths, scales share fewer and fewer notes with the first scale of the series. Halfway around the circle, that is, six scales away, the scales begin to come closer again and share more and more notes with the initial scale. Not only is the note six semitones from any given note the furthest note, but the scale based on it is also the furthest scale—that is, the least similar.

1,	3,	5,	6,	8,	10,	12	
8,	10,	12,	1,	3,	5,	<u>7</u>	1 note different
3,	5,	<u>7</u>,	8,	10,	12,	<u>2</u>	2 notes different
10,	12,	<u>2</u>,	3,	5,	<u>7</u>,	<u>9</u>	3 notes different
5,	<u>7</u>,	<u>9</u>,	10,	12,	<u>2</u>,	<u>4</u>	4 notes different
12,	<u>2</u>,	<u>4</u>,	5,	<u>7</u>,	<u>9</u>,	<u>11</u>	5 notes different
<u>7</u>,	<u>9</u>,	<u>11</u>,	12,	<u>2</u>,	<u>4</u>,	<u>6</u>	6 notes different
<u>2</u>,	<u>4</u>,	6,	<u>7</u>,	<u>9</u>,	<u>11</u>,	1	5 notes different
<u>9</u>,	<u>11</u>,	1,	<u>2</u>,	<u>4</u>,	6,	8	4 notes different
<u>4</u>,	6,	8,	<u>9</u>,	<u>11</u>,	1,	3	3 notes different
<u>11</u>,	1,	3,	<u>4</u>,	6,	8,	10	2 notes different
6,	8,	10,	<u>11</u>,	1,	3,	5	1 note different

Figure 2.4
The twelve major scales following the circle of fifths.

In summary, there are two special characteristics about the interval of the fifth.

(1) Moving by this interval, a sequence of notes is created in which each of the twelve notes will be arrived at once before any note is arrived at a second time. This sequence is known as the circle of fifths. (This is seen in the leftmost column of the above table.)

(2) Given the Western scales, there is a difference of only one note between the scale of any given note and the scale of its fifth. (This is seen in the difference between the successive rows of the above table.)

The History of Western Music Viewed as an Exploration of the Circle of Fifths

The 500 years of Western music between 1400 and 1900 can be viewed as an exploration of the circle of fifths, an exploration of the expressive possibilities of a system of music based on the special characteristics of the interval of the fifth. It is also an exploration of the musical structures that can be built exploiting these expressive possibilities.

As music evolved from a single voice to multiple voices, initially all the notes of all the voices were always from the same scale. Writing music using predominantly the notes of a given scale is called writing in the *key* of that scale. It was not until the early part of the sixteenth century that *chromatic passages* began to appear in music, that is, passages in which a series of notes might include several from outside the notes of a single scale. And as composers began to use notes from more than one scale, they developed a technique, called *modulation*, for switching between the notes from one scale and those from another.

The gentlest manner of modulation is to switch to the notes of the scale beginning on the fifth of the initial scale.[7] In this way, only one new note is introduced. However, in the sixteenth century, such a novelty would have been seen not as a subtle change in the music but rather as a bold departure into new worlds. The whole point of switching keys would have been to make a dramatic change that had to be perceived in order to achieve expressive impact in the music. The possibility of moving from one set of notes to another, of modulating from key to key, opened up new expressive possibilities for composers to explore.

At first these explorations were limited. Composers would make a quick switch to another key and then return again. And then maybe three or five switches before returning to the original key. Composers seemed compelled to develop the new expressive potential that modulation made possible.

However, these composers' adventurous explorations were not welcomed by the Church. There was a growing concern that these musical "tricks" presented too many distractions from the religious text and the content of church services. By the middle of the sixteenth century there was a strong reactionary movement to curb these deviations from the purer music of previous centuries, particularly in the context of the religious renewal of the Counter-Reformation.

Among the actions of the Council of Trent (a series of meetings held between 1545 and 1563 that codified the Counter-Reformation) was the formulation of measures for purging church music of these unwelcome deviations. A simpler form of music was prescribed. Catholic church music, it was decreed, should stick to the same set of notes. The music of the composer Giovanni Pierluigi da Palestrina was held up as the paradigm of this purer form. Palestrina's harmony represented the complete studied avoidance of chromaticism; virtually all the notes come from the same key. As a result, the music has a quality of purity and clarity that was felt to exemplify the spirit of the mass, without distracting from its ritual and text.

However, not to be suppressed, composers soon began again to explore this new expressive resource. The most notorious of the deviant composers of the late Renaissance was Carlo Gesualdo, prince of Venosa (1560–1613). Gesualdo's first book of madrigals was published in 1594, the year that Palestrina died, also the year of Shakespeare's *Romeo and Juliet*. Gesualdo used *all* twelve notes—that is, all the notes of all the scales—in his music. Though the madrigals were secular music and, therefore, were not subject to the Church's prohibition, he also wrote intense church music in this style.

Gesualdo was part of a school of experimental composers in northern Italy that explored sequences and combinations of notes that would not be heard again until 300 years later in the music of Wagner. If not for his extraordinary experiments that resulted in a profoundly expressive music, Gesualdo is remembered as a jealous husband who axed his wife and murdered her lover.

Tonality as the Basis for Structuring Music

Tonality, the use of the fifth and traveling the circle of fifths, became the basis for *structuring* compositions. In Walter Piston's classic text on harmony, he explains:

Tonality, then, is not merely a matter of using just the notes of a particular scale. It is more a process of setting forth the organized relationship of these notes to one among them which is to be the tonal center. Each scale degree has its part in the scheme of tonality, its tonal function.[8]

The use of keys and modulations shaped the form of a composition. Tonality organized the flow of the music.

As a composition unfolded, composers began to switch from one scale, or key, to another closely related scale and would conclude the composition by returning back to the original scale. The easiest way to do this was to move from the original key to the key of the fifth of the original key. During the course of a composition, a composer could subtly introduce an extraneous note, the note that distinguishes the scale of the fifth from the original scale, and then drop the note of the original scale that isn't found in the scale of the fifth.

In this manner, the key of the composition would change from the original to the key of the fifth.

Composers became more and more daring as they searched for new means of expression. They would not only switch to the key of the fifth, but move around the circle in the other direction to the key to which the original key was the fifth (though still only one note away). By the seventeenth century, the European courts shared the patronage of Western music with the Church; many secular patrons welcomed such harmonic experimentation. The doors were open to study just how great the scope of a structure built on tonality and the circle of fifths could be.

Throughout the eighteenth and nineteenth centuries, the major-minor tonality was the dominant underlying support of music. By this time, all the harmonies of a composition were organized in relation to the base key, called the *tonic*, with temporary modulations to other keys. An explicit theoretical foundation was described in Rameau's *Treatise on Harmony*, published in 1722, but this type of tonal organization had already been in use for at least 40 years and had been foreshadowed in the music of the Renaissance, especially that written in the latter half of the sixteenth century.

New forms extended into large musical structures using new techniques built on tonal organization with a clear "tonic-dominant" (that is, first-note-to-its-fifth) relationship. Grout explains the development of music based on this relationship.

The final perfection of the fugue, as well as of all the other large musical forms characteristic of the late Baroque, was inseparable from the full development of the major-minor system of tonality with its hierarchy of keys, which made possible a systematic use of key relationships in the musical design of long movements.[9]

From this time until the early twentieth century, periods of music can be seen as the exploration of structures extending further and further around the circle of fifths.

Mozart and Haydn explored the fifth of the fifth to the fullest. Both of the best-known musical forms of this classical period—the sonata and the symphony—are, again, based on the first-note-to-its-fifth relationship. Generalized very simply, both begin with the exposition of a theme in the base key. Then a second theme is introduced in the key of the fifth. After this formal introduction of the themes, the bulk of the movement consists of *developing* various relationships between the themes and different keys. Ultimately, the movement concludes with the first and second themes both played in the initial key of the movement. This overall structure of a movement is known as *sonata form*:

Theme 1 (in the base key), Theme 2 (in the key of the fifth),
Development of themes (with modulations to various keys),
Theme 1 (in the base key), Theme 2 (in the base key).

Beethoven explored the fifth of the fifth of the fifth and beyond. After his Symphony no. 3, *Eroica,* with its extended development sections, the development section assumed prime significance in a musical structure. Themes were transformed and combined to explore the full potential of the harmonic and melodic universe. Schumann and then Brahms, Wagner, Bruckner, and Mahler each went a step further. The explorations became even more extensive and the compositions grew in size and complexity throughout the nineteenth century, culminating in the massive works of Wagner, Bruckner, and Mahler.

The explorations progressed further and further along the circle of fifths until, hearing a note, one could not determine to which set of notes it related. The original set? The set of notes of the fifth? The fifth of the fifth? The fifth of the fifth of the fifth? Ultimately such descriptions seemed as contrived to a musician or composer as they seem nonsensical to a nonmusician. And they are. The context of any given set of notes changed so frequently that any note could appear at almost any time. Effectively, all twelve notes were equal. The progression of notes and the relationships from which they may have been derived were so difficult to determine, and were obscured by such complex and rapidly changing underlying harmonies, that the tonal structure of the music was virtually unintelligible. The harmonic structures that had been the basis of Western music for centuries collapsed. They were no longer used to build musical structures.

The whole course of late romantic music, especially in Germany, tended to this collapse of tonality as the underlying structure of music. The dissolution of classical tonality begins in the works of

Schubert and Chopin and continues in the works of Liszt. Melodies and chord progressions using all twelve notes and in which no tonal center or underlying set of notes can be perceived began to appear in the work of Wagner and Strauss.

At first these passages were unusual and rather short. But by the early twentieth century, in the works of Strauss and Mahler, the experiments became bolder and the explorations longer. Schoenberg explored the extreme possibilities of using all twelve notes within the limits of tonality in *Gurre-Lieder* and his String Quartet no. 2. Finally, he cut loose altogether from a key center. In his *Pierrot Lunaire,* rather than regarding some notes as alien to the original key, he treated all twelve notes as of equal rank.

Conclusion

For 500 years tonality was the basis for *structuring* music. It was the foundation for musical form, the rationale for the relationships between the notes of a composition.

The interval of the fifth is at the very foundation of tonality. The first and fifth notes of a scale are the anchors in the harmony of tonal music. And it is the circle of fifths that provides the framework for building larger musical structures.

But for early twentieth-century composers, inheritors of these harmonic traditions, tonality was no longer effective as a structuring device for creating a piece of music. Music was faced with a great challenge; some other device was needed.

Some composers experimented with new approaches to tonality. Debussy, Ravel, and others experimented with exotic alternatives to traditional tonality, using modes and the pentatonic, whole tone, and other nontraditional scales and chords. Busoni and Strauss, who influenced Hindemith and Weil, developed a new simplicity that was intended in some ways as a return to Bach. Others, such as Stravinsky and Bartok, created an entirely new aesthetic driven by rhythm and folk melody.

Still others, such as Schoenberg, Webern, and Berg, found themselves virtually unable to write music. These composers, one day to be seen as innovators by the post-World War II avant-garde, were in a sense the ultimate traditionalists. They clung to traditional tonality as their basis for writing music; with its collapse in the early years of this century, their works became mere 20-second compositions. The massive musical structures that characterized the works of Wagner, Bruckner, Strauss, and Mahler at the turn of the century collapsed into small musical fragments. Without the logic and structure of harmony, every note written was the result of a difficult struggle to follow one note with another.

3   *Nāgārjuna*

After Pāṇini, the interest in language in India continued to flourish. Although Pāṇini's *Aṣṭādhyāyī* was the definitive grammar of Sanskrit, other linguists carried the studies of language into new domains. For example, the Indians developed dictionaries not unlike our modern thesaurus. These dictionaries contained lists of words of approximately the same meaning and words used in similar contexts, sometimes with brief definitions. Beyond the structural aspects of vocabulary and syntax, Indian linguists went on to study the meaning, or semantics, of language and even the representation of knowledge.

Indian interest in language spread to philosophy, and there was considerable speculation about the relationship between a word and the thing it represented. The Mīmāṃsā school, perpetuating the verbal mysticism of the Vedic period, maintained that every word was the reflection of an ideal prototype, and that its meaning was eternal and inherent in it. Their opponents, especially the logical school of the Nyāya, supported the view that the relationship between words and meaning was purely conventional.

Nāgārjuna and Differentiation

It was in the context of this tradition that Nāgārjuna, considered one of the subtlest dialecticians of all time, founded a school of philosophy in India around 150 A.D. known as the Mādhyamaka.[1] It flourished throughout the period of Buddhism in India, into the sixteenth century, and continues today in Tibet.

The core tenet was that salvation was to be found in the exercise of wisdom, which was understood by the Mādhyamaka as the contemplation of *śūnyatā*, emptiness. *Śūnyatā* is neither affirmation nor negation, neither existence nor nonexistence.

As *śūnyatā* was often discussed in terms of what it was not, the philosophical teachings of Nāgārjuna were often thought of as negativist. Focused on nothingness or emptiness, they were often thought of as nihilist.

The opening paragraphs of Nāgārjuna's *Mādhyamakakārikā* presents the core of his philosophy:

Without cessation, without origination, without annihilation, without eternity, without unity, without diversity, without coming and without going.
I bow to the Buddha, the best of teachers, who has taught *pratītyasamutpāda* [dependent origination], liberation, the calming of all verbal differentiation.[2]

Nāgārjuna's philosophical discourses are based on the supposition at the foundation of the Buddha's teaching: "the Lord, who has understood both being and non-being, denied 'It is,' 'It is not,' and both positions together." Nāgārjuna's discourses are a thorough exploration of the implications of another very subtle fundamental Buddhist concept, dependent origination, and the related theories of causality.

In Buddhism, all things are subject to the law of causality, all things are dependent for their origination. That is, they are the effect of some cause. In Nāgārjuna's discourses, if something is dependent, then it lacks its own intrinsic nature.

That nature which is dependent is devoid of an intrinsic nature.... If things were by their own nature they would be even without the aggregate of causes and conditions. But they are not so. Therefore, they are said to be devoid of an intrinsic nature, and hence, empty.

Rather than interpreting his conclusion as "things do not exist," Nāgārjuna's point can be understood as "things do not exist independent of causation." They are devoid of an entirely independent existence and lack their own intrinsic value. They exist dependently and are, therefore, empty.

However, the purpose of *śūnyatā* in Nāgārjuna's teaching is more subtle. Its purpose is to calm all verbal differentiations. Interpreting *śūnyatā* as nonexistence is itself an interpretation in terms of verbal differentiations.

Who differentiates the Buddha, who is imperishable and beyond verbal differentiations, all those are destroyed by their verbal differentiations.

Śūnyatā is beyond verbal differentiation: "not conditioned by others, calm, not differentiated by verbal differentiations, beyond discursive thought, without diversity." Understanding the essence of *śūnyatā* leads to liberation, *nirvāṇa*.

By the destruction of actions and passions there is liberation. Actions and passions are the results of discursive thought, and those discursive thoughts are produced by verbal differentiation. But verbal differentiation is destroyed in emptiness (*śūnyatā*).... Liberation is the calming of all representations, the calming of verbal differentiation.... Those who apprehend the existence and non-existence of entities do not see the liberation which is the calming of appearances.

Nirvāṇa is *śūnyatā*: *nirvāṇa* is completely beyond differentiation. "The Lord is not conceived as existing, not existing, both or neither. There is nothing whatsoever differentiating *saṃsāra* [not-*nirvāṇa*] from *nirvāṇa*. There is nothing whatsoever differentiating *nirvāṇa* from *saṃsāra*." To the extent that both completely lack inherent existence, there is no differentiation between *saṃsāra* and *nirvāṇa*, between earthly existence and bliss.

Nāgārjuna's *Mādhyamakakārikā* concludes:

Śūnyatā is a refuge from all philosophies.... I bow in adoration to Gautama [Buddha], who, possessing compassion, taught the True Doctrine for the destruction of all philosophies.

Dignaga's Theory of Apoha

Under the influence of Nāgārjuna's teachings, the Indian logician Dignaga developed a theory of meaning based on the concept of *apoha* in approximately 400 A.D. *Apoha* can be translated as differentiation.

In Dignaga's theory, the meaning of a word consists of its repudiation of what it is not. For instance, using a popular Indian example, the meaning of "cow" is defined as that which is not "not-a-cow." Hence, "cow = not-not-cow." The ability to distinguish a cow is based on its differentiation from all cases of "not-cow." We know what a thing is by cognizing what it is not; indeed it is only perceived to exist to the extent that it is cognized or differentiated from other things.

Imagine a language with four colors: blue, red, mauve, and green. Imagine that anything either blue, red, mauve, or green is called "colored." Then anything that is *not* blue, red, mauve, or green is called "not-colored." Blue is defined as not-red, not-mauve, not-green. Red is defined as not-blue, not-mauve, not-green. And so on.

Like the philosophy of Nāgārjuna, this could be thought of as negativist. It was argued, however, that to define "A" in terms of "not-A" presupposes "A," in a positive sense. "Not-A" implicitly says "A" *is*.[3]

Color Table 1

Plate 1 is a table of twelve colors, each labeled and numbered. This table, as well as the tables that follow, illustrate some ideas that are central to this chapter. The sequence of tables represents a simple puzzle.

The colors of plate 1 relate to one another in a number of ways. It is common to consider that blue, color **1**, provides a sharp contrast with red, color **4**, but that they are nonetheless well suited together. On the other hand, pink, color **10**, is generally considered to clash with yellow, color **5**.

The Beginning of Modern Linguistics

The first known reference in Europe to Sanskrit is from the end of the sixteenth century. It is found in a letter of an Italian, Filippo Sassetti, who wrote from India about the resemblances between some Sanskrit and Italian words.

The beginning of modern linguistic science can be said to have been in 1786. It was in this year that a judge from the British court in India, Sir William Jones, presented a now famous paper to the Royal Asiatic Society in Calcutta. In it he convincingly established for the first time that Sanskrit, Latin, Greek, and other European languages were all from the same family. Jones stated:

The Sanskrit language, whatever be its antiquity, is of a wonderful structure; more perfect than the Greek, more copious than the Latin, and more exquisitely refined than either; yet bearing to both of them a stronger affinity, both in the roots of verbs and in the forms of grammar, than could possibly have been produced by accident; so strong indeed, that no philologer could examine all three without believing them to have sprung from some common source, which, perhaps, no longer exists. There is a similar reason ... for supposing that both the Gothic and the Celtic had the same origin with the Sanskrit.[4]

With the discovery of Sanskrit and Jones's insight, the systematic study of the resemblances and historical links between different languages began, a discipline known as comparative linguistics. Equally important, with the translation of Sanskrit texts European linguists discovered the Indians' work on semantics, grammar, phonology, and phonetics. Indian phonetics, for example, was far more advanced than any European work. The Europeans discovered in the Indians' work an understanding of language and techniques for its study that provided a foundation for new work in Europe. In general, European linguists took over from where the Indian linguists had left off.

In the nineteenth century, the study of language in Europe focused on comparative linguistics. The task of linguistics became the search for similarities and, in effect, the search for evidence substantiating that there was a common source for all of the Indo-European languages. An even more ambitious goal was to find the source of *all* languages, the "original" human tongue. Sanskrit was the key to this search, for it made clear similarities among the three oldest known languages—Sanskrit, Greek, and Latin—that were not evident when comparing just Greek and Latin.

Two of the earliest Sanskrit grammars published in English were W. Carey's *Grammar for the Sanskrit Language* in 1806 and C. Wilkins's *Grammar of the Sanskrit Language* in 1808. Both Carey and Wilkins studied with living pundits in India. Franz Bopp's *The Sanskrit Conjugation System* of 1816 compared the conjugation system of Sanskrit with Germanic, Greek, and Latin.

During the first half of the nineteenth century, the most important work in comparative linguistics was by Jacob Grimm. His work reflected a swelling national pride in Germany and included a study of the German language, a study of German mythology, and, in collaboration with his brother Wilhelm, a German dictionary and a collection of German folk tales, *Grimm's Fairy Tales*. Jacob Grimm's *Germanic Grammar* outlined a series of nine correspondences between different Indo-European languages, known as Grimm's law. Grimm demonstrated that Germanic languages have a *t* where Latin, Greek, and Sanskrit have a *d*; an *f* where they have a *p*; a *b* where Latin has an *f*, Greek a *ph*, and Sanskrit a *bh*; and so on.

Color Table 2

In the second color table (plate 2), the order of the twelve colors has been changed. The ordering of the twelve colors is arbitrary. Now, color **6** (blue) is in sharp contrast but well suited with color **9** (red), while color **8** (pink) clashes with color **2** (yellow).

Ferdinand de Saussure

In December 1878, Ferdinand de Saussure, 21 years old, published his *Memoir on the Primitive Vowel System in Indo-European Languages*. This work has been described as "the most splendid work of comparative philology ever written."[5] At the time, Saussure was a student of Indo-European languages—studying French, German, English, Latin, Greek, and Sanskrit—at the University of Leipzig, a center of linguistic study in Europe. He had earlier abandoned his studies of physics and chemistry at the University of Geneva to pursue linguistics. Saussure's thesis at Leipzig was to be on the use of the genitive case in Sanskrit.

Today, Ferdinand de Saussure is recognized as the founder of modern linguistics. Saussure defined a new science, semiology, the science of signs, of which linguistics is a subset. He developed an analytical view of language in terms of its structure that is applicable not only to the study of language and signs, but to human behavior in general. The influence of his ideas in the twentieth century has extended to art, architecture, philosophy, literature, and anthropology. Interestingly, Saussure transformed twentieth-century thinking without ever writing anything directly discussing his ideas of greatest significance. Furthermore, his life remains for the most part undocumented. He lived a rather unadventurous life personally, and as far as is known he had no major intellectual crises or decisive moments of insight.

After teaching for a decade in Paris, Saussure moved back to Switzerland in 1891 to assume a professorship at the University of Geneva, where he taught Sanskrit and general linguistics. However, unlike Leipzig and Paris, Geneva was not a center of linguistic study. Saussure wrote less and less, and for the most part faded into obscurity. Between 1906 and 1911, while he was a professor at the University of Geneva, he gave three courses of lectures on general linguistics. After his death in 1913, his students decided that his work and ideas should not be lost. However, Saussure had kept few notes, and there was no manuscript that outlined his theory. So his students gathered *their* notes and assembled what was published in 1916 as Saussure's *Course in General Linguistics*. It is this *Course in General Linguistics* that is the basis for Saussure's tremendous influence on twentieth-century thinking.

Saussure's View of Language as a System

Saussure rejected the then prevailing historical and comparative focus of linguistics. For him comparative linguistics was inadequate because it failed to recognize the structural nature of language. Saussure felt comparative linguists did not ask the critical question: What was the significance of the relationships they had discovered?

As the Indo-European languages diverged, the pronunciation of the languages, that is, the sounds themselves, had changed from language to language. Where Latin and Sanskrit begin a word with *s*, Greek begins it with *h*. Where Latin and Greek have *o*, Sanskrit has *a*. Where Gothic and Old English have *f*, Latin, Greek, and Sanskrit have *p*. Comparative linguistics recognized that a single Indo-European language had evolved over centuries into a family of languages.

But what was significant to Saussure was not that specific words looked alike among these languages, but that there were *regular correspondences in the positions of sounds throughout the system*. He realized that this reflected a common underlying system or set of rules for combining sounds. What he found important was not the evidence of historical evolution that the similarities between the languages revealed, but that the Indo-European languages shared a system. Rather than viewing language in a historical context, Saussure was interested in understanding the system underlying a language that enabled communication *at any given point in time*. He developed a view of language that recognized that what defines a language and makes it a basis for communication is its *system*.

For example, there are a number of vocal sounds at the foundation of any spoken language. Thirty-five are used in English, 27 in Italian. (The groups of contrasting sounds in a spoken language are called *phonemes*.) All speakers of English, whether in New York, Edinburgh, or Calcutta, share the same system of sounds. Pronunciation differs from speaker to speaker. Though consonants such as *m* and *n* generally are pronounced similarly by all English speakers, the vowel *a* varies from New York to Edinburgh to Calcutta.[6] However, even though the specific pronunciation a speaker uses for these sounds may vary, what all the speakers of English share when they pronounce the word *man* is that the sounds of the word—*m, n,* and *a*—occupy the same *position* in the system. They all contrast the vowel in *man* with a different vowel in *men*. And they do not contrast this vowel with the vowel sound in other words such as *can* and *fan*.

All speakers of English share the same system for combining sounds into words. The system prescribes how sounds may be grouped together to form words, which sounds may begin words, and which sound sequences are permitted. The system defines the positions a sound may take within the complete system: for example, the sound of *a* in *man* is not found at the end of English words.

More generally, Saussure recognized that language consists of a number of linked systems and he saw structure in it at all levels. Among the different Indo-European languages, in addition to regular correspondences in sounds there are structural correspondences that can be seen in features of grammar and syntax. For example, in the Germanic branch of the family (including English) there are two main ways of putting a verb in the past tense. One is changing the root vowel, as in *I sing* and *I sang*. The other is by adding a *d* or *t* to the ending, as in *I love* and *I loved*. In German, we have the corresponding *ich singe* and *ich sang*, and *ich lebe* and *ich lebte*; in Swedish, *jag sjunger* and *jag sjong*, and *jag lever* and *jag levde*. This again reflects a common underlying system.

Within English, system is seen in the way words are constructed from smaller parts. *Quick*, *slow*, and *happy* can be combined with *ly* to form *quickly*, *slowly*, and *happily*. System is found in the way verbs change their form for different grammatical purposes—*talk*, *talks*, *talking*, *talked*—and in singular and plural: *boy* and *boys*. It is also found in the rules for combining words into sentences (syntax).

Saussure and Differentiation

Saussure proposed the study of language in terms of *structure*. He saw the linguist's job as the definition of the elements of a language, the relations between them, and their rules of combination. "The linguist must take the study of linguistic structure as his primary concern, and relate all other manifestations of language to it."[7]

At the center of the study of language, Saussure identified the *linguistic sign*. Noises can be said to be part of language only if they communicate ideas. And for noises to communicate ideas, they must be part of a system of conventions that relates noises to ideas. Saussure defined the linguistic sign as the combination of the noise —the *signifier*—and the idea or object it signifies—the *signified*. Language is a system of signs.

The essential feature of the linguistic sign is that it is arbitrary. A particular combination of a signifier and a signified is an arbitrary entity. That is, there is no natural or inevitable link between the signifier and the signified. The signifier *tree* refers to a living organism made of wood, with leaves, and so on—the signified. But this object could also be referred to by any number of other noises than *tree* and still be understood as long as others speaking the same language knew the convention. A tree could be referred to by the noise *stub*, the French word *arbre,* or the Sanskrit word *vṛkṣa*. The fact that different languages use different noises to refer to the same concept or object suggests the arbitrary nature of the sign.

Saussure suggested that the linguistic sign could not be viewed independently of the complex system of contrasts implicitly recognized by a community of speakers. The interpretation of a sign is made only by contrast with other signs, which together form a structured system. Roy Harris, commenting on Saussure, explains: "Saussure's linguistic sign, being intrinsically arbitrary, can be identified only by contrast with other coexisting signs of the same nature, which together constitute a structured system."[8]

Color Table 3

In plate 3, the choice of language for describing the colors is changed. Sanskrit is substituted for English.[9] In this case, *kāla*, color 6, is in sharp contrast but well suited with *dhūmra*, color 9; *pāṃsuvarṇa*, color 8, clashes with *hārita*, color 10.

Defined in Relation to Other Members of the System

The study of language in terms of structure, known as structuralism, is interested only in the relationships between objects. Objects are diacritically defined—that is, by opposition to one another. As a result, a structure is simply a set of relationships between objects—on an abstract plane. What the objects are is arbitrary in terms of the structure.

In fact, not only is the signifier arbitrary, but the signified also is arbitrary. There is no underlying set of universal concepts that each language refers to with a different set of noises. The very concepts of one language differ significantly from the concepts of another. Each language articulates and organizes the world differently.

For example, the words *fleuve* and *rivière* are signifiers of French, but not of English. And *river* and *stream* are English and not French. More importantly, the conceptual planes against which these words are understood in English and French are different. In English, a *river* is defined in relation to a *stream* only in terms of size—it is larger. However, in French a *fleuve* is defined by the fact that it flows into the sea, whereas a *rivière* does not. Size is not an issue; a *rivière* may be larger than a *fleuve*. Thus, these words are not simply different utterances referring to some shared underlying universal concepts. They are in fact different concepts. French and English provide different ways of viewing, segmenting, and interpreting the world. If this were not the case, translation would be the simple substitution of one word for another. The difficulty in translating between languages is in fact that the concepts and meanings of words in one language may have no equivalent in another, or at least no exact equivalent.

That the concepts of different languages are arbitrary ways of dividing a continuum suggests not only that there are not some fundamental underlying entities to which they refer, but also that a language's concepts are defined in relation to other members of the system. The concept of a stream is defined in terms of the differences between a *stream*, a *river*, a *rivulet*, and so on. In Saussure's words:

> We discover not *ideas* given in advance but *values* emanating from the system. When we say that these values correspond to concepts, it is understood that these concepts are purely differential, not positively defined by their content but negatively defined by their relations with other terms of the system. Their most precise characteristic is that they are what the others are not.[10]

Though there was no historical link, 1,500 years later Saussure's philosophy recalls Nāgārjuna's regarding the importance of differentiation, and Saussure's words echo Dignaga's interpretation of *apoha*.

Meaning Emanates from the System

Meaning is often thought of in terms of what words refer to. The meaning of the word *horse* is a horse, the four-legged animal that exists in the "real" world. However, in a view of language as a formal system, a *horse* may be defined by what it is not—that is, it is not a *cow, cat, dog,* or *tree.*

In a traffic light, there are three colors: red, green, and yellow. What they mean is defined by their relationship to one another. Red is *not-green-or-yellow.* Yellow is *not-green-or-red.* Green is *not-yellow-or-red.* The referential meaning we decide to assign to each of these is quite arbitrary. Green could equally easily indicate stop, red proceed. The interpretation of green as proceed and red as stop is entirely based on custom. In a formal system, it is the relationships that count. Add another color to the light, for example, blue, and all the relationships will be redefined.

In language, there are many examples where items contrast with one another. There are the pronouns *I, he, she, it, we, you, they.* If one is added or removed, all of the others will change their formal meaning. Words form sets, and the meaning of a word depends on the other words in the set with which it can be contrasted.

An example of a set is the degrees of temperature: *hot, warm, cold.* Add *tepid* and *cool* and the meaning of all the others changes. Warm is now not just *not-cold* but also *not-tepid.* The definition of warm is different.

In the set of *captain, major, colonel,* and other ranks, the meaning of each term depends on its *position* in the hierarchy. Add a new rank and the meaning of all the others changes. Some become lower in rank, others even higher.

Another set is colors. *Red, green, blue.* Add *azure, light green, dark blue,* and *turquoise* and the meaning of the others changes. It is interesting to note that different languages and cultures divide the spectrum of colors differently. The Latin *caeruleus* includes both dark blue and dark green. Eskimo has over 20 terms for English's white. Similarly, the colors of Sanskrit cannot be exactly matched to the colors of English. The number and definition of colors is based on custom, interests, and other factors, and varies from language to language.

In a structuralist view of meaning, it is not necessary to have a referent for each sign. Meaning, or "sense," can be discussed in terms of structure. Though the actual underlying world may have been a necessary condition for the development or design of language, it is not a necessary condition to understand how it *functions.* Words are understood by their place within a system of other words that are in opposition to them and circumscribe them.

Meaning is a question of positional value. In a structuralist view of language, one is not concerned with the referents of words or objects, but rather with values that emanate from a system. Every value is defined by positions and differences within a system of relationships. The sense of a word is defined by its place in a system of relationships that link it with other words. They are defined diacritically; it is the relationships that count. In Saussure's words:

Linguistic system being what it is, wherever one begins one will find nothing simple, but always and everywhere this same complex equilibrium of reciprocally defined or conditioned terms. In other words, language is a form and not a substance.[11]

Structure operates in language at all levels. At the lowest levels, there are relationships between the sounds that make up words. It is a system of diacritically defined relationships between sounds that distinguishes *bed* from *bad*, *bid*, *bud*, and *bode*; or *bread* from *dead*, *fed*, *head*, *led*, and *red*. It is the opposition of a given sound to others that could replace it in the same context. Structure and diacritically defined relationships are found in word structure. For example, *-ly*, *-less*, and *-ship* are all suffixes that could follow the word *friend*, whereas *-er* cannot. And *friend* relates to *partner* and *professor* to the extent that all may be followed by *-ship*.

In addition to the relationships between individual words, there are also relationships between units that define how they may be combined to form sequences. At this level of relationships, referred to as *syntax*, diacritically defined relationships determine how classes of items may follow one another in a given sequence. For example, *he frightened* may only be followed by certain types of sequences, such as *George* or *the man standing on the corner*, but not by *the stone* or *purple* or *in*.[12]

Language is a system where elements are entirely defined by their relationship to one another within the system *at all levels*. At each level, one can identify elements that contrast with one another and that combine to form higher-level units that, again, one can identify in contrast with other elements at *that* level. In fact, at each level of structure one identifies the units or elements precisely by their ability to differentiate units of the level immediately above them. The principles of structure *at all levels* are essentially the same. This viewpoint is the essential foundation of structuralist thinking.

Structuralism Applies to All Systems of Expression

Saussure proposed that a structuralist view is applicable to *all* systems of meaning. From a structuralist view, any form of communication, in order to succeed as a form of communication, must have an underlying system of discernible and differentiable distinctions and conventions. As a result, any form of communication can be studied in terms of its formal structure.

The applicability of structuralism to the study of human and social behavior, of which language is just one example, is based on the assumption that such behavior has meaning within a societal context. The meaning of a given behavior is based on a shared underlying system of norms. Saussure explains:

By considering rites, customs, etc. as signs, it will be possible, we believe, to see them in a new perspective.... Every means of expression used in a society is based, in principle, on a collective norm—in other words, on convention. Signs of politeness, for instance, often have a certain natural expressivity (one thinks of the way a Chinese prostrates himself nine times before the emperor by way of salutation), but they are nonetheless determined by a rule; and it is this rule which leads one to use them, not their intrinsic value.[13]

Saussure envisaged a new science. "We can imagine a science which would study the life of signs within society ... we call it semiology."[14] The science of semiology, the study of signs, can be applied well beyond the domain of language. During this century, a whole school of structuralists has emerged concerned with the structural analysis of a number of nonlinguistic "languages." Since World War II, anthropologists, literary critics, and others have seen in structural linguistics a model and methodology that could be applied to their own disciplines.

For example, in 1961 Claude Lévi-Strauss defined anthropology as a branch of semiology and recognized Saussure as the pioneer who had laid the foundations for this structuralist view. Lévi-Strauss applied structuralist principles to the study of myth, undertaking an enormous study of the myths of various cultures to demonstrate how there was an underlying formal system in myths. The significance of various myths could only be understood by contrasting them with other myths to reveal this underlying system of codes and conventions.

In a structuralist view, a society's rites and customs are meaningful only in terms of its shared assumptions and conventions. A marriage ceremony only derives meaning in terms of the institutionalized framework in which it occurs. An observer from a different culture might describe what occurs during a ceremony, but doesn't understand the meaning of the various acts unless they are placed in the broader context of social conventions. The exchanging of rings is meaningful only within the social conventions that ascribe meaning to it. In another simple example, in the game of soccer, someone kicks the ball between two posts. Someone from another culture may observe the action but will not understand its significance unless he or she is familiar with the conventions or rules of soccer. The significance of kicking the ball between the two posts must be contrasted with hitting it with one's head (another legal way to score), kicking it off to the side, or picking it up and carrying it by hand between the posts.

In a structuralist view of a representational visual form of communication such as painting, the meaning of the visual image is not derived from what it represents but rather from the conventions for how it represents it. A structuralist approach to understanding painting will try to make explicit the codes that allow for a meaningful representation through an iconic process. For example, in a portrait or a still life of fruit on a table that is realistic or even photographic in its representation of the subject, the meaning of the painting is derived from how the subject is represented: how accurately, with what expression, with what surroundings for the subject, in what lighting. It is not the fruit in itself that is interesting (although the choice of fruit and its arrangement may be significant, given still life conventions), but the way the fruit is painted. In nonfigurative or abstract painting, where there is no obvious interpretation of the subject, there are still conventions that enable its interpretation. If painting is to be called a language, it is because, like all language, it has an underlying system of conventions that permit communication.

Others, such as Roland Barthes and A. J. Greimas, have pioneered the structuralist analysis of literature. Such approaches suggest that a poem or a novel has meaning only with respect to a system of conventions with which the reader is familiar. In a poem, the choices between words, sentences, and different modes of presentation will be made on the basis of their effect, and the very notion of their effect is based on a system of conventions and expectations that guide a reader through a text. Rhymes or the lack of them derive their effect based on a system of conventions and expectations. Poetic rhythmic patterns such as iambic pentameter are based on conventions that establish expectations. It is this underlying set of conventions that makes poetry a vehicle for expression that is distinct from ordinary speech.

The goal of structuralism is to formalize and make explicit these underlying rules and conventions.

Color Table 4

In plate 4, the twelve colors with the twelve Sanskrit labels and the translations of the labels into English reveal an error. What is not evident in plate 3, except to those familiar with Sanskrit, is that the Sanskrit words are misplaced against the colors.

There was an expectation that the labels would be associated with the color swatches, not with the numbers. But the translator was unaware of this. The significant relationships were mistaken to be between the original labels of each color swatch and the numbers, between blue and pink and **1** and **10**. The Sanskrit labels of plate 3 were positioned according to the relationships between the original English labels and the *numbers* of plate 1. The labels were interpreted as referring to the numbers, not the colors.

The relationships can be thought of in terms of a cube with colors, English labels, Sanskrit labels, and numbers on four (of the six) different sides. In plates 1 and 2, changing the relationships on one side, the ordering of the colors, also changed another side with the English labels in an isomorphic manner (that is, the same structure of relationships was reflected). The structures of two sides—the colors and English labels—were linked. The third side—the numbers—was not linked to the others and did not change. Two sides, therefore, shifted isomorphically and one side stayed the same.

In the case of the third color table, the Sanskrit labels were mistakenly ordered corresponding to the numbers, not to the reordered colors. The structural correlations were maintained between the twelve Sanskrit labels and the twelve numbers—between the wrong sets. The wrong sides were linked. When the colors were reordered, the Sanskirt labels, linked to the numbers, did not get repositioned. One side shifted and two stayed the same. In the analogy with a cube, rather than the numbered side of the cube being the anchor while the labels shifted isomorphically with the colors, instead only the side with colors changed.

A simple error. After all, "blue" is a word for a color, but could just as easily have been the word for the number **1**—the relationship between the signifier and signified is arbitrary.

Color Table 5

The same structural transformation that reordered the colors and English labels in plates 1 and 2 is applied to the now independent side of numbers in plate 5. In this view of four sides of the cube, it can be seen that the Sanskrit labels and the English labels are now correctly linked to the colors. The numbers shift position. The colors, the Sanskrit, and the English remain in their original positions.

Conclusion

Sanskrit was the key that opened the way to modern linguistics. The discovery of Sanskrit made visible the common basis underlying Sanskrit, Greek, and Latin. For Saussure, this revealed a common underlying *formal system*. With a view of language as a system, Saussure established structuralism.

The essence of the structuralist view is that the key to studying language is the distinctions and relationships that emanate from the underlying system—and that this view is applicable to *all* systems of meaning. All languages (in the broader sense) can be studied in terms of formal structure. Even the most expressive and subtlest languages can be studied in terms of formal structure, including the languages of literature, poetry, painting, sculpture, and music.

Language is a system of relationships. Differentiation makes it possible to perceive these relationships. Differentiation rests at the foundation of Saussure's view of language. Similarly, differentiation is at the core of Nāgārjuna's philosophy and Dignaga's theory of *apoha*.

Meaning is defined by relationships. What something refers to is understood in the context of a web of relationships, in terms of what it is and is not, and of how each of the other pieces in the web relates to all the others. Meaning is defined by relationships in this massively complex web.

6 is *not* 1, 2, 3, 4, 5, 7, 8, 9, 10, 11, 12.

Blue is defined by the fact that it is not red, green, yellow, pink, purple, gray, or any other color. Blue is well suited to red. Yellow clashes with pink. These relationships give blue, red, yellow, and pink a *place* within a complete system of relationships.

Structuralism tries to understand the web of relationships that underlie and make possible a system of communication. At the center of such a study of a language are the *differentiating* and *structuring* operations by which the elements of a language derive meaning.

This reflects directly on the mind's ability to derive meaning by differentiating. Perception itself is a process of differentiation. To perceive something is to differentiate it from what it is not. Just as language and thought are tightly interwoven in consciousness, the mind's ability to differentiate is also at the heart of consciousness.

Nāgārjuna's philosophy also addresses the web of relationships that are at the center of discursive thought. But the goal of Nāgārjuna and his followers was to understand the nature of verbal differentiation in order, ultimately, to transcend it. Nāgārjuna understood the massively complex web of relationships that is the product of a differentiating consciousness. In understanding being and nonbeing, and that there is neither without the other, Nāgārjuna followed his path to enlightenment, not conditioned by others, calm, beyond verbal differentiations, beyond discursive thought, without diversity.

4   *The Second Viennese School*

Through the first decade of the century, Arnold Schoenberg found the composition of extended works to be more and more difficult. His music was deeply rooted in the traditions of tonality. Without tonality as a basis for writing music, his compositions were increasingly sustained purely by direct emotional expression without the support of traditional musical structures. However, Schoenberg eventually exhausted this draining source of inspiration. Finally, by 1917, he was no longer creating any new compositions.

Schoenberg published no music for several years, but he returned to the music scene in 1923 with new ideas. He had developed a new foundation for composition that could replace tonality, a "method of composing with twelve tones which are related only with one another." In Schoenberg's method, each of the twelve notes of the scale is equal in importance to the others. He proposed that the twelve notes could be ordered in a unique *series* that could be thought of like a theme and used as the core material for a composition. Schoenberg went on to suggest that the twelve notes should be ordered so that each note occurs once and only once in the series. In a composition, the notes of the series would be used in the order they occur in the series, over and over and over.

There was a new method to determine the relationships of the notes of a piece. Using the same series of notes over and over for an entire composition provided a means for unifying a complete work, analogous to the role tonality had played before. The role of each note was determined by its position within a series, and the role of a given occurrence of the series was determined by its position within the larger structure of the composition. In analyzing a composition, *every* note could be numbered as the *n*th note of the *y*th occurrence of the series.

Schoenberg's method of composition is known as *serialism*. It was to be extremely influential in musical thought for the 40 years that followed his first works using this method in the early 1920s. Schoenberg and two disciples of his new musical doctrine, Alban Berg and Anton Webern, established a foundation for a new music.

Mozart, Beethoven, and Schubert, the great masters of classical music, had lived in Vienna between 1780 and 1830. Schoenberg, Berg, and Webern, who were also centered in Vienna, are often referred to as the *Second Viennese School*.

Arnold Schoenberg

This invention of a new technique was made not by a radical young innovator but by a man who, in 1923, was 49 years old. Nor was this seemingly mechanical and mathematical system for writing music invented by a man obsessed with abstractions and divorced from life. Rather, Schoenberg is described as having been a "fiery-tempered, hoarse-voiced, chain-smoking, bald-headed little man, this dynamo of nervous energy ... the battleground of barely governable emotions."[1] He lived in Vienna at a time when a collection of brilliant individuals in a broad array of disciplines—including Sigmund Freud, Ludwig Wittgenstein, Adolf Loos, and Oskar Kokoschka—each found a need to rethink the basic language of their disciplines.

Schoenberg had begun playing the violin at the age of eight or nine and composing soon after. But his parents were not particularly interested in music. His family belonged to the poorest level of the petite bourgeoisie; his father owned a small shoe shop and hoped Arnold would become an engineer. When his father died, he had to begin work at 15 as a clerk in a bank to support his family. Finally, five years later in 1895, the bank went bankrupt and Schoenberg committed himself to composition in spite of his family's lack of enthusiasm.

In 1897, Schoenberg's String Quartet in D Major became his first piece to be publicly performed. It was well received: "It seems to me that a new Mozart is growing up in Vienna."[2] His musical language developed rapidly. Two years later, he wrote *Verklärte Nacht* (Transfigured Night), which met a cooler reception. This was modern music that went beyond Wagner in chromatic intensity.

In 1901, Richard Strauss, Germany's most recognized living composer, was impressed by Schoenberg's next work, *Gurre-Lieder*. Strauss helped Schoenberg find work and encouraged his compositions. In 1903, upon hearing *Verklärte Nacht*, the Austrian composer Gustav Mahler also became a staunch supporter.

However, Schoenberg's works found increasingly unreceptive public audiences. By 1908, a performance of his String Quartet no. 2 was met with whistling, jeers, and catcalls. A review of this concert politely concluded that the composer was "tone-deaf and thus, musically, *non compos*."[3] Although audiences were impressed by the intensity of his compositions, they were baffled by the distant explorations of tonality and chromaticism.

In his personal life Schoenberg was experiencing intense distress. In 1908, his wife Mathilde had moved in with an expressionist painter and teacher named Richard Gerstl, nine years Schoenberg's junior. Schoenberg pleaded with her to return to him and their family. She left Gerstl, who killed himself shortly thereafter at the age of 25.

In the years following 1908 and preceding the outbreak of war, Schoenberg wrote *Erwartung, Pierrot Lunaire,* and other milestone compositions. These works are often described as "expressionist" music, which, like expressionist painting, was considered to be a direct reflection of troubled psychological states. Schoenberg wrote in a letter of 1910, "Art is the cry of distress uttered by those who experience at first hand the fate of mankind."[4] (During this same period, Schoenberg undertook painting in the expressionist style. Three of his paintings were included in the first Blaue Reiter exhibition in Munich, with works by Wassily Kandinsky and Franz Marc.)

Schoenberg's intense emotional state resulted in free-form streams of intense, feverish music. His instrumental works virtually stopped; all of his major works were now vocal works, where the text helped shape the flow of musical events. His compositional language evolved to one of complete chromaticism, freely using all twelve notes. His works had no solid tonal foundation; his direct emotional expression propels them from their first note to their last. Schoenberg described his music of this period in a letter to Richard Strauss as "without architecture, without structure ... an ever-changing, unbroken succession of colors, rhythms and moods."[5] (At this same time, Strauss found Schoenberg's music to be incomprehensible and described it to others as the work of a man needing psychiatric care.)

In the years just before World War I, Schoenberg found that he could no longer compose works driven purely by his intense emotional energy. Between 1913 and 1922 he completed only one ten-minute work, his *Four Songs* (opus 22). With a compositional language of complete chromaticism without tonal support structures, and having exhausted the emotional expressiveness of a few years earlier, Schoenberg now had no basis from which to compose.

Finally, between 1920 and 1923, he formulated his theory of composing with twelve notes. His first composition to use a complete series of twelve notes was the fifth of his *Five Piano Pieces* (opus 23), from 1923. This was followed by the serial compositions *Serenade* (opus 24) and *Suite for Piano* (opus 25). Schoenberg was liberated to compose again. He found a new basis for composition, a new musical logic. He wrote in 1923, "I find myself positively enabled to compose as freely and fantastically as one otherwise does only in one's youth."[6]

The Series

The circle of fifths is an example of a series. Each of the twelve notes in the circle occurs once before any other is repeated.

Circle of fifths: **1, 8, 3, 10, 5, 12, 7, 2, 9, 4, 11, 6**
Series position: 1 2 3 4   5 6   7 8 9 10 11 12

A serial composition using the series of the circle of fifths would repeat the notes of the circle in order. Serialism, however, was to become the basis for *new* music languages. The circle of fifths represents the very essence of tonal music. It is, therefore, not the most appropriate series to illustrate the serial composition process. It is also not appropriate due to its simplicity—all the intervals between successive notes are of seven semitones. Such simplicity is uncharacteristic of how serial techniques were generally used.

The series from Schoenberg's opus 23, the first serial composition, is more suitable.

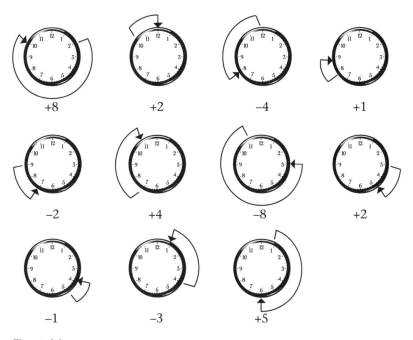

Figure 4.1
Moving on the clock's dial by the intervals of the opus 23 series.

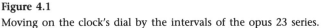

Opus 23 series: 2, 10, 12, 8, 9, 7, 11, 3, 5, 4,   1,   6
Series position: 1   2   3   4   5   6   7   8   9   10 11 12

Looking at this series, we see that the intervals are not always a fifth, +7. They are +8 (i.e., 10 – 2), then +2 (i.e., 12 – 10), then –4, +1, –2, +4, –8, +2, –1, –3, +5. (See figure 4.1.)

The particular sequence of notes that forms a given series is entirely the choice of the composer. And, as the series is a basic building block, the composer's choice of a series shapes the overall composition. In this way, the series functions somewhat like a traditional theme in music.

One can imagine that a composition where twelve notes are repeated over and over might become a little dull. However, Schoenberg's system allowed a number of transformations of the twelve notes in the series. The notes could be played forward, backward, upside-down, or backward and upside-down—the same four transformations used with themes and motifs by Machaut 600 years earlier, by Bach 200 years earlier, and by Beethoven 100 years earlier.

Furthermore, the series could be transposed to start on a different note while maintaining the same structure, that is, while maintaining the same sequence of intervals between the notes. This transformation is just like the transposition of a scale—also a technique common in music for hundreds of years.

A serial composition, then, becomes like a perpetual variation on the series. There can be up to 48 different manifestations of the series, each of the four transformations—forward, backward, upside-down, and backward and upside-down—being possible with the series beginning on any of the twelve notes. In addition, there was scope to vary rhythm, dynamics, timbre, orchestration, texture, and so on.

A new musical language was born. Nonetheless Schoenberg's ideas on music should not be seen as a total break with tradition. They are in fact an evolution following from the collapse of tonality, and his techniques of manipulation are well grounded in traditional music techniques. Given the extreme complexity of turn-of-the-century chromatic music, with musical structures in which no tonal center was actually *perceptible*, it was a logical progression to abandon keys, tonal centers, and harmonic progressions altogether. Rather than regard notes as chromatically altered in a complex scheme of relationships between fifths of fifths of fifths or whatever, it made sense to simply treat all twelve notes as of equal rank.

The Four Versions of a Series

Using Schoenberg's series, let's look at the four different versions of the series: the original (forward), backward, upside-down, and backward and upside-down.

The starting point is the original series.

Original
Opus 23 series: **2, 10, 12, 8, 9, 7, 11, 3, 5, 4, 1, 6**

This series is then subjected to a number of transformations in order to derive the other versions of the series.

From the original, it is easy to create the backward version of Schoenberg's series:

Backward

Opus 23 series: 6, 1, 4, 5, 3, 11, 7, 9, 8, 12, 10, 2

The transformation of the original to derive the upside-down version is more involved. In music, playing something "upside-down," also called inversion, is defined in terms of intervals. We can use the analogy of the watch's dial to illustrate this. If the original interval moves *forward* 8 notes on the clock, from **2** to **10**:

then the inversion moves *backward* 8 notes, from **2** to **6**:

Given a set of intervals, the process of inversion consists of changing each + to − and vice versa. The same intervals are heard in the same order, but in the other direction. Given that the intervals from the original opus 23 series are:

+8, +2, −4, +1, −2, +4, −8, +2, −1, −3, +5,

those of the inversion are:

−8, −2, +4, −1, +2, −4, +8, −2, +1, +3, −5.

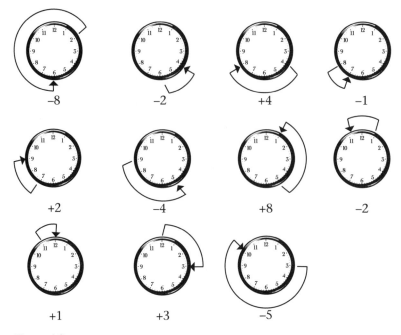

Figure 4.2
Taking the intervals of the opus 23 series and going in the other direction.

Applying the latter intervals starting from the first pitch of opus 23, we derive the inversion or upside-down version of Schoenberg's series. (See figure 4.2.)

Original
Opus 23 series: **2, 10, 12, 8, 9, 7, 11, 3, 5, 4, 1, 6**

Upside-down
Opus 23 series: **2, 6, 4, 8, 7, 9, 5, 1, 11, 12, 3, 10**

To perform the transformation of the series to backward and upside-down, we start with the backward version of the original series:

Backward
Opus 23 series: **6, 1, 4, 5, 3, 11, 7, 9, 8, 12, 10, 2**

We can see that the intervals are

−5, +3, +1, −2, +8, −4, +2, −1, +4, −2, −8.

The upside-down version of the backward version of the series inverts the intervals of the backward series, so that the intervals of the backward and upside-down series are:

+5, −3, −1, +2, −8, +4, −2, +1, −4, +2, +8.

Starting with note 6 and applying this sequence of intervals, we arrive at the backward and upside-down version of the series:

Backward upside-down
Opus 23 series: 6, 11, 8, 7, 9, 1, 5, 3, 4, 12, 2, 10

In summary, there are four versions of the Schoenberg series.

Original
Opus 23 series: 2, 10, 12, 8, 9, 7, 11, 3, 5, 4, 1, 6

Upside-down
Opus 23 series: 2, 6, 4, 8, 7, 9, 5, 1, 11, 12, 3, 10

Backward
Opus 23 series: 6, 1, 4, 5, 3, 11, 7, 9, 8, 12, 10, 2

Backward upside-down
Opus 23 series: 6, 11, 8, 7, 9, 1, 5, 3, 4, 12, 2, 10

The Late Years

Schoenberg had developed a new system for writing music that effectively rid twentieth-century European musical tradition of its tonal basis for musical structures. Yet Schoenberg's music was still deeply rooted in the structure of classical music. He combined his new system for deriving the notes of a composition with musical forms that were traditional, like canons, minuets, and so on. Themes are recognizable, the rhythmic pulse has a classical feeling. The works have shape, direction, and a sense of climax and release. The music still sounded like a part of classical tradition, and it was. Consequently, Schoenberg—the inventor of a technique that was to radically change music in the twentieth century—has been rejected by audiences tuned to the tonal traditions of the nineteenth century as too progressive and by the avant-garde of the postwar years as too conservative.

In July 1921, Schoenberg declared to a friend, announcing his discovery of a new compositional system, "Today I have discovered something which will assure the supremacy of German music for the next hundred years."[7] In 1933, he was forced to leave his teaching post at the Berlin Academy as part of the Nazi purge of Jewish elements from German culture.

His brother Heinrich was killed by injection in a Nazi hospital. His cousin Arthur died in a concentration camp. Several of his pupils met violent deaths in the Holocaust. He himself escaped and spent his last years in the United States, frequently ill and living in cultural isolation in southern California. He died in 1951.

Alban Berg's Serialism

Alban Berg began his studies with Schoenberg in 1904, at the age of 19. He has emerged as the composer of the Second Viennese School with perhaps the widest audience; among his works are the twentieth century's two greatest operas, *Wozzeck* and *Lulu*.

Berg's explorations of serialism were imbued with a passionate and emotional feel that was not unlike the music of the late romantics in spirit. As a result, his music is warmer and more humane than Schoenberg's. However, the underlying process of compositions such as *Lulu* and the *Lyric Suite* was serialism, not tonality.

Berg's first serial composition in 1925 was a setting of a poem. The series from this setting was also used in the first movement of his next work, the *Lyric Suite* for string quartet. The series is:

Lyric Suite series 1:   6, 5, 1, 10, 8, 3, 9, 2, 4, 7, 11, 12

Looking closely at the intervals of the first six and second six notes of the series, one sees that the series is *symmetrical*. The second six notes are the backward and upside-down version of the first six.

−1, +8, −3, +10, −5, +6, +5, −10, +3, −8, +1.

As a result, the backward and the backward and upside-down versions of the series are identical with the original and upside-down versions (though six notes are transposed).

The *Lyric Suite* has two other series in other movements of the quartet. These are:

Lyric Suite series 2:   **6, 1, 8, 3, 10, 5, 12, 7, 2, 9, 4, 11**
Lyric Suite series 3:   **1, 3, 5, 6, 8, 10, 7, 9, 11, 12, 2, 4**

It's also interesting to take a look at the intervals of these two series.
The intervals of the second series are:

–5, +7, –5, +7, –5, +7, –5, –5 +7, –5, +7

The second series is the circle of fifths, starting on **6**! (Keep in mind
that the intervals of –5 and +7 are effectively the same—from any
given point on the clock, whether you go forward +7 or backwards
–5 you will arrive at the same note.)
The intervals of the third series are:

+2, +2, –1, +2, +2, –3, +2, +2 +1, +2, +2

As with the first series, with both these series the backward and
backward and upside-down versions of the series are the same as the
original and upside-down versions. Upon further inspection, one no-
tices in addition that the set of the first six notes (**1, 3, 5, 6, 8, 10**)
and the set of the last six notes (**2, 4, 7, 9, 11, 12**) *of all three series*
are the same sets of notes, just ordered differently. All three series
share the same two *hexachords*, that is, the same two sets of six
notes. All of these ties form a basic web of relationships that create
the building blocks and unity of the composition.

Berg's serial works are characterized by the use of a series mixed
with nonserial passages and movements. Sometimes he would use
more than one series in a movement, which Schoenberg did not do.
And, as in the *Lyric Suite*, his series had no backward or backward and
upside-down versions.

These are characteristics of Berg's rigorous and systematic, if idio-
syncratic, manner of using serialism as the foundation for his work.
And although the formal structure may not have been based on the
rules of tonality, Berg, like Schoenberg, continually merged the two
worlds, with compositions built on series somewhat paradoxically
based on the very roots of tonality: major and minor chords, the
circle of fifths, strong tonal centers, and so on.

Even in his last work, the Violin Concerto written in 1935, Berg
uses his series in such a way that all of the instruments are playing
fifths, that very fundamental interval of tonal music. It opens with
the clarinet and harp doubling one another playing fifths:

Clarinet   —, 6, 1, 8, 8, 1, 6
Harp   11, 6, 1, 8, 8, 1, 6

The concerto continues with a solo violin, also playing fifths, alternating with the doubling clarinet and harp.

Berg died at 50 on Christmas eve, 1935, of an infection related to an insect sting.

Anton Webern's Music

The music of Anton Webern represents a totally different direction in the exploration of serialism. Webern's works were of extreme economy and concentration.

Webern also began his studies with Schoenberg in 1904 and was an enthusiastic supporter of Schoenberg's ideas. Beginning at the limits of tonality in the style of the turn of the century, Webern found intense economy a necessity given the difficulty of building larger structures without a tonal foundation. By 1910, his works were brief sequences of fleeting aphoristic gestures. His concision resulted in complete works that consisted of the statement of only a few motifs, chords, and ostinatos. He avoided repetition. Webern said, "While working I had the feeling that once the 12 notes had run out, the piece was finished.... This may sound incomprehensible, but it was immensely difficult."[8]

The results were compositions, such as his *Five Pieces for Orchestra*, in which each piece or movement lasts less than one minute. The fourth of the *Five Pieces* is the closest he came to a twelve-note composition—it had 27 notes, counting repeated attacks of the same note as a single note. (Although the first twelve notes present each note of the semitone scale once and only once, this composition is not serial.) Figure 4.3 shows the *complete* fourth movement—all 27 notes!

Two phrases pass fleetingly, the first played by the mandolin, the second by the trumpet and trombone. A single chord played by the harp accents the mandolin phrase. The viola and clarinet each play a note softly in the background while the brass "sweetly" sing the second phrase. The piece slows down as it already begins to conclude. Several different instruments each softly repeat notes, as if echoed, as the piece ends with a phrase played by the violin. Every

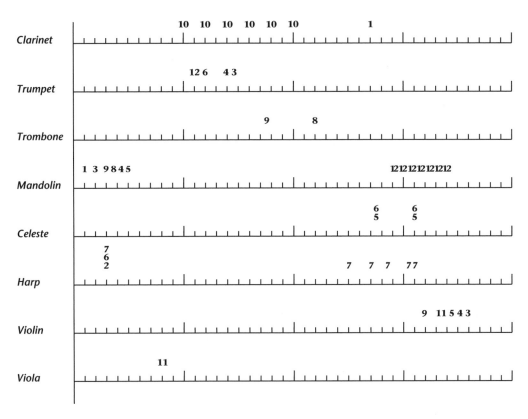

Figure 4.3
Transcription of the complete fourth movement of Webern's *Five Pieces for Orchestra*, op. 10, no. 4.

note is played softly (*p*), very softly (*pp*), or very very softly (*ppp*). There is no rhythmic pattern. The orchestration varies from phrase to phrase and even from note to note. The one-minute movement leaves a disembodied ghostly impression.

Another example of Webern's compressed compositions is found in his *Three Pieces for Piano and Cello* (opus 11) from 1914. This work lasts 2 minutes and 30 seconds. Every note on the piano uses either a different attack or a different dynamic. Every phrase of the cello uses a different type of tone production. It has a Zen-like concentration where every detail and every gesture are significant.

By 1914, Webern, like Schoenberg, found it difficult to compose without using a text as the basis for the compositional structure. For ten years, Webern composed only vocal works; only in 1924 did he return to purely instrumental music, after Schoenberg had introduced

the compositional methods of serialism. Webern's first serial composition, and first instrumental work since 1914, was the tiny *Kinder-
stück* for piano, a simple exercise in serialism with the series repeated
always in the same form.

Webern did, however, develop complicated and intricate serial
works. For example, the series in his *Concerto* (opus 24) is built from
four groups of three notes, where each group is a different version of
the original three notes.

Concerto (opus 24)
series: **12, 11, 3, 4, 8, 7, 9, 5, 6, 1, 2, 10**

Using the first three notes as the original set, a sort of miniseries,
there follow the set backward (and transposed), then backward and
upside-down, and lastly just upside-down. The intervals found between the three notes of each set show this clearly:

1st set (**12, 11, 3**):   −1, +4
2nd set (**4, 8, 7**):   +4, −1
3rd set (**9, 5, 6**):   −4, +1
4th set (**1, 2, 10**):   +1, −4

Webern's brevity and concision remained even after his total adop-
tion of serialism. (Unlike Schoenberg and Berg, he never composed a
nonserial work after 1924.) With only one early exception, he wrote
no compositions of more than five minutes. His entire oeuvre can be
heard in four hours.

Webern's works represent a new language, a new approach to music. He was not a tonal composer using serialism to create quasi-tonal
compositions. Whereas Schoenberg and Berg still fell back on their
classical and romantic roots to compose, and their music feels like
an extension of that tradition, Webern's broke with it. Schoenberg
used classical forms, such as the minuet, complete with frequent
repetition, traditional rhythmic structure, and Brahmsian orchestration. Webern's music is concentrated without repetition, without
rhythm, and without traditional orchestration.

Webern died on September 15, 1945, after being shot in error by
an American soldier just after the war. He became the hero, and his
music the departure point, for young composers looking to develop
new musical languages after World War II.

Conclusion

Tonality, rooted in the circle of fifths, was a highly formal foundation that dominated the composition process for centuries. The formal basis of tonal music was explicitly understood and extensively analyzed, discussed, and studied. Numerous treatises were written on harmony and counterpoint. One of the best known is J. S. Bach's last work, *The Art of Fugue,* written between 1749 and 1750 but never completed. In it, Bach takes a theme and plays it backward, upside-down, and backward and upside-down. He also demonstrates a number of other very formal manipulations of musical material. Studying *The Art of Fugue,* one develops a clear understanding of the abstract nature of musical structures and the almost mathematical nature of the musical techniques of harmony and counterpoint.

Serialism is also a highly formal foundation that has had a major influence on composers for much of the twentieth century. Schoenberg's techniques are formal and explicit. They can also be understood in terms of an abstract system, and the mathematical nature of the techniques of serialism should be apparent.

All music can similarly be viewed as a formal abstract system. Even music that may seem like noise or that is based on randomness and chance must have an underlying system. To the extent that music is a form of communication between composer and listener, it must have an underlying shared set of rules that makes communication possible.

With the end of the war in 1945, the banner of serialism was left to be carried by a new generation. Schoenberg was ill, living in cultural isolation in southern California. Webern was dead. Berg had died in 1935. Schoenberg, Berg, and Webern had developed the foundation for a new musical language.

5 *Kandinsky*

On January 1, 1911, Wassily Kandinsky attended a concert that included performances of Schoenberg's second string quartet and *Three Piano Pieces*. On January 18, Kandinsky wrote a letter introducing himself to Schoenberg with the explanation: "What we are striving for and our whole manner of thought and feeling have so much in common that I feel completely justified in expressing my empathy."[1] It was to be the beginning of a lifelong friendship.

Kandinsky had a striking personal vision of the place of art in society. He saw the artist's drive to express and create as a fundamentally spiritual activity. Kandinsky felt that a spiritual revolution was on the verge of emerging throughout Europe, and he envisioned artists as the leaders and prophets at the forefront of this revolution. Amid the considerable diversity of the avant-garde, he sought to bring together artists from across Europe and from all the disciplines of the arts who shared a similar vision.

In 1912, Kandinsky and Franz Marc, another painter pioneering new means of expression, published *Der Blaue Reiter Almanac*, a manifesto for their work and a forum for similarly minded artists, composers, and others. Marc wrote in it:

We believe that we stand today at the turning point of two long epochs.... There is a new religion arising in the country, still without a prophet, recognized by no one.... But the artistic style that was the inalienable possession of an earlier era collapsed catastrophically in the middle of the nineteenth century. There has been no style since.... The first works of a new era are tremendously difficult to define. Who can see clearly what their aim is and what is to come? But just the fact that they *do exist* and appear in many places today, sometimes independently of each other, and that they possess inner truth, makes us certain that they are the first signs of the coming new epoch—they are the signal fires for the pathfinders. The hour is unique. Is it too daring to call attention to the small unique signs of the time?[2]

In an article by Kandinsky, the two processes that were at the center of the artistic revolution are described.

1. Disintegration of the soulless, materialistic life of the nineteenth century, i.e. the collapse of the material supports that were considered the only solid ones and the decay and dissolution of the various parts.
2. Construction of the spiritual and intellectual life of the twentieth century that we experience and that is already manifested and embodied in strong, expressive, and distinct forms.

These two processes are the two aspects of the 'modern movement'.[3]

Like Schoenberg in music, Kandinsky was pioneering new means of expression in the visual arts. In 1910 Schoenberg had crossed a critical juncture at which his works abandoned tonality, to be driven only by direct emotional expression without the use of traditional musical structures. In 1910 Kandinsky was on the verge of a similar breakthrough in the visual arts, his paintings driven only by direct emotional expression without the traditional foundation of representational content. It was this quality of Schoenberg's music, driven by an inner world and abandoning established forms, that immediately attracted Kandinsky.

New visual languages were emerging that were nonrepresentational, that were *abstract*, and Kandinsky was the first painter to create such "abstract art."

Wassily Kandinsky

Kandinsky had already conceived his specific artistic goal and mission when he arrived in Munich in 1896. What shaped this vision were two experiences he had had while still living in Moscow.

I experienced two events which left their stamp on my whole life, and at the time shook me to the roots of my being. One was the Moscow exhibition of the French Impressionists—first and foremost Claude Monet's *Haystack*—and the other a performance of Wagner's *Lohengrin* at the Court Theatre.

Up till then I had known nothing but realist art.... And suddenly for the first time I saw a picture. The catalogue told me that it was a haystack: I couldn't tell it from looking. Not being able to tell it upset me. I also considered that the artist had no right to paint so indistinctly.

I had the dull sensation that the picture's subject was missing. And was amazed and confused to realize that the picture did not merely fascinate but impressed itself indelibly on my memory and constantly floated before my eyes, quite unexpectedly, complete in every detail....

Lohengrin, on the other hand, seemed to me to be a complete realization of this Moscow of mine.... All my colors were conjured up before my eyes. Wild, almost mad lines drew themselves before me. I did not dare to tell myself in so many words that Wagner had painted 'my hour' in music. But it was quite clear to me that painting was capable of developing powers of exactly the same order as those music possessed.[4]

Kandinsky was born in Moscow on December 4, 1866, to an aristocratic family. His father had been born in Siberia but his family had been deported to the east, to the Mongolian frontier, for failing to provide the Grand Duke with fresh horses when he was traveling in the area. His father was a successful tea merchant and his wealth enabled Kandinsky to pursue a distinguished academic career. Studying political economy and law at the University in Moscow, Kandinsky was appointed lecturer in jurisprudence in 1893, a year after graduating, and three years later was offered a professorship at the University of Dorpat in Estonia. However, having painted since his youth, Kandinsky decided at 30 to dedicate his life to painting and moved to Munich.

At the time, Munich was a mecca for talented artists. It was the center of the Jugendstil, the German school of *art nouveau*, a style that Kandinsky followed after finishing his studies in 1901. He also became preoccupied with bold stylized wood-block prints. He explored impressionism, traveled widely, and won awards including the Grand Prix in Paris in 1906.

Kandinsky spent a year in Paris between 1906 and 1907 and attended many of the early fauve exhibits. The fauves were a group in Paris—among them André Derain, Henri Matisse, Maurice de Vlaminck, and Georges Braque—whose work was characterized by the use of bright primary colors. In fact, the fauves were the first to give color primacy over all other elements of painting; their influence on Kandinsky was reflected in the liberation of color in his work.

His paintings of this time use dramatic colors and reflect the importance of color over form. In 1908, he wrote:

Houses and trees made hardly any impression on my thoughts. I used the palette knife to spread lines and splashes of paint on the canvas, and made them sing as loudly as I could. That fateful hour in Moscow rang in my ears, my eyes were filled with the strong saturated colors of the light and air of Munich, and the deep thunder of its shadows.[5]

Kandinsky's work was dominated by strong combinations of red, yellow, blue, and green. Forms were described summarily by means of planes, dots, or short strokes. Subjects lost their representational function and now were merely a framework for contrasting bold colors. The paintings became studies in the harmony of color (see *Blue Mountain*, plate 6).

One day a chance experience moved him further toward his goal:

I had just come home when I suddenly saw an indescribably beautiful picture, suffused with an inner radiance. I stood gaping at first, then I rushed up to this mysterious picture, in which I could see nothing but forms and colors, and whose subject was incomprehensible. At once I discovered the answer to the puzzle: it was one of my own pictures that was leaning against the wall on its side.... Now I knew for certain that the object harmed my paintings.[6]

With this discovery, Kandinsky moved rapidly to paintings without subjects, or where the subject was a mere pretext. Landscapes became areas of color, and the forms dissolved into structural elements without perceptible transitions. Analysis of the forms of objects contributed nothing to the understanding of the picture and was in fact distracting. Kandinsky's work was directed by his instinct, by the feeling an experience aroused in him which he tried to reproduce in a painting. And that feeling, rather than the representational subject, became the painting's "content."

From 1909 on Kandinsky painted in a nonrepresentational style. Although subjects, especially of a biblical nature, may have been part of the basis or conception of the paintings, they were not easily discernible and were not meant to be interpretable. (It has been suggested that Kandinsky at this time used a visual language in which certain shapes were in fact symbolic representations of various images: a horse and rider, a troika of three horsemen, lovers, ghosts, and so on.)

Color became purely expressive, not associated with any representational function. In his *Improvisation 7* (1910), Kandinsky's sketches show that he first created the imagery using linear forms, noting where he would use different colors. In the final painting, however, his colors are applied independently of the underlying drawing. Kandinsky separated color and drawing, treating them as two separate abstract properties with independent functions.

Kandinsky painted the first completely abstract works in 1910 (see *First Abstraction,* plate 7). He placed colors down against planes and spheres. No center of gravity was created. No representational structure supported the paintings. *With a Black Arc* (1912) is an arrangement of abstract planes overlapping and intersecting one another (see plate 8).

Concerning the Spiritual in Art

A painting, the subject matter apart, consists of line and composition, brushwork, light and color, rhythm and expression. A painting is built from the relationships between these elements that create the visual image. To the extent that visual art is a communicative system independent of its representational content, these elements have their own rules of operation and interrelation. Even in the most realistic rendering in a Dutch portrait, the essential visual expression is the line and composition, the brushwork, the light and color, and the rhythm.

Abstract art concentrates on these dimensions of painting to the exclusion of all else. There is no subject (at least, none to which an object corresponds in the material world), only relationships between the abstract elements that create the visual image. There is form and color. There is the pigment of the paint.

To better understand how Kandinsky could view painting in terms of just these elements, independent of a subject, and still feel he had a rich expressive medium, it is insightful to consider the depth of his experience of them. This is reflected, for example, in his description of color coming from a tube of paint.

Joyous, thoughtful, dreamy, self-absorbed, with deep seriousness, with bubbling roguishness, with the sigh of liberation, with the profound resonance of sorrow, with defiant power and resistance, with yielding softness and devotion, with stubborn self-control, with sensitive unstableness of balance came one after another these unique beings we call colors—each alive in and for itself, independent, endowed with all necessary qualities for further independent life and ready and willing at every moment to submit to new combinations, to mix among themselves and create endless series of new worlds.[7]

To Kandinsky, the elements of painting, the subject matter apart, offered a world of a depth that would permit endless exploration and expression. In 1911 he published a book that set out his goals for a new painting. *Concerning the Spiritual in Art* defined the principles on which much of modern art was to develop.

In the beginning of the book Kandinsky writes of the role artists must play in society. He describes them as explorers of the world of the spirit, with a mission to uncover and express inner truths. Artists pioneer new territory, and others, through their efforts, share in their discoveries and thereby also move forward in a spiritual journey. Artists through their work must "show the way to the spiritual food of the newly awakened spiritual life."[8] Although this view may seem rather elitist, the central point for Kandinsky was that the role of the artist was a *spiritual* one.

In the remainder of this book, Kandinsky discusses his radically new view of painting and the explorations of abstraction that were about to begin. Painting, as he says, "has two weapons at her disposal: color and form." Both color and form, Kandinsky insists, have direct effects on the viewer, which he describes in spiritual-psychological terms. On seeing colors,

in the first place one receives *a purely physical impression* ... but to a more sensitive soul, the effect of colors is deeper and intensely moving. And so we come to the second main result of colors: *their psychic effect.* They produce a corresponding spiritual vibration, and it is only as a step towards this spiritual vibration that the elementary physical impression is of importance.... Color is a power which directly influences the soul. Color is the keyboard, the eyes the hammer, the soul is the piano with many strings. The artist is the hand which plays, touching one key or another, to cause vibrations in the soul....

Form, in a narrow sense, is nothing but the separating line between surfaces of color. That is its outer meaning. But it has also an inner meaning, of varying intensity, and properly speaking, *form is the outward expression of this inner meaning.... So it is evident that form-harmony must rest only on the corresponding vibration of the human soul.*[9]

Form can stand alone representing an object or as a purely abstract limit to a space or surface. Color, however, cannot stand alone. It must have boundaries of some kind. When red is presented in a painting, it must have a limited surface, divided off from other colors. As a result, there is an essential connection between color and form, and these two attributes of painting have an influence on one another. "A yellow triangle, a blue circle, a green square, or a green triangle, a yellow circle, a blue square—all these are different and have different spiritual values."[10] The impact of an element in painting, therefore, consists of the impression of the color of an element, its form, and its combined color and form.

Kandinsky continues with a thorough analysis of color. He proposes "two great divisions of color ... into warm and cold, and into light and dark."[11] Kandinsky discusses the attributes of color: "Warm colors approach the spectator, cold ones retreat from him." He discusses individual colors. Yellow, "the typically earthly color," has an "aggressive character." Blue is "the typical heavenly color" and has an "active coolness." Green is "restful." Red is "warm." Vermilion "is a red with a feeling of sharpness, like glowing steel which can be cooled by water." Kandinsky derives a list of antithetical colors, opposing yellow to blue, white to black, red to green, and orange to violet. (See figure 5.1.)

What is crucial in this color analysis is that Kandinsky attributes properties to color formerly associated only with objects. Describing blue as "heavenly" does not seem terribly surprising, given our natural association of blue with the sky. Significantly, however, blue is given tangible and emotive qualities *in a completely nonrepresentational context*.

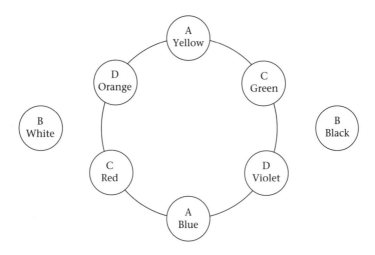

Figure 5.1
"The antitheses as a circle between two poles," after an illustration in Kandinsky's *Concerning the Spiritual in Art*, figure III, p. 43.

Lastly, Kandinsky discusses the problem of composition, the creation of the whole from its various elements:

Nothing is absolute. Form-composition rests on a relative basis, depending on (1) the alterations in the mutual relations of forms one to another, (2) alterations in each individual form, down to the very smallest. Every form is a puff of smoke, the slightest breath will alter it completely.... The adaptability of forms, their organic but inward variations, their motion in the picture, their inclination to material or abstract, their mutual relations, either individually or as parts of a whole; further the concord or discord of the various elements of a picture, the handling of groups, the combinations of veiled and openly expressed appeals, the use of rhythmical or unrhythmical, of geometrical or non-geometrical forms, their contiguity or separation—all of these things are the material for counterpoint in painting.[12]

With this new systematic approach to the elements of painting, he concluded, "we have before us the age of conscious creation." *On the Spiritual in Art* had tremendous and widespread influence on artists in the first part of the century.

The Spread of Abstract Art

Kandinsky had already organized two short-lived artists' groups before he and Franz Marc formed Der Blaue Reiter in 1911—one of the seminal groups of twentieth-century art. Der Blaue Reiter organized exhibitions not only of their own works but also of works by Arp, Braque, Kirchner, Klee, Nolde, and Picasso. In 1912 the publication of *Der Blaue Reiter Almanac,* an anthology edited by Kandinsky and Marc, became a rallying point for a new era in the arts. In this anthology folk art, primitive art, Asian and African art, and medieval woodcuts were shown alongside works by Picasso, Braque, Derain, Kandinsky, and Marc. Kandinsky and Marc heralded a new spiritual age in the arts and championed the symbiotic and integrated nature of all the arts. Articles included discussions of the arts and music in Germany, Russia, and other parts of Europe. Musical compositions by Schoenberg, Webern, and Berg were included.

Nor were these the only artists interested in the new possibilities of abstraction. In the second decade of the century, abstract painting spread throughout Europe and Russia. Painters such as Robert Delaunay, Marcel Duchamp, Francis Picabia, and Paul Klee experimented with color and abstract form. In particular, Piet Mondrian in Holland

and Kasimir Malevich in Russia developed very formal abstract styles that were precise and geometric.

In 1913, Malevich's *Black Square* created an uproar in the art community. A black square on a white ground, the impact of this painting was in its simple two-dimensional nonobjective nature. His *Eight Red Rectangles* (1915) was composed of geometric elements placed against a white ground. He developed the use of flat geometric elements, some small, some large, overlapping, with bright colors against a white background. His work evoked a strong sense of movement.

For Malevich, color and form were "the essence of painting which the subject has always killed."[13] He, on the other hand, killed the *subject* with an abstract visual language characterized by the extreme use of lines and forms and geometrical shapes.

In 1917, Mondrian began to work with colored squares and rectangles; within a year he had developed a style characterized by the asymmetrical arrangement of various-sized rectangles and the use of only the three primary colors (red, yellow, and blue) and three noncolors (black, white, and gray). This became the core of his painting for the next 25 years, as Mondrian explored the dynamic placement of the elements in relation to one another.

The Russia Years

In August 1914, with the outbreak of war, Kandinsky was given 24 hours to leave Germany. With his departure from Munich, his explorations of paintings as directly transcribed bursts of emotional energy ended. The years between 1914 and 1921, which Kandinsky spent in Russia, were not productive ones for him. During this time he painted a total of only 40 works. Kandinsky had difficulty adjusting to the Moscow art world. In Munich he had defined the avant-garde, and his opposition had perceived him to be a revolutionary. To the militant and younger avant-garde of Moscow, Kandinsky, nearing 50, seemed reactionary. New schools of thought abounded, including acmeism, to-be-ism, Scythism, neoprimitivism, all-ism, rayonism, cubo-futurism, and constructivism.

By the 1920s, two polarized perspectives on art were emerging. Kandinsky and others such as Malevich believed that abstract art had a key role in affecting the spiritual life of viewers. Another school of artists known as constructivists, led by Vladimir Tatlin, saw this as a romantic anachronism that did not address the needs of the day in the postrevolutionary Soviet Union. The constructivists championed "utilitarian functions." They proposed using "real materials in real space" with the objective of taking "the shortest path to the factory."[14] Nonfunctional abstract art such as Kandinsky's was increasingly unwelcome in the pragmatic Soviet state, and the avant-garde dispersed.

Kandinsky left Russia and returned to Germany, joining his former friend Paul Klee at the Bauhaus in Weimar. Founded by Walter Gropius in 1919, the Bauhaus was a multidisciplinary school, much as Kandinsky had imagined years earlier. It included painters, sculptors, architects, craftsmen, potters, and typographers. In this new environment, Kandinsky settled down to painting once again.

Parallels between Kandinsky and Schoenberg

Kandinsky's development and progress parallel that of Schoenberg in certain respects. Both developed their basic techniques at the turn of the century. Both made their first breakthroughs—abandoning the fundamental traditions of their arts to develop new foundations—in the decade before World War I, and both made their second breakthroughs—establishing new formal theoretical foundations for their arts—in the 1920s.

While Schoenberg discovered the world of atonal music, Kandinsky discovered the world of abstract painting. The dissolution of the object corresponds to the dissolution of tonality. With the traditional foundations of their arts abandoned, in the prewar years both created works that relied on emotional expressiveness without the aid of larger formal structures. But both men found their personal lives disrupted by the war and both found their creative output nearly ended for some years.

It was in the early 1920s that Schoenberg made his second breakthrough in his development as a composer with his new technique of "composing with twelve notes related only to one another." His first composition using the twelve-tone technique was completed in 1923. With a new formal foundation, Schoenberg again began to compose productively. No longer writing music driven purely by his intense energy, Schoenberg had developed a formal, almost mathematical system as his new method of composition.

It was also in the years following the war that Kandinsky developed a new formal theoretical foundation for painting that became the basis for a new and extremely productive period for him. He painted three works in 1922, 19 in 1923, and 24 in 1924. In addition he made a large number of drawings and watercolors. In 1925, he produced 40 paintings, returning to his productivity of the Munich years.

Kandinsky developed a formal pictorial language based on geometric forms. His work became more precise. Elements in his paintings had crisper outlines. His paintings were now based almost exclusively on pure forms such as circles, half-moons, crescents, intersecting lines, and other geometric shapes. At the same time he restricted himself to the use of primary colors. All of this was a distinct contrast from the freer and more directly expressive approach of his earlier works.

At the heart of this new direction were his theories of pure form documented in *Point and Line to Plane*, published in 1926 as part of the Bauhaus collection, in which he codified his rules of composition for the visual arts.

Kandinsky's "Point and Line to Plane"

If Kandinsky's *On the Spiritual in Art* was his definitive exploration of color, *Point and Line to Plane* was his definitive exploration of form and composition, which were only superficially addressed in the earlier book. A similar shift of emphasis is evident in his painting from the prewar to the postwar years.

Kandinsky defined the point as "the smallest elementary form or the proto-element of painting."[15] He explored the implications of this definition—at a certain size, a point becomes a plane. And he discussed the possibilities of different kinds of points, each with its own sound or spiritual vibration.

The line, created by movement, is the antithesis of the point. It represents movement, in contrast to the "self-contained repose of the point."[16] A line can be characterized by the tension and the

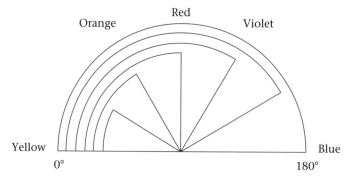

Red

Orange   Violet

Yellow   Blue

0°   180°

Figure 5.2

"System of typical angles—colors," after an illustration in Kandinsky's *Point and Line to Plane*, figure 28, p. 73.

direction of the force by which it is created. There are different kinds of straight lines, each with different temperatures. Vertical lines are warm, horizontal lines are cold, diagonal lines tend to one or the other depending on their position. From straight lines one can create angular lines. Like different kinds of lines, different angles have different temperatures. Red, being the midpoint between yellow and blue, correlates with the right angle. Acute angles tend to yellow and obtuse angles to blue. (See figure 5.2.) Furthermore, a geometric right-angled object—a square—is red. A triangle, yellow. A circle, blue. (See figure 5.3.)

Kandinsky went on to discuss complex angular lines, curved lines, and wavelike lines. He considered the effects of emphasis and direction. And he briefly touched on "the different ways of using several lines and the nature of their reciprocal effect, the subordination of individual lines to a group of lines or to a *complex of lines*."[17] (See figure 5.4.) Kandinsky discussed lines that are found in other arts—music, architecture, dance, and poetry—and in nature: trees, crystals, leaves, plants, the ligament tissue of rats, and lightning. He discussed planes and their different types.

Ultimately, Kandinsky discussed the process of composition using all of these elements. By positioning the various elements, the artist can achieve different effects. A horizontal format tends toward cold, a vertical toward warmth. Where the eye is led upward, the effect is "free and light," downward is heavy and dense, leftward adventurous, to the right reassuring. The effect of elements in a composition

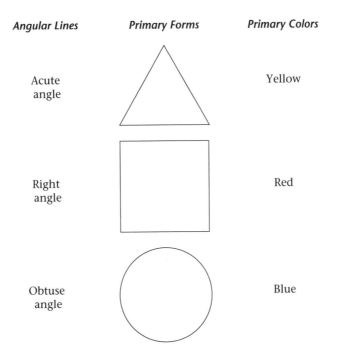

Angular Lines	Primary Forms	Primary Colors
Acute angle		Yellow
Right angle		Red
Obtuse angle		Blue

Figure 5.3
"Acute angle, right angle, obtuse angle," after an illustration in Kandinsky's *Point and Line to Plane*, figures 30–32, p. 74.

varies depending on their position. They may be calmer or tenser, lighter or heavier, depending on whether they are positioned at the top or bottom or left or right.

Kandinsky's geometric style pervaded his work during the 1920s, when he taught at the Bauhaus. (See plates 9–12.) This style was first seen in *Circles on Black* (1921). Another example, considered by Kandinsky to be his most important postwar painting, was *Composition VIII* (1923). In these works he used the circle as he had previously used the horse. For Kandinsky, "the contact of the acute angle of a triangle with a circle is no less powerful in its effect than that of the finger of God with the finger of Adam in Michelangelo's painting."[18]

Kandinsky and Schoenberg Diverge

Schoenberg established an explicit foundation for a new musical language. Kandinsky set out to establish an explicit foundation for new visual languages. It was their common vision in their respective arts

Figure 5.4
"Some simple examples of rhythm" and "Repetition," from Kandinsky's *Point and Line to Plane*, figures 50–58 and 59–61, pp. 94–95.

that was at the core of their friendship in the years before the war. Kandinsky was completely isolated in Russia between 1914 and 1921 and had no communications with Schoenberg during this period. It was not until 1922, after his return to Berlin, that they renewed their correspondence.

Kandinsky's and Schoenberg's backgrounds were radically different. Kandinsky was of aristocratic descent, well educated and well traveled, while Schoenberg was of a poor working class Jewish family. That they should become close friends is testimony to their shared ideas. However, these differences ultimately undermined their relationship. In 1923, Schoenberg reacted strongly to indications that Kandinsky was anti-Semitic. In the correspondence that followed, Kandinsky, hoping to have Schoenberg join him at the Bauhaus, explained that though "I reject you as a Jew ... I assure you that I would be so glad to have *you* here in order to work *together!*"[19]

Schoenberg had begun to reembrace Judaism, at least partly in response to the growing anti-Semitism in Germany. He explained in his letter responding to Kandinsky that "when I walk along the street and each person looks at me to see whether I'm a Jew or a Christian, I can't very well tell each of them that I'm the one that Kandinsky and some others make an exception of, although of course that man Hitler is not of their opinion."

Ironically, Kandinsky would also be the victim of Nazi oppression. Perceived as a home to anarchists and revolutionaries, the Bauhaus was persecuted and evenutally forced to close permanently. In 1933 Kandinsky left for France, settling at Neuilly and remaining there for the rest of his life. These years marked a third distinctive period in his creative thinking. His paintings were of imagined worlds filled with fantastic and dreamlike creatures, animal shapes, amoebas, and flying figures. Having taken the concrete world to the abstract, in this last period Kandinsky took the abstract world and made it concrete. (See, for example, his *Sky Blue*, plate 13.)

Kandinsky died on December 13, 1944.

Conclusion

For Kandinsky, the process of visual composition involved establishing a complete and coherent system of visual elements in dynamic relationships, with no element treated in isolation. Given that each element has its own "inner nature" and "force," to Kandinsky "a composition is nothing other than an *exact law-abiding organization* of the vital *forces* which ... are shut up within the elements."[20]

Kandinsky's ultimate aim was to define a grammar for a language of visual harmonies and dissonances. While still believing in emotional expressiveness, he acknowledged the necessity of conscious control. He wanted to uncover the universal laws that applied to visual languages:

The progress won through systematic work will create an elementary dictionary which, in its further development, will lead to a "grammar" and, finally, to a theory of composition which will pass beyond the boundaries of the individual art expressions and become applicable to "Art" as a whole.[21]

Kandinsky recognized the abstract nature of music and consciously sought to develop a similar foundation for the visual arts. Just as music can be seen as an abstract system relating elements realized in sound, Kandinsky saw the visual arts as an abstract system relating elements realized in visual form.

Music seen as an abstract language, however, had a tradition that went back centuries. In music, the essential elements, notes, were clear. There was extensive theory that considered musical structures in terms of the relationships between sounds in temporal sequences. The visual arts had not been thought of in such atomistic terms. Kandinsky had to define the basic elements for visual languages, which he defined as colors, points, lines, and planes. And he had to define ways of thinking about the structures built out of these elements.

Not only the first abstract painter, Kandinsky was also the first to conceive of a visual language in abstract terms. Kandinsky was a visionary; his vision was of an explicit grammar for a visual language.

blue
1

green
2

orange
3

red
4

yellow
5

black
6

azure
7

gray
8

purple
9

pink
10

white
11

brown
12

Plate 1
Twelve colors, labeled and numbered.

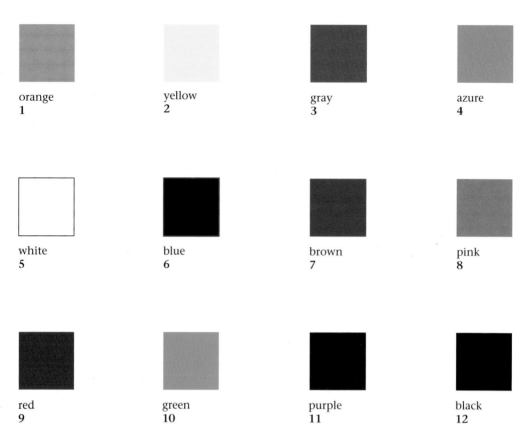

orange
1

yellow
2

gray
3

azure
4

white
5

blue
6

brown
7

pink
8

red
9

green
10

purple
11

black
12

Plate 2
Twelve colors, reordered, labeled, and numbered.

nila
1

harita
2

kasaya
3

rakta
4

pita
5

kala
6

nilakasavarna
7

pamsuvarna
8

dhumra
9

patala
10

sukla
11

kapisa
12

Plate 3
Twelve colors, twelve Sanskrit labels, and twelve numbers.

nila
blue
1

harita
green
2

kasaya
orange
3

rakta
red
4

pita
yellow
5

kala
black
6

nilakasavarna
azure
7

pamsuvarna
gray
8

dhumra
purple
9

patala
pink
10

sukla
white
11

kapisa
brown
12

Plate 4
Twelve colors, twelve Sanskrit labels with the Sanskrit translated into English, and twelve numbers.

nila
blue
6

harita
green
10

kasaya
orange
1

rakta
red
9

pita
yellow
2

kala
black
12

nilakasavarna
azure
4

pamsuvarna
gray
3

dhumra
purple
11

patala
pink
8

sukla
white
5

kapisa
brown
7

Plate 5
Twelve colors, labeled in Sanskrit and English and numbered.

Plate 6
Wassily Kandinsky, *Blue Mountain* (1908–1909). Solomon R. Guggenheim Museum, New York, gift of Solomon R. Guggenheim, 1941. Photo: David Heald, copyright The Solomon R. Guggenheim Foundation, New York.

Plate 7
Wassily Kandinsky, *Untitled–First Abstraction* (1910). Musée National d'Art Moderne, Centre Georges Pompidou, Paris, bequest of Nina Kandinsky. Copyright Centre Georges Pompidou.

Plate 8
Wassily Kandinsky, *With a Black Arc* (1912). Musée National d'Art Moderne, Centre Georges Pompidou, Paris, bequest of Nina Kandinsky. Copyright Centre Georges Pompidou.

Plate 9
Wassily Kandinsky, *Circles on Black* (1921). Solomon R. Guggenheim Museum, New York. Photo: David Heald, copyright The Solomon R. Guggenheim Foundation, New York.

Plate 10
Wassily Kandinsky, *Dream Motion* (1923). Solomon R. Guggenheim Museum, New York, gift of Solomon R. Guggenheim, 1938. Photo: David Heald, copyright The Solomon R. Guggenheim Foundation, New York.

Plate 11
Wassily Kandinsky, *Composition VIII* (1923). Solomon R. Guggenheim Museum,
New York, gift of Solomon R. Guggenheim, 1937. Photo: David Heald, copyright
The Solomon R. Guggenheim Foundation, New York.

Plate 12

Wassily Kandinsky, *Yellow-Red-Blue* (1925). Musée National d'Art Moderne, Centre Georges Pompidou, Paris, bequest of Nina Kandinsky. Photo: Philippe Migeat, copyright Centre Georges Pompidou.

Plate 13

Wassily Kandinsky, *Sky Blue* (1940). Musée National d'Art Moderne, Centre Georges Pompidou, Paris, bequest of Nina Kandinsky. Copyright Centre Georges Pompidou.

Plate 14
Harold Cohen, *Herb with Wall Hanging* (1992). A drawing created by AARON and colored by Harold Cohen. Photo: Becky Cohen.

Plate 15

Harold Cohen, *Stephanie and Friend* (1993). AARON created and colored a drawing displayed on a computer screen, which Cohen used as a color sketch for this painting. Photo: Becky Cohen.

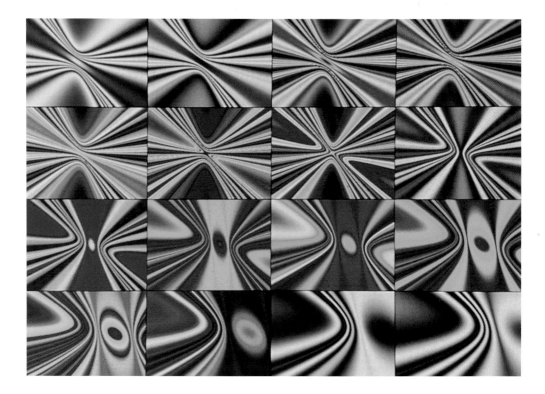

Plate 16
Domains from Brian Evans's *Color Study #7* that illustrate form and color transitions over time.

6   *Postwar Serialism*

Serialism dominated European musical thinking in the years following World War II. In the aftermath of the war, many young composers wanted a new beginning. Serialism was seen as "pure" and rigorous. Banned by the Nazis, its acceptance was also a repudiation of the Nazis. Serialism was to be the foundation for their search for a new music language. A young Frenchman, Pierre Boulez, was the leader of this search.

Schoenberg was not a rebellious youth at the time he invented serial composition. However, in 1945, when Pierre Boulez heard serial music for the first time, he was rejecting much of his cultural heritage. He had abandoned Catholicism and attended meetings of the Communist Party. He mocked the grand music of the past with distorted performances on the piano.

Boulez led a group of Paris Conservatory students in booing the French premiere of two works by Igor Stravinsky. Stravinsky's work, branded by the Germans as decadent, was celebrated in postoccupation Paris, but to Boulez it represented neoclassicism rooted in the music of the past. Boulez proclaimed that the musical life of the past would not return, that neoclassicism was dead, and that he would search for a new language.

Serialism was to be at the core of this new language. For Boulez, the experience of hearing serial music for the first time was "a revelation."

Here was a music of our time, a language with unlimited possibilities. No other language was possible. It was the most radical revolution since Monteverdi, for all the familiar patterns were now abolished. With it, music moved out of the world of Newton and into the world of Einstein. The tonal idea was based on a universe defined by gravity and attraction. The serial idea is based on a universe that finds itself in perpetual expansion.[1]

Pierre Boulez

Boulez had studied with Olivier Messiaen at the Paris Conservatory in 1944. Messiaen, a very influential French composer, approached composition from a nontraditional orientation. He wrote music based on medieval modes and Gregorian melodies rather than traditional tonal harmony; he was a specialist in Asiatic rhythms; and he was fascinated by exotic bird songs and based complete compositions on his transcriptions of them. In the extremely conservative world of the Paris Conservatory, he was a maverick whose classes provided a forum for experimentation and exploration. Although Boulez would later deny it, Messiaen was the first major influence on him as a composer.

It was only a year later that Boulez discovered the German serialist composers and experienced his "revelation." Among these composers, he quickly rejected Schoenberg and embraced Webern. "I had discovered elaborate rhythms through both Messiaen and Stravinsky. Webern thought primarily in terms of pitches. The two things had to be unified." Boulez had committed himself to formulate a new theoretical system that would serve composers in the future as tonality had served them in the past. He resolved "to strip music of its accumulated dirt and give it the structure it had lacked since the Renaissance."[2] He made serialism the basis for his new musical language.

Boulez composed his first serial composition in 1946, his Piano Sonata no 1. Two years later, he completed his Piano Sonata no. 2, a virtuosic tour de force that had a tremendous influence on other young postwar composers. Traditional melody disappeared. There were no themes. Any trace of traditional harmony was eliminated. The piano was used as a percussive instrument; performance directions indicated were "savage," "brutal," and "violent." With the music anchored in a strict serial system ordering the pitches, Boulez turned to rhythm to create a sense of wild delirium.

With serialism and violent rhythm as his tools, Boulez developed a new language that could be used to crush the life out of romanticism and the music of Schoenberg. Boulez rapidly established a preeminent position among the young avant-garde with his piano sonatas, the vocal work *Le Visage nuptial* based on a passionate text by René Char, and the *Sonatine* for flute and piano. He also sat at the center of a web of important personal alliances.

In 1949, the American composer John Cage visited Paris and became a friend of Boulez. Cage was a student of Schoenberg during his last years in California. While a student of Zen Buddhism in D. T. Suzuki's class at Columbia University, Cage wrote *Sonatas and Interludes for Prepared Piano*. This work used a piano prepared with nails, paper, and other items fixed to the strings to create a variety of percussive sounds and timbres not previously associated with the piano. Both Boulez and Cage used the piano as a new percussive instrument and explored rhythm at the expense of harmony. When Cage returned to the United States later that year he enthusiastically promoted Boulez's music.

Boulez met a young Belgian composer, Henri Pousseur, in 1951. Pousseur showed Boulez a work for three pianos, for which Boulez proposed changes that Pousseur later incorporated. Boulez shared his works with Pousseur and, by Pousseur's account, helped him "to understand that Webern was not an end but a beginning."[3]

In January 1952, Boulez made a strong impression on a young German, Karlheinz Stockhausen, who had come to Paris to study at the Conservatory. Boulez was also impressed by Stockhausen. Stockhausen showed him his first serial composition, *Kontra-Punkte*; here too Boulez suggested a number of changes that Stockhausen incorporated. Boulez said, "We talked about music all the time—in a way I've never talked about it with anyone else."[4] When Stockhausen returned to Germany in 1953, he established an avant-garde music movement in Cologne. Stockhausen, Pousseur, and many others followed Boulez in embracing serialism and Webern as the basis for a new music.

Foundations for a New Music

Schoenberg's original theory was for a "method of composing with twelve tones which are related only with one another." Its focus was on the twelve *tones*. Although the notes of Schoenberg's compositions were derived from the series, he used classical forms for compositional structures, and his melodic structures, rhythmic structures, dynamics, phrasing, and orchestration were also traditional. Serialism for Schoenberg was a way of organizing notes.

In Webern's work, however, the postwar composers saw the potential to apply serial techniques to control elements other than pitch (even though Webern himself did not actually do so). Webern's compressed technique had led him to craft every note; often, each note had a different duration, a different dynamic, and a different attack. Though his techniques were directly influenced by the contrapuntal techniques of Renaissance composers, to the postwar composers his music seemed a total break with the forms of the past.[5]

Messiaen was the first actually to apply quasi-serial techniques to much more than just the notes, in particular to the organization of durations, dynamics, and modes of attack. The pitch structures of his compositions, however, were based on modes and other techniques that owed more to the composers of the Renaissance than to Schoenberg.

Messiaen's *Quatuor pour la Fin de Temps* demonstrates the formal dissociation of rhythm and harmony. It was composed in 1940–1941 under somewhat unusual circumstances. Captured by the Germans in 1940, Messiaen was a prisoner of war in a camp in Görlitz, Germany. At the camp there were a clarinetist, a violinist, and a cellist. The clarinetist and the violinist had their instruments; the cellist was given a cello, lacking one string, by the Germans. The work was written for these instruments and piano. A piano, an out-of-tune upright with many malfunctioning keys, was made available by the Germans for the work's first performance, given in the prison camp on January 15, 1941, in front of an audience of 5,000. Messiaen said of the performance, "Never have I been listened to with such attention and understanding."[6]

What is particularly interesting in the *Quatuor* is the formal process Messiaen used to compose the piano part in the first movement. The piano part, with the cello, creates a sustained rhythmic foundation over which the clarinet and violin perform solo phrases that are derived from birdsong. The piano part consists of two completely independent elements: a progression of 29 chords that is repeated over and over, and a rhythmic pattern of a series of 17 durations that is also repeated over and over. As the lengths of the two progressions are different, the chord progression and harmony are completely dissociated from the rhythmic pattern. The result is a piano accompaniment that seems to drift. The structural relationship between the chord progression and rhythmic pattern is illustrated in figure 6.1. Although it does not use Schoenberg's particular technique of twelve-note serialism, the movement is similarly built on a technique of mathematically rigorous repetition. What is striking is that the formal compositional process was applied to *both tones and durations.*

In 1949, in a work entitled *Mode de valeurs et d'intensité*, Messiaen extended such formal processes to the dynamics (i.e., loudness) of the notes and to their timbre. Again, his technique is effectively the same as applying serial processes. A melodic series of 36 notes repeats over and over, as do a series of 24 durations, a series of seven attacks, and an additional series of dynamics. *For the first time, formal techniques were applied to determine the structuring of all of the key musical elements.*

The 36 notes of the pitch series were organized into three groups of twelve notes, in each of which the twelve pitches occurs once. Following is group 1.

4, 3, 10, 9, 8, 7, 5, 2, 1, 11, 6, 12

Each group of notes was then assigned a series of durations. The duration series for the first group, given a duration of time called *d*, was:

1d 2d 3d 4d 5d 6d 7d 8d 9d 10d 11d 12d

(Thus each duration in the series is longer than the preceding one by the time *d*.)

The second and third duration series are the same except that the starting value of *d* was twice as long for the second series and four times as long for the third series. In total, 24 different durations were

Chords	1	2	3	4	5	6	7	8	9	10	11	12	13	14	15	16	17	18	19	20
Duration	1	2	3	4	5	6	7	8	9	10	11	12	13	14	15	16	17	1	2	3
Position	1	2	3	4	5	6	7	8	9	10	11	12	13	14	15	16	17	18	19	20

Chords	21	22	23	24	25	26	27	28	29	1	2	3	4	5	6	7	8	9	10	11
Duration	4	5	6	7	8	9	10	11	12	13	14	15	16	17	1	2	3	4	5	6
Position	21	22	23	24	25	26	27	28	29	30	31	32	33	34	35	36	37	38	39	40

Chords	12	13	14	15	16	17	18	19	20	21	22	23	24	25	25	26	27	28	29	1
Duration	7	8	9	10	11	12	13	14	15	16	17	1	2	3	4	5	6	7	8	9
Position	41	42	43	44	45	46	47	48	49	50	51	52	53	54	55	56	57	58	59	60

Chords	2	3	4	5	6	7	8	9	10	11	12	13	14	15	16	17	18	19	20	21
Duration	10	11	12	13	14	15	16	17	1	2	3	4	5	6	7	8	9	10	11	12
Position	61	62	63	64	65	66	67	68	69	70	71	72	73	74	75	76	77	78	79	80

Figure 6.1
Messiaen's chord sequence and duration sequence in the piano part for the first movement of his *Quatuor pour la Fin de Temps*.

organized in the three series. (The first six durations of the second series are found in the first series, and the first six durations of the third series are found in the first and second series.)

There was a series of 7 dynamics, from very very soft to very very loud:

ppp pp p mf f ff fff

Lastly, there was a series of twelve different modes of attack.

Influenced by their teacher, Messiaen, and by the potential they saw in Webern's work, the postwar composers extended the concept of the series and serial manipulation to all of the elements of music.

Serial techniques were used to organize note durations. Different durations were ordered, numbered as members of a series, and then assigned to notes in forward or backward order. Transformations were applied to the durations, lengthening or shortening them. The techniques of serialism were also applied to the dynamics of notes (from *ppp* to *fff*), as these were ordered as members of a series, and to modes of attack.

When Schoenberg died in California in 1951, Boulez wrote an article entitled "Schoenberg Is Dead!" It was an epitaph to Schoenberg in which Webern was crowned as the true creator of a new language.

Boulez's "Structures"

In 1952, Boulez wrote *Structures*, the definitive model of serialism in its most complete application. Boulez planned the work to be like *The Art of Fugue*—Bach's didactic masterpiece on the techniques of counterpoint—for the serial language. Scored for two pianos, the work became a milestone in postwar music.

Boulez used the same pitch series as Messiaen had used in his *Mode de valeurs et d'intensité,* a recognition that he had been strongly influenced by his former teacher. Messiaen's series also gave him an impersonal basis for his composition. "What I was after was the most impersonal material. Personality had to be involved, of course, in bringing the mechanism into action, but then it could disappear after that."[7]

Once Boulez had defined the rules, the "mechanism" could run its own course. The process of composition was effectively automated.

Define the series that control each musical element. Define how these series and controls interact. And then, let the process follow its course.

In *Structures*, Boulez defined a very intricate process. There is perpetual transformation. No pitch ever recurs with the same duration, the same dynamic, or the same attack.

The pitch series is:

4, 3, 10, 9, 8, 7, 5, 2, 1, 11, 6, 12

The duration series, given a duration of time called *d*, is:

1d 2d 3d 4d 5d 6d 7d 8d 9d 10d 11d 12d

Boulez defined twelve very fine gradations of dynamic, from very very very soft to very very very loud:

pppp ppp pp p quasi-p mp mf quasi-f f ff fff ffff

Boulez also defined twelve different modes of attack, representing different ways of performing a note on the piano. These included *legato*, a smooth playing where one note is held until the next one is hit, and various degrees of shortened playing such as *staccato* (where the note is shortened by about $\frac{1}{2}$), *mezzo staccato* (where the note is shortened by about $\frac{1}{4}$), and *staccatissimo* (where the note is shortened by about $\frac{3}{4}$). Other attacks indicated different degrees of accentuation when hitting the note, such as *sforzando* for a very forceful attack and *mezzo forte* for a somewhat forceful attack. Boulez derived orderings for the dynamics and for the modes of attack using tables developed from the series.

Boulez then defined a set of processes that determined the overall structure of the composition, ordering the different series for notes, durations, dynamics, and attacks. He defined the first piano part as the progression of four versions of the note series: the original series followed by the backward, the backward a second time, and then the backward and upside-down. The second piano part's progression is the upside-down series followed by the backward and upside-down, the backward and upside-down a second time, and then the backward. Each note series is assigned one dynamic for the complete series, following a dynamic series. So, in the first piano, the first series is all very very very loud, *ffff*, and the next *mf*. In the second piano, the first series is somewhat soft, *quasi-p*, the next very very soft, *ppp*. Modes of attack were assigned in the same way; one mode of attack was applied to the first series, another to the second, and so on, in an order determined by the series of the modes of attack. Every pitch, every dynamic, every duration, and every mode of attack for every note is determined by a defined process.

Boulez wrote the following about Messiaen, but it might also have been about himself:

He wants discipline, a discipline that transcends his own personality and refers only to itself, implying its own justification by means of a numerical order that has to be obeyed. He wants as it were to decipher in his own way the secrets of the universe, just as a scientist can transcribe natural laws in numerical terms. In this way a composition strictly observing numerical laws would reflect a transcendent order in which personal desires have no place and are annulled by explicit laws that override any individual purpose. 8

Stockhausen, Leader of the Avant-Garde

By the time Boulez completed *Structures*, he was convinced that serialism was the only basis for the new music language: serialism as the control of pitch, durations, attacks, dynamics, everything. To Boulez, anyone who did not feel this necessity was missing the point and was a composer without consequence. "Everything he writes will fall short of the imperatives of his time."9

Cage, however, had taken another path. He too was looking for ways to take personality out of the composing process, but he was exploring the use of chance, randomness, using the *I Ching* and other techniques influenced by Asian thought. Cage tossed a coin as part of the composition process. Cage wrote a composition, *Imaginary Landscapes*, for twelve radios and 24 performers—one to hold each radio, one to tune it. This composition represented an almost complete loss of control, given that it is impossible to predict what will be broadcast during a performance at some future time and location. Cage wrote *4:33*—the duration a pianist sits at the piano without touching the keyboard. In this piece, reflecting Zen influence, the music is the sound of the environment—random and arbitrary sounds—during that particular moment in time. To Boulez, the very thought of chance, of not controlling every element in the greatest detail, was abhorrent. Boulez broke his relationship with Cage and they had virtually no contact thereafter. (Cage died in 1992.)

More significantly, Stockhausen soon went his own way. In the early 1950s, Boulez and Stockhausen were the leaders of serialism in Europe. After returning to Germany from Paris, Stockhausen worked at the West German Radio (WDR) and began composing electronic compositions. Using sine wave generators, he applied serial techniques to build up the structures of the individual sounds themselves. Serial techniques were also used to organize these sounds into a composition; the composition was unified from the lowest level of the sounds themselves to the highest level of the complete sound structure.

Like Boulez, Stockhausen aimed to dismantle the conventions of rhythm and meter just as they had undone classical tonality. His *Zeitmasse* was composed using a new technique, "discontinuous time." Tempos were controlled by the limits of a player's breath or the player's ability to articulate rapidly. Boulez and Stockhausen had discussed breaking from strict meter, but while Boulez was considering the idea, Stockhausen wrote a ground-breaking work.

Stockhausen then developed the idea of "controlled chance." In *Klavierstück XI*, there are 19 groups of notes, sections of music, each ending with instructions on how to perform the next group—fast, slow, loud, soft. The performer randomly moves from one group to the next following the performance instructions at the end of each sequence, combining chance and control. (Boulez, in the composition *Le Livre* that he based on Mallarmé, also began to explore the random ordering of segments. However, he explained this as a natural evolution of *his* music.)

Stockhausen produced the first major electronic work in the avant-garde world, *Gesang der Jünglinge*. After *Zeitmasse* and *Klavierstück XI*, he then wrote the massive orchestral work *Gruppen*, where three orchestras surround the audience, each playing at different speeds. By 1958, he was established as the innovator and the leader of the postwar composers.

Boulez, on the other hand, wrote few new works and began to pursue conducting instead. Boulez said, "I came to trust Stockhausen's music more than anything else. I felt he could solve all the problems, that it was no longer necessary for me to address myself to them."[10] The relationship between Boulez and others in avant-garde music circles became more and more strained. Abusive words were exchanged in meetings and in published essays. Boulez gradually withdrew from the leadership of the European avant-garde.

He began to conduct regularly with the BBC Symphony in London, the New York Philharmonic, and the Cleveland Orchestra. In 1977, after eight years as music director of the New York Philharmonic, Boulez became the director of a new music research institute in Paris, IRCAM, the Institute of Research and Coordination in Acoustics and Music, where his task was to lead research aimed at applying technology and computers to open the next frontiers in music. He retired from IRCAM in 1992 to focus again on composing.

Conclusion

Schoenberg thought of his serial method as one for organizing notes. Even Webern, though more important for the postwar serialists, applied serial techniques only to the organization of notes. Messiaen was the first to apply very formal techniques not only to durations but, with *Mode de valeurs et d'intensité*, to dynamics and attacks. Boulez, following the path established by Messiaen, controlled all aspects of the composition in his *Structures* with serial techniques.

The postwar serialist composers created music languages in which every element influencing the content of a musical expression was controlled by explicit and formal rules: pitch, duration, attack, dynamic. To the extent that any attribute was considered important in music, these composers wanted to make explicit the rules governing its organization. They organized the macrostructure of the composition. They organized even the microstructural components of a sound built out of sine waves.

The significance of their vision was in the comprehensive nature of it: formal and explicit rules were used to organize every element at every level of a complex hierarchical system. Their music was totally abstract.

7 Chomsky

In 1957, a young American linguist published a book that was to be as significant to the future of linguistics as had been the discovery of Sanskrit or the publication of Saussure's *Course in General Linguistics*. Noam Chomsky, working at MIT, proposed ideas in *Syntactic Structures* that radically changed how linguists view language.

Pāṇini created the first grammar. His grammar not only described the Sanskrit language but also defined rules that could be used to *generate* words in Sanskrit. Like Pāṇini's grammar from 2,500 years earlier, at the heart of Chomsky's new approach were new types of grammars whose rules could be used not only to describe a language but also to generate sentences in a language. He called these *generative grammars*.

Given that not only language but also music, the visual arts, and all other vehicles of expression can be thought of as abstract systems, Chomsky's work on language can be extended to provide a framework for describing these vehicles of expression.

Early Twentieth-Century Linguistics

The focus of European linguistics in the nineteenth century, following the discovery of Sanskrit, was principally historical. Linguists searched for similarities between the different Indo-European languages to better understand how each language, thought to be originally from the same source, had developed in a different manner over the centuries. They aimed to uncover links between different languages and how languages had influenced one another.

In the first half of the twentieth century, influenced by Saussure, linguistics shifted from a primarily historical perspective, interested in how languages had evolved over time, to a *synchronic* perspective, interested in the structures that enabled a given language to function *at a given time*. The goal of linguists was to analyze the structure of language.

At the beginning of the twentieth century, the primacy of science led scholars in other disciplines to seek the same rigor in their disciplines. Leonard Bloomfield, a prominent American linguist, proposed that the study of language structure should be rigorous and "scientific." To Bloomfield, this meant a process that begins with data collected through experience and observation. "Science shall deal only with events that are accessible in their time and place to any and all observers."[1] This empirical approach was the accepted norm in all disciplines of the "hard" sciences, such as physics, chemistry, and biology. It was rooted in philosophical traditions that dated to the seventeenth and eighteenth centuries with Francis Bacon, John Locke, George Berkeley, and David Hume.

Bloomfield was also influenced by behaviorism, a scientific school of thought that proposed that the behavior of any organism, from amoeba to human, could be described in terms of the organism's response to stimuli in its environment. He believed that language was a type of behavior and that what linguists aimed to do was document the manifestations and forms of this behavior.

As a result, Bloomfield and his followers described sentences, seen as manifestations of language behavior, in great detail. They analyzed expressions of spoken or written language—publicly observable phenomena. And they focused on developing disciplined ways of studying language.

In the tradition of Saussure, their goal was to establish a set of "elements, and the statement and distribution of these elements relative to each other."[2] Sentence structure was viewed in terms of what is known as *constituent analysis*, an approach that describes how sentences are constructed by breaking them down into their component parts, each with defined roles in the language: nouns, verbs, adjectives, subjects and predicates, compound structures, prepositional phrases, appositives, subordinate clauses, connectives, and so on. The words were then linked together in trees representing relation-

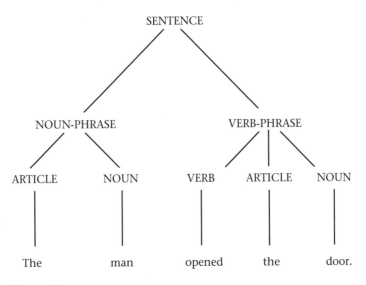

Figure 7.1
Example of a "tree" representation of the structure of a sentence.

ships between these constituent parts in structures of increasing size and complexity.

This approach to linguistics was based on observation and description. It made no attempt to provide an explanatory theory for the behavior or for the intellectual mechanisms that enabled such behavior. Bloomfield was an empiricist.

The Creativity of Human Language

In contrast to this tradition, Chomsky was a rationalist, building a theory on ideas produced by inductive rational thinking. Rather than focus on the externally visible manifestations of language—actual observable expressions—his interest was in what it is inside the mind that makes language possible, what enables the mind to create and interpret an infinite variety of expressions.

Chomsky's stress was on the creativity of human language: the ability speakers of a language possess to create and understand expressions that have never been created or heard before, a theoretically infinite variety of sentences. He wanted to understand how children could learn a complex and rich system of rules from exposure to only a limited body of examples, and within just a few years.

Chomsky aimed to describe the "living" capability by which speakers of a language produce and understand sentences. And he felt that any theory of grammar had to reflect this creative faculty, lest it fail to address the essential nature of language.

In this view, English, like other languages, consists of an infinite number of expressions, only a small fraction of which will ever be spoken. Though a grammatical description may be supported or validated by a finite set of examples, these are only a small sample of all the sentences that may be spoken in the language. Chomsky was interested not in describing the structure of a particular given sentence, but rather in describing the overall processes by which *all* sentences could be described. For him, therefore, a grammar should create or *generate* all the sentences of the language and should not distinguish between existing expressions and potential expressions of the language. This property reflects the creative aspect of language. Chomsky's approach to grammar is both analytic, permitting the understanding of given expressions, and creative, to the extent that it can be used to create new expressions.

Although a language's set of sentences is infinite, it is not unconstrained. Language is a rule-governed behavior, constrained within limits set by the rules of a grammar. To Chomsky, grammars are the *rules* that define how expressions in a language may be created.

It was Chomsky's view of language as a rule-based system that took linguistics beyond Saussure's view of language as a system of interrelated elements. Saussure and the Bloomfieldians had not conceived of the possibility that a finite set of rules could be constructed that would generate an infinite number of sentences. Twenty-five centuries after Pāṇini, Chomsky "invented" generative grammars—the application of rules in successive stages in a specified order to create linguistic expressions.

Generative Grammars

Chomsky's approach to grammatical description brought mathematical rigor and precision to linguistics. His basic assumption was that the rules of a grammar and the conditions under which they operate must be precise and completely explicit. They must be *formalized*.

And they must be capable of generating all (and of course only) the sentences of the language.

Consider the following algebraic expression: $2x + 3y - z$. Given that x, y, and z can be any number, the expression will generate an infinite set of values. For a particular set of values, say $x = 2$, $y = 3$, and $z = 5$, the expression will generate only the value 8 as a result. The expression is explicit, precise, and unambiguous. This was the type of precision Chomsky sought for describing linguistic processes.

Chomsky represented the rules of a grammar in the form of *rewrite rules*. They take the form

[NOUN → *man*],

where the arrow is interpreted as an instruction to replace (or rewrite) the character string occurring to the left of the arrow with the character string to the right of the arrow. This rule in effect says: "Wherever there is 'NOUN,' replace it with '*man.*'" (The character string may be an actual word from a language's vocabulary, represented here in italics, or a more abstract entity represented in capital letters.)

Often, a rule allows more than one possible substitution for the character string found to the left of the arrow. For example,

[NOUN → *man . woman . boy . girl . baby*]

offers five alternative choices (each separated by a period) for the substitution of "NOUN." The period can be read as "or." This rules says: "Wherever there is 'NOUN,' replace it with '*man*' or '*woman*' or '*boy*' or '*girl*' or '*baby.*'"

A language (i.e., the set of all its possible sentences) is generated from a set of rules and a set of character strings. The generative process begins by taking one of the rewrite rules and searching among the set of character strings for one that matches the left-hand side of this rewrite rule. When a match is found, it is replaced by a string from the right-hand side of the rule. (If there is more than one possible choice on the right-hand side, then one is chosen—for now, let's assume the choice is random.) Then the search continues for additional matches among the set of character strings. When there are no further matches, the next rule is used, again searching for matches among the set of character strings.

This process continues until the set of character strings has been compared to all of the rewrite rules and all possible substitutions have occurred. What remains at the end of this process is a set of character strings consisting only of the elements that cannot be replaced. A sentence is generated!

For example, below are four rewrite rules that define a very simple language:

Rule 1: [PHRASE → ARTICLE, NOUN, VERB]
Rule 2: [ARTICLE → *A . The*]
Rule 3: [NOUN → *man . boy*]
Rule 4: [VERB → *runs . ran*]

Initiating the generative process with the character string "PHRASE" and applying Rule 1, "PHRASE" is replaced with "ARTICLE, NOUN, VERB." (A rule may also rewrite one character string with a sequence of several character strings, separated here by commas.) Then, applying Rule 2, "ARTICLE" is replaced by either "*A*" or "*The*." Applying Rule 3, "NOUN" is replaced by either "*man*" or "*boy*." Finally, applying Rule 4, "VERB" is replaced by either "*runs*" or "*ran*." "*A*," "*The*," "*man*," "*boy*," "*runs*," and "*ran*" do not appear on the left-hand side of any of the rewrite rules. Therefore, the rewriting process ends when they are arrived at. Using these rules, the following eight phrases—the entire set of possible sentences in this simple language—can be generated:

A man runs.
A boy runs.
The man runs.
The boy runs.
A man ran.
A boy ran.
The man ran.
The boy ran.

In *Syntactic Structures* Chomsky demonstrated how different types of rewrite rules that are increasingly more powerful can be used to develop precise descriptions of complex languages. He also formalized the generative properties of alternative systems of grammatical description, characterizing each by the types of rules it allowed.

Chomsky showed how grammars, using just a small number of rules, could generate an infinite variety of sentences.

The Search for Universal Grammars

Chomsky's ideas about grammar are part of a centuries-long tradition of linguistic and philosophical investigation. Linguists have long sought to discover the universals underlying *all* language. Philosophically minded linguists in the Middle Ages, influenced by the rediscovery of Aristotle's works in western Europe, were the first to be interested in the theoretical basis for grammars.

Latin was the foundation for all education in the Middle Ages, and the focus for grammarians. The Latin grammars of Donatus and Priscian, developed in the fourth and fifth centuries, respectively, were the basis of education in the Middle Ages (and remain the basis for today's grammars of Latin). Priscian's comprehensive grammar was nearly a thousand pages and eighteen books long. However, it was only a descriptive grammar of Latin.

Stimulated by Aristotle, William of Conches (twelfth century) suggested that the study of language at the time failed to ask *why* language had developed the elements and categories so well documented and described by these Latin grammars. William of Conches was from a school of linguistic philosophers known as the "speculative grammarians" that developed an elaborate theory of language and mind. They were interested in the causal basis for the various parts of language.

Greatly simplified, their theory proposed that the mind abstracts properties from things in the world using different modes of understanding. The mind then ascribes meaning to various vocal sounds by relating them with these abstracted things and their properties—the sounds function as words. This enables the mind to communicate the abstractions it derives from understanding the world. It was suggested that the various modes of understanding and the different types of properties of things in the world were the basis for the different categories of words that exist in languages.

From their efforts came the concept of an underlying universal grammar. Earlier grammarians had not made universal claims. These new philosophical grammarians proposed that linguistic and mental processes were shared by all men. They stated that grammars were fundamentally one and the same in all languages and that differences were merely superficial.

However, the study of language by the speculative grammarians was based almost exclusively on Latin and Greek, two very similar languages. The view of the speculative grammarians that all languages were fundamentally the same fell into disfavor with the discovery of more and more languages that clearly were very different in their grammatical structures and semantic categories.

Some 500 years later, in France in the seventeenth century, a school of "rationalist grammarians" appeared who were also interested in the underlying unity of the grammars of different languages and the role of language in communicating thought. They believed that much of the grammar of Latin—still the departure point for all scholars in Europe—was shared by all languages. The examples in their studies drew on Latin, Greek, Hebrew, and modern European languages. Like their medieval predecessors, these scholars also related word classes to thought processes. They considered nouns, articles, and pronouns as "objects" of thought, whereas verbs were seen as a "manner" of thought.

The rationalists were interested in identifying what was common between languages and between different statements below the surface level. Reflecting an approach influenced by formal logic, they suggested that the proposition "the invisible God has created the visible world" was related to "God, who is invisible, has created the world" and to the three propositions "God is invisible. God created the world. The world is visible." They suggested that, at a deeper level, these three surface representations were fundamentally the same. That is, each of the three surface representations expressed the same three logical propositions, but in different ways.[3]

In the eighteenth century, the focus of linguistics shifted to comparative work following the discovery of Sanskrit, and the search for universal grammars again fell out of favor. In fact, a diametrically opposed view, articulated by eighteenth-century linguists such as Herder and Humboldt and later by Saussure, suggested that different languages and their different ways of structuring the world resulted in fundamentally different ways of interpreting the world. Jacob Grimm proposed that language shaped the different world views not only of individuals but also of nations. In a nationalistic interpretation, Grimm associated the development of German as a distinct language with the development of independence by his early German ancestors.

It was not until Chomsky that universals in language again became a central issue for linguistic studies.

Deep Structure

In *Syntactic Structures* Chomsky demonstrated that different types of grammars—which he referred to as finite-state, context-free, and context-sensitive—could be used to describe the structures of natural language. But he found that they intuitively did not seem to reflect *the way the mind might generate such structures*. To do this, Chomsky introduced a new type of grammar, which he called a *transformational grammar*. At its foundation are the concepts of *deep structure* and *surface structure*.

Chomsky suggested that language has a deep structure that represents its essential structure, and a surface structure that represents a specific instantiation of this deep structure. These concepts of deep structure and surface structure radically increased this new grammar's ability to describe language structures in a way that reflects a more intuitive model of the mind's language faculty.

Chomsky proposed that the mind is endowed with certain innate capabilities for communication upon which specific languages are built. These core capabilities are logically anterior to any given language and, indeed, are the necessary condition for the existence of language. In his view, the mind is endowed with a basic faculty that enables the conceptualization of fundamental structures that are at the foundation of language—Chomsky's *deep structures*. Chomsky asserted that these fundamental linguistic structures are shared by all languages at a deep level and that differences in languages are differences at a surface level. These deep-level structures, shared by all languages, are effectively language universals. "The trick is to find the fundamental rules of all languages—a formidable but reachable goal."[4]

In a transformational grammar, there is a deep structure representation of the essential content or meaning of an expression. This deep structure is then subjected to a set of transformational processes that ultimately result in the representation of this deep structure in a surface-level form—as an expression in a language.

An essential element of this deep-level representation is that the same deep structure can be realized in different ways to form different surface-level representations. A single deep structure can be the basis for generating different sentences in English. The sentences "The man runs," "The man ran," "The man does not run," and "Does the man run?" share the same deep structure, which undergoes a transformation for the present or past tense, to a negative or interrogative statement, and so on.

What is especially interesting is that the same deep structure can also be the basis for generating what is essentially the same sentence in different languages. The deep structure of the sentence "The man runs" is the same for the French "L'homme court" or the German "Der Mann lauft." They all share the same deep structure. Only the surface structure changes. And these deep structures are shared not only by Indo-European languages, but by *all* languages, including Asian and African languages that share no similarity in surface structures.

Transformational Grammars

Transformational grammars start by representing language at the level of its deep structure. In the process of generating a sentence, this deep structure is then transformed into different forms that represent the same essential structure. Transformational grammars describe first the essential structure and then the transformations to be applied to generate its surface structure. Rewrite rules generate the basic form of an expression and transformational rules then process and transform the basic components of the expression into a refined final form.

Chomsky introduced the concept of a transformational processing stage because he felt that the processes of natural language could not be simply and clearly represented with other grammars. For example, it is possible to account for tense in the generation of a sentence with a context-sensitive grammar by ensuring that all the verb endings are appropriate to the context. However, it is simpler and more intuitive to think of a sentence as a *kernel sentence*, and of tense being applied as a transformation to the complete kernel sentence. With a transformational rule, a transformation for tense may be applied to a string of several elements at once.

For example, rewrite rules could first generate the kernel phrase

the man open the door.

This kernel phrase can then be marked off as a complete phrase to be transformed (the transformation is designated with the "@" symbol):

@past-tense (the man open the door),

yielding the final sentence

The man opened the door.

The benefit of this is clearer with a compound sentence, such as

the man open the door and go through it.

In the transformational stage, the whole sentence is transformed to the past tense:

@past-tense (the man open the door and go through it)

to generate

The man opened the door and went through it.

Combining other transformations, such as whether the subject and verb of the phrase are singular or plural, makes the power of transformations even clearer. The transformation of

@present-tense (@plural (the man open the door and go through it))

results in the sentence

The men open the door and go through it,

or, in the singular form,

The man opens the door and goes through it.

In addition to tense and number, other transformations can be defined such as whether a phrase is *negative, interrogative, passive,* and so on. The following are further examples that could be generated from the same kernel phrase but with different transformations applied:

The man didn't open the door and go through it.
Did the man open the door and go through it?
Didn't the men open the door and go through it?
Wasn't the door opened and gone through by the man?

Extending Generative Grammars to Other Forms of Expression

Grammars, formalized descriptive systems, can also be applied to other languages or forms of communication. A conclusion from Saussure's work is that, to the extent that there is a vehicle of communication, by definition there is an underlying system. Without an underlying system, there could be no way for another to discern information from the communication. Given that we accept that music, art or even architecture can communicate ideas, they are languages. And, to the extent that they are languages, they can be represented as formalized systems with grammars, given that one can make explicit the rules of a given language.

Chomsky's notion of rule-governed creativity can be projected to other vehicles of communication—to languages other than natural languages. Though Chomsky himself did not do so, others have extended his work using generative grammars for the description of other forms of expression, such as music and the visual arts.

Grammars and Music

Music, a language that is subject to formal rules that can be made explicit, can be described with grammars. For example, it is possible to describe a sonata form using rewrite rules.[5]

The classical form of a sonata movement consists of three sections. The first section is an *exposition*, where two themes are presented. This is followed by a *development*, where the themes are contrasted and varied and the harmonic possibilities (of the circle of fifths) are explored. The movement is concluded with a *recapitulation*, where the two themes are returned to in their original form as presented in the exposition. This is often referred to by musicians as an "ABA" form. Rewrite rules can express this high-level form in simple terms.

Rule 1:   [SONATA → A, B, A]
Rule 2:   [A → THEME 1, THEME 2]
Rule 3:   [B → DEVELOPMENT OF THEMES]

Starting with the string "SONATA," the following structure is generated:

THEME 1, THEME 2,
DEVELOPMENT OF THEMES,
THEME 1, THEME 2.

Other rules can continue the process of rewriting to ultimately define themes, the thematic development, and so on.

Just as with languages, the power of transformations can also be applied to the description of grammars for music. Grammars can include *musical* transformations. For example, transposition, that is, starting a sequence of notes (or intervals) on a different note, can be represented by a transformation:

@key-*"note"* (THEME).

The simplest view of a sonata form is as an "ABA" structure. However, there is a fundamental difference between the A *before* the development and the A *after* the development. Generally, in sonata form, the first time the themes are presented in the exposition, before the development, the first theme is in the base key and the second theme is in the key of the *fifth*. However, after the development, during which the themes are contrasted and played in many different keys, both themes are played in the recapitulation in the base key, representing the resolution of the conflict or tension of these two themes and keys as presented in the exposition. It is this tension between the two themes and keys that is at the heart of sonata form.

The essential tension of sonata form can be formally represented using context-sensitive rewrite rules and musical transformations. Now, when started with "SONATA," rules can generate the kernel form:

@key-base (THEME 1), @key-of-fifth (THEME 2),
DEVELOPMENT OF THEMES,
@key-base (THEME 1), @key-base (THEME 2).

Before the development, the two themes are in opposing keys. After the development, the two themes are both in the base key. Again, other rules continue the process of rewriting to ultimately define the themes and so on. Once this is done, the emerging sonata material will then be processed by transformations that place the themes in appropriate keys depending on their position within the sonata.

Additional transformations, such as playing a sequence of notes backward, forward, upside-down, and backward and upside-down, allow for the simple description of all forms of a series:

SERIES
@backward (SERIES)
@upside-down (SERIES)
@backward-upside-down (SERIES)

Grammars and Visual Languages

It is also possible to describe the rules of visual languages in the form of grammars. One way of describing visual languages is in terms of what are called *shape grammars*, that is, grammars that are well suited for describing visual shapes. These grammars were first developed by Stiny and Gips in 1975.

Using rules not unlike the rewrite rules of Chomskyan natural language grammars, the following example demonstrates how the rules of a shape grammar can be specified. The following is a rule that specifies the rewriting of a line.

Like Chomskyan rewrite rules, this rule indicates that whenever the shape found on the left-hand side of the rule is encountered, a line in this case, it should be replaced by the shape on the right-hand side of the rule.

Starting the rewrite process with a square and applying the rule to each of the four sides, the following rewrite takes place.

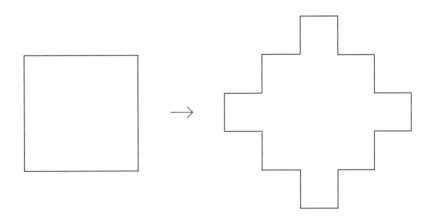

This example is a very simple rule. Shape grammars can be defined with rules of much greater complexity and subtlety, with which it is possible to formally and explicitly describe rich visual languages.

Conclusion

In search of the universal underlying basis of language, Noam Chomsky introduced twentieth-century linguistics to generative and transformational grammars. His work can be traced back to Pāṇini's generative grammar of Sanskrit from 2,500 years earlier. Reintroducing a rationalist view of language processes, Chomsky's work can also be seen as part of a tradition of linguistics that links ancient Greece to the speculative grammarians of the Middle Ages and the rationalist grammarians of seventeenth-century France. Like Chomsky, these earlier rationalist schools also developed a view of language operating at both deep and surface levels.

What is particularly interesting about Chomsky's approach is that it focuses on the "creative" aspects of language. Chomsky wanted to understand how people could create (and understand) expressions that have never been created before. He saw language as rule-governed creativity. *His generative grammars are an explicit, precise, and unambiguous way of describing rule-governed creativity.*

Extrapolating this notion of rule-governed creativity, Chomsky's generative grammars can be extended to natural language, music, the visual arts, and other vehicles of expression. They can be applied to linguistics, to Kandinsky's goal of defining a grammar for visual languages, and to the description and automation of explicit music languages such as that in Boulez's *Structures*. Chomsky's grammars are a method for describing not only natural language but potentially all vehicles of expression.

8 *Coda*

Units with Positions in a System

By the first half of the twentieth century, the study of language had arrived at structuralism: the study of language as a formal system. Saussure's view of language as a system of relationships between abstract elements—a system "of reciprocally defined or conditioned terms"—has dominated linguistics. Language is looked at in terms of *units* with *positions* in a *system*.

To the extent that language is looked at in terms of its structure, it is seen as a purely *abstract* system. The object of study is not what or how utterances relate to concrete objects in the "real" world. The referential function of language is put aside. The object of study is the relationships between the elements of a language and the resulting structure.

The structure of language is seen as independent of the medium in which it is expressed. English, for example, can be represented in both spoken and written form. Both forms are recognized as the same language. But the *units* that represent the different media—sounds or letters—are different. It is only the structure that both forms have in common. The language system itself is independent of the medium in which it is realized. It is in this sense also that language is seen as a purely abstract system.

Similar views in terms of abstract structure have also emerged of other forms of communication and expression. Kandinsky developed a new foundation for visual languages. He developed an abstract art based on "the mutual relations of forms one to another." Visual languages are understood in abstract terms. Kandinsky saw visual languages in terms of abstract *units* with *positions* in a *system*. Today, abstraction is taken for granted as part of the vocabulary of the visual arts.

Music has long been understood in abstract terms. Tonality is a structured system of relationships between notes that are treated as abstract elements. Walter Piston described tonality as "the process of setting forth the organized relationship of these notes to one among them." Tonality is an abstract system for *structuring* music.

The abstract nature of music is even more explicit in Schoenberg's "method of composing with twelve tones which are related only with one another." By the second half of the twentieth century, some composers had arrived at total serialism. Every element of music—every note, every dynamic, every duration, every attack—was subject to organization by a formal process. Music is often viewed in terms of abstract *units* with *positions* in a *system*.

By the 1950s, linguists viewed language in abstract terms, artists had developed abstract visual languages, and music was seen as a very formal abstract system.

All Languages of Expression Can Be Seen in Abstract Terms

These views of other forms of communication and expression were, at least initially, not influenced by Saussure. Kandinsky formulated his views of abstract art and Schoenberg formulated his views of serial music unaware of Saussure. Saussure's *Course in General Linguistics* was first published in 1916, while Kandinsky, isolated in Russia, was formulating his ideas on abstract art and Schoenberg was developing his ideas on serialism in Germany. The similarity in these views of communications systems in abstract terms reflects a broader intellectual trend to formal systems that has influenced many disciplines.

Natural language and music have longest been studied in terms of their forms and structures. But all vehicles of communication can be the subject of formal description, including spoken languages, music, and the visual arts. Any form of communication must have an underlying system of discernible and differentiable distinctions and conventions. And any such system can be studied in terms of its formal structure. In fact, a structuralist view of language is not that a language has structure, but that a language is structure.

All vehicles of communication can be looked at in terms of abstract *units* with *positions* in a *system*. All can be understood as abstract systems.

Chomsky's Generative Grammars

Chomsky's interest was in the "creative" aspects of language. He created a view of language as a rule-based system in which grammars are seen as the *rules* that define how expressions may be *generated* in a language. His breakthrough was the description of formal and explicit grammars that could be used to precisely describe *and* generate expressions in a language. In particular, he developed the concept of transformational grammars that represent the processes of language in terms of deep and surface structures.

The formal descriptive capabilities of the generative grammars outlined by Chomsky can also be applied to the description of other languages. Any language can be described if its rules can be made explicit. And these grammars need not be only descriptive, but also can be generative. What is remarkable about these generative grammars is that, using just a small number of rules, an infinite set of expressions can be created. With a larger set, it is possible to create rich and varied expressions reflecting both complex structures and subtle nuances—in natural language, music, and the visual arts.

Conclusion of Part I

As a result of Saussure's work, language is viewed as a formal system. And all forms of communication—all semiotic systems, all vehicles for communicating ideas—are viewed as languages. Kandinsky imagined "grammars" for visual composition. Boulez developed explicit grammars and music composition techniques that could be automated. Chomsky developed techniques for, first, formally and explicitly describing languages, and, then, generating expressions in a language so described.

By the 1950s, linguists, artists, composers, and others viewed their expressive languages in abstract terms and were creating formal and explicit descriptions of their languages. It was also in the 1950s that another breakthrough was made: the development of computers.

Computers are the ultimate manipulators of abstract structures. The widespread views of languages as abstract systems combined with the ability to create precise descriptions with generative grammars forms a foundation for developing expressive systems *with* computers. Given this foundation, the development of the computer opens new avenues for exploring creative processes and developing new vehicles of expression.

Part I has described how the developments of linguistics, music, and the visual arts have evolved formal views of language.

Part II will look at how, using computers, pioneers have experimented with the formal description and automatic generation of language, music, and the visual arts, as well as new media such as virtual reality. These efforts reflect the convergence of the development of the computer and the different ideas and disciplines presented in part I.

We are on the verge of a new age of creative expression. It represents a direct continuity with centuries of tradition in linguistics, music, and the visual arts.

Interlude

♮**whoawhap!** *It's morning and the night bird sings its song.* ♮**whoawhap!** ♮**whoawhap!** *These are the last sounds before the bird goes silent for the day.* ♮**whoawhap!** ♮**whoawhap!** *A momentary pause.* ♮**whoawhap!** *The bird sings at regular intervals—a few times per hour—throughout the night. Only one bird is close. Crisp.* ♮**whoawhap!** ♮**whoawhap!**

Fainter and more distant, a second bird also sings. ♮**whiawhoop** ♮**whiawhoop.** *A pause.* ♮**whiawhoop.** *Several minutes pass. Again, it sings* ♮**whiawhoop** ♮**whiawhoop.** *Pause.* ♮**whiawhoop.** *There is a third, still fainter.* ♮*whooa* ♮*whooa* ... ♮*whoawhap!* ... ♮*whooa* ♮*whooa* ... ♮*whoawhap!* And fainter yet, a fourth ... and a fifth.*

It would be a long journey through the jungle to the furthest ♮**whoawhap!** *Crisp. Close. Daylight would break first.*

Sleeping to this rhythm, or awakening at any time, there is always the night bird's song. ♮*whooa* ♮*whooa* ... ♮*whoawhap!* ... the night's quiet* ... ♮**whiawhoop** ♮**whiawhoop.**

At dawn, the rhythm changes to a cacophony of morning birds. All other sounds are lost in the din. The morning outburst subsides. It is time for a walk to the fields.

Some hours later, the daily afternoon rain has just stopped. The earth still sizzles and pops as it absorbs the damp. Gurgles and trickles can be heard from little rivulets in the distance that drain the field. Slowly, the sounds of the rain fade. Rather than silence, the decrescendo reveals a soft humming.

At first the crickets seem like a soft monotonic drone. It's a few minutes before any of the individual crickets are perceptible. But then you are listening to a fragment of one cricket's voice. [CRICK CRICK CRICK] ... *pause* ... [CRICK CRICK CRICK CRICK CRICK] ... *pause* ... [CRICK CRICK CRICK CRICK] ... *pause* ... *Your ear drifts to another cricket. At a slightly slower tempo and not to a synchronized beat, but still well paced:* [CH CH] ... [CH CH CH] ... [CH] ... [CH CH] ... [CH] ... [CH CH] ... [CH]. *You distinguish another cricket, somewhat faster:* [CHRICK CHRICK CHRICK CHRICK CHRICK] [CHRICK CHRICK CHRICK CHRICK] [CHRICK CHRICK CHRICK] [CHRICK CHRICK CHRICK CHRICK CHRICK CHRICK]. *And then listen to a fourth cricket, more moderate:* **[CHICK CHICK] [CHICK CHICK] [CHICK CHICK] [CHICK CHICK] [CHICK].** *Soon you pick out a fifth and then a sixth* ... ***[CRICKA CHRICKET] [CRICKA CHRICK CHRICKET]*** [CH CH CH CHA] ... *It is the start of a tremendous crescendo of crickets.*

Each cricket can be heard playing alone as a soloist. There are two that you hear together against the support of the less distinct drone. At different paces and with different patterns, groups of 2s, 3s and 4s versus groups of 4s, 6s and 7s. It is difficult not to lose one or the other back into the drone. But as one fades back into the drone another or two take its place. You concentrate on two voices ... [CH CH] [CH CH] [CH] ... [CHRICK CHRICK CHRICK][CHRICK CHRICK CHRICK CHRICK CHRICK] ... [CH CH CH] ... [CHRICK] ... [CH CH CH CHA] ... *Then three* ... [CH CH CHA] [CHRICK CHRICK CHRICK] *[CHACH CHACH]* [CH CHA] *[CACHRICK]* [CH CHA] *[CHACH CHACH]* ... *five* ... [CHRICK CHRICK CHRICK] *[CRICKA CHRICKET]* [CH CH CH] *[CACHRICK]* [CHICK CHICK] *[CRICKA CHRICKET]* [CH CHA] [CH CH CHA] *[CRICKA CHRICK CHRICKET]* [CHICK CHICK CHICK] [CH CH CH] *[CACHRICK]* ... *A cacophony of percussive instruments, each playing to its own tempo, rhythm and frequency, each with a slight variation in timbre.*

You concentrate. There is a cricket. And then another. There are groups of 2s, 3s and 7s. Each group is clear and distinct with its part in the sym-

phony. Each cricket is distinctly heard. One. Two. Several. You concentrate. Ten. You concentrate. Tens. You concentrate. Hundreds. Thousands. Hundreds of thousands. Every [CHRICK], *[CACHRICK] and* [CH CH CHA] *is heard as itself and as a part of the complete cacophony. Every interplay of rhythms, of timbres, the groups and subgroups is completely heard. You concentrate. You are listening to the vibration of a million crickets and know each and every component of that overwhelming crescendo. You become that crescendo. You are that crescendo. You are that vibration....*

Perhaps an hour has passed before you hear the first birds of the afternoon. Many birds sing.

By evening, you hear the first night bird ♮**whoawarp tada** *... a long pause ...* ♮**whoawarp tada**. *The night bird's song has a sound very different from the rest of the day. A sleepy almost tropical sound, it seems a little odd in the surrounding environment, like a tabla in a symphony. However, the lazy and relaxed quality of the* ♮**whoawarp** *overcomes any feeling that this sound does not fit in. Instead it becomes the timekeeper of a beat that is hundreds of times slower than the crickets that pace the afternoon. Its regular recurrence is heard three or four times an hour not only through the early evening but throughout the night until early morning.* ♮**whoawhap!** ♮**whoawhap!**

The crickets can still be heard softly humming throughout the night. Early morning is again the time of the birds. By midday there is the whisper of a breeze, and the sky darkens as a prelude to the regular afternoon rain. A couple of drops ... then all that is heard is the downpour on the dry ground. A drone, and then individual drops heard, one then another, then two and three together. The crescendo now is of a timbre totally unlike the crickets that will emerge later in the day. It is afternoon. The timbres, patterns, rhythms, frequency and beats are distinctively afternoon.

You follow the hours of the day. Not tracking the angle of the sun or following the hands of a watch carefully tuned. But through each vibration. Each minute, each day of a beat that measures on a scale that is both immeasurable and inconceivable.

II   *Structure Manipulators*

9 *Calculus Ratiocinator*

The Thirty Years' War (1618–1648) marked a major turning point in the fundamental structure of Europe, leaving much of the continent in a state of devastation. The Elbe and Rhine regions of Germany were depopulated; cities were entirely destroyed, German commerce and industry ruined. Even more significant for the future development of Europe, it marked the end of religious ideologies as the primary political force there.

The political profile of Europe was dominated by the powerful Catholic Hapsburgs. Two powerful Hapsburg empires, one centered in Austria and the other in Spain, held influence across much of the continent, from Italy to Hungary to the Netherlands to Portugal. The Thirty Years' War began as a war of ideology between the Protestant Reformation and the Counter-Reformation, with the Hapsburgs committed to the defense of Catholicism against the Reformation.

The war started in Bohemia, part of today's Czech Republic. Prague was its capital. Though it had been under Hapsburg rule since 1526, most of its population was Protestant. The Hapsburg rulers introduced Jesuits to Bohemia with the aim of returning the country to Catholicism. Religious tension remained high for decades; finally in 1618, Protestant nobles revolted and threw two imperial councilors out the window of the Hradcin Castle in Prague. They deposed Catholic King Ferdinand II, soon to be head of the Austrian Hapsburg empire, and elected the Protestant Frederick V to the Bohemian throne. The revolt quickly spread to other Hapsburg dominions, including the Upper Palatinate and Translyvania. As might be expected, the Hapsburgs objected to Frederick V. The Hapsburg armies proceeded to devour the territories of Bohemia and the Upper Palatinate. Frederick was forced to resign after a brief reign and became known as the Winter King.

But the war didn't end there. It became entangled in international political and economic rivalries as Denmark, fearing the rise of the Hapsburgs in northern Germany, came to the support of the Protestants. England provided aid and sent a few thousand soldiers to support the Danes. The Danish armies, however, were soundly defeated by the Hapsburg forces.

Then, in 1629, Ferdinand II issued the Edict of Restitution that declared void all Protestant titles to land previously taken from church establishments. The edict would have had a disastrous effect on German Protestantism. Gustavus II of Sweden now joined the war. Ferdinand's control of Germany provided him access to the Baltic Sea; Gustavus was fearful that Ferdinand's maritime designs might threaten Sweden's control of the Baltic.

As the war grew, the alliances did not divide consistently along religious lines. When Protestant Sweden intervened in Germany, it was funded by Catholic France, under the leadership of Cardinal Richelieu, who was also concerned with the increasing power of the Hapsburgs. Saxony, ruled by Elector John George I who had Lutheran sympathies, initially sided with the Hapsburgs, but then demonstrated its independence and joined the Swedes in 1631. The Saxons then made a deal for peace with the Hapsburgs in 1635 that gained them power over Upper and Lower Lusatia. The Swedes, particularly motivated by this betrayal of loyalties, then invaded Saxony and thoroughly devasted it. France entered the war directly, unwilling to see the Hapsburgs retain power. Catholic Bavaria, between Bohemia, Austria, and Saxony, also joined the Protestant forces to thwart the Hapsburgs.

The war now involved most of Europe. France and the United Provinces of the Low Countries (today the Netherlands, Belgium, and Luxembourg) fought the Spanish. France and Spain also struggled for power in Italy. Portugal revolted against Spain. Austria invaded France—later to be repulsed, with French forces advancing to just outside of Vienna. In 1645, the Swedes were defeated by the Hapsburg forces. Successful campaigns were followed by resounding defeats. Invasions were repelled. Alliances shifted. Europe was in a state of chaos.

Finally, the Peace of Westphalia brought a conclusion to the war in 1648. In the end, the Spanish Hapsburg empire was broken; control of the Netherlands and Portugal was lost. The Austrian Hapsburg empire was shaken. But the greatest impact of the Thirty Years' War was not the shifting of alliances or even the end of Spanish power; it was the destruction of the whole underlying political system. The Holy Roman Empire was a mere shell. Out of this chaos, sober republics and mercantilist-minded absolutist states emerged.

Gottfried Wilhelm Leibniz

Gottfried Wilhelm Leibniz was born into this chaos on July 1, 1646, two years before the Peace of Westphalia. Leibniz is considered "one of the most imposing figures in the history of Western thought."[1] Among his accomplishments, he laid the foundation for modern logic, developed breakthroughs in the architectures of the first calculating machines, and proposed the idea of a machine capable of reasoning.

Leibniz independently invented differential and integral calculus at the same time as Newton. He is renowned for his works in philosophy. His manuscripts address a broad array of subjects including law, theology, politics, political and economic history, architecture, and technology. And he was knowledgeable in physics, chemistry, astronomy, alchemy, geology, archaeology, literature, and linguistics.

Leibniz's interest in logic was motivated by an idealistic vision. A pacifist in the wake of the wars that had devastated Europe, Leibniz believed logic could enable sufficient clarity and precision in discourse so that disputes and disagreements could be peacefully resolved. Leibniz believed that misunderstanding was at the root of disputes and disagreements, even of wars, and that the inadequacy of language was at the root of misunderstandings between people. He concluded that it was necessary to bring the clarity and precision of mathematics to language and discourse. He felt that to be able to understand what someone has said without ambiguity, it is necessary to clearly define the terms of the discourse. To this end, he aimed to define any and all components of a discourse so that there was a

Figure 9.1
Gottfried Wilhelm Leibniz (1646–1716).

satisfactory and unambiguous answer to the question: "What does that mean?"

Leibniz saw in the symbols used in algebra and geometry, and rules for their combination and manipulation, the potential to develop a universal logic. He conceived of a formal symbol system that could bring clarity and precision to language, unambiguously representing knowledge, thought, and ideas. Like many linguists before and after him, his goal was to find a universal basis for language.

He concluded that if language could be made to reflect more accurately the structure of the world people were arguing about, then resolving disputes would become a straightforward process of performing logical operations in a symbol system to derive an unambiguous conclusion. It would only be necessary for people "to take their pencils in their hands, to sit down to their slates, and say to each other (with a friend to witness, if they liked): Let us calculate."[2] Though such a view might seem naive today, Leibniz followed a philosophical tradition that accepted that rational thought could settle all arguments, a tradition that dated to the Greek skeptics and was revived with the rationalist philosophy of Descartes.

Logic in the Quest for Peace

Leibniz's first project to apply logic to politics was concerned with the election of a king of Poland. King John Casimir of Poland had abdicated the throne in 1668. Leibniz, then working with a German diplomat, decided to develop a "proof" that his candidate for the kingship, Count Philipp Wilhelm von Neuburg, was indeed the only *logical* candidate. Under the penname of a purported Polish aristocrat, Leibniz produced a 360-page treatise to that effect. Basing his argument on the social and economic affairs of Poland, Leibniz developed 60 propositions and 25 logical proofs to support his deduction "that the king should be from outside Poland and should not be a member of the Piast family."[3] This deduction in turn led to the final conclusion—that only the German Count Philipp Wilhelm von Neuburg could be king.

The mission was not successful—the Piast Michael Wisniowiecki was selected as king. One might consider it naive, even for a 22-year-old, to think that such a series of deductions could really influence the results of an election. But Leibniz would continue to point proudly to this work as a demonstration of how mathematical reasoning could be used in politics and diplomacy.

His next big project in a similar vein involved King Louis XIV of France, who in 1671 was sending menacing signals toward his neighbors, particularly Holland. The Germans were also afraid of his potential aggression. Therefore, Leibniz, now with a diplomatic charter to represent Germany, developed several hundred pages of arguments to persuade King Louis to attack Egypt instead. The gist of the argument was that the conquest of Cairo would be "the greatest of the possible projects, and the easiest of the great ones."[4] Leibniz was invited to Paris to present his argument—but before he arrived England declared war on Holland and France immediately followed suit. (When Napoleon attacked Egypt over a hundred years later, Leibniz was blamed for the idea!)

Leibniz took on other seemingly unattainable goals, such as reconciling the Catholic and Protestant churches. In 1686 he examined Catholic and Protestant doctrines and attempted to demonstrate that the differences between them were small. He concluded that, as a result, the differences should be easy to resolve.

Lingua Philosophica

These projects were part of Leibniz's much more ambitious vision: the development of an artificial language, a *lingua philosophica*, that could be used to represent human thought. He aimed to develop a language of reasoning, and he wanted to provide a clear articulation of its rules.

In 1666 Leibniz suggested that the process of reasoning could be broken down into smaller and smaller elements until it was reduced to a few basic ones, much like factoring a number into its primes. He proposed that there is a set of elemental concepts, "first terms," by means of which all other concepts are defined.

Man, for example, is a complex concept that is defined by other concepts it contains. *Man* is an *animal*. The concept of *man*, therefore, is defined in terms of other concepts, such as *animal*. *Animal* in turn is defined as a *living thing*, which in turn is defined in terms of other concepts until one arrives at unanalyzable elemental concepts—first terms. Leibniz's Law of Expressions stated that "the expression of a given thing is to be composed of the expressions of those things the ideas of which compose the idea of the given thing."[5] A complex concept is composed of a web of simpler ones.

Leibniz aimed to develop a way to represent the basic elements of thought symbolically, much as symbols are used in mathematics. This set of signs—a universal symbolism he called a *characteristica universalis*—would hold a one-to-one isomorphic correspondence to the concepts that they represent. This symbolic representation of concepts was to be the foundation for his precise reasoning system.

Leibniz thought that it was the way in which some concepts contained others that made reasoning possible. For example, in the statement "Every animal is a living thing," the concept of *animal* contains *living thing*. Similarly, in the statement "Every man is a living thing," the concept of *man* contains *living thing*.

Given the set of first terms, Leibniz suggested that it was possible to draw conclusions by applying methods of logic. For example, here are two statements and a conclusion.

If every animal is a living thing,
and every man is an animal,
then, every man is a living thing.

Given the set of basic elements represented symbolically, this logical deduction could be represented as:

If   A := B

and   C := A

then C := B.

Here, "A" represents the concept of "every animal," "B" represents "living thing," "C" represents "every man," and ":=" is read as "implies."

Leibniz envisaged that logical operations could be performed on the basic elemental concepts of thought much like the mathematical manipulation of numbers. He asserted that "all truths can be demonstrated *solo calculo*, or solely by manipulation of characters according to a certain form, without any labor of the imagination or effort of the mind, just as occurs in arithmetic and algebra."[6] The result is a system that reduces reasoning to a mechanical process. He called this the *calculus ratiocinator*, the reasoning calculus, as opposed to the differential and integral calculus he also invented.

An even bolder part of Leibniz's vision was that, given an unambiguous representation of the structure of the world and the rules of logic, the reasoning process could be executed automatically, whether by pen and paper or *by a machine*. His idea of a *reasoning machine* was very original, if again somewhat naive with respect to the complexity of the task. But the excitement of such a possibility was stimulated by the technological developments of the seventeenth century, a time of discovery when almost anything seemed possible. Leibniz himself developed breakthroughs at the leading edge of technology: the first calculating machines.

The First Calculating Machines

Several independent efforts in Europe had recently led to the building of *calculating* machines. Based on state-of-the-art engineering techniques using the most sophisticated gear wheels developed for clocks, the first calculating machine was developed in 1624 by Wilhelm Schickard. Another very early gear train calculator was developed in 1642 by the French mathematician Blaise Pascal. (Unlike Leibniz, Pascal was convinced that reason could not resolve man's difficulties. A religious man, he believed that "the heart has reasons of which reason itself knows nothing.")[7]

Among his other contributions, Leibniz also developed mechanical calculators that pushed the state of the art forward. In 1685, he proposed a calculator that used a variable-toothed gear wheel to achieve multiplication in a single operation, rather than through multiple additions as was necessary in earlier designs. These calculating machines provided him concrete evidence that, given symbolic representations of thoughts and strict reasoning rules, it should be possible to build mechanical reasoning machines.

The task, then, that Leibniz conceived was to make explicit the relationships between concepts, ultimately permitting the automated manipulation of these concepts by methods of logic to derive various conclusions. He was the first to conceive of mechanizing thought. However, Leibniz, who undertook many projects, never completed this one. The pursuit of a reasoning machine didn't resurface until a few hundred years later, ultimately to become the goal of a new scientific discipline that emerged in the 1950s: artificial intelligence.

The "Analytical Engine"

The computer is the enabling technology for research aimed at Leibniz's vision of mechanizing thought. Its invention represents the culmination and convergence of many intellectual achievements that have roots that can be traced back directly to Leibniz.

Following the initial work of Pascal and Leibniz, various experiments in the development of mechanical calculators continued through the eighteenth century. These calculating machines worked by establishing a starting set of numbers on which an operation would be performed—for example, by setting the starting positions of gears or dials—and then letting the calculating machine perform its operation to generate a result. It was a process that conceptually consisted of a *single* set of starting inputs and the performance of a *single* operation from which a result would be generated.

In the 1830s, an Englishman, Charles Babbage, conceived of the Analytical Engine, generally regarded as the first machine to embody concepts of modern computer architecture. This was to be a machine where the results of a given operation could be fed back into the machine and used for a subsequent operation. Babbage described a machine that could "combine together general symbols in successions of unlimited variety and extent."[8]

Babbage's machine, like today's computers, had a *central processor* to which numbers were brought and operated on and from which results would emerge. (Babbage called it a "mill," where numbers metaphorically are the grain entering the mill to be ground into flour, the refined result of the computation.) Connected to the central processor was a storage area where numbers were kept to be sent to the central processor and where results also were stored.

But probably the most significant innovation of Babbage's Analytical Engine was the facility to have a predetermined series of operations programmed to automatically execute in sequence. Joseph Jacquard had recently developed sequence control techniques for controlling patterns in the process of weaving. Using punch cards, a Jacquard loom could be directed to automatically execute certain operations to create predetermined and extremely complex patterns. Babbage, using Jacquard's sequence control techniques, envisioned the programming of a sequence of instructions that each indicated what numbers should be retrieved from storage for a given operation, the operation to be performed, and where the result should be stored. Even more striking, Babbage proposed that the execution of the sequence of operations might change depending on the results generated by earlier operations.

Hindered by the limits of the mechanical technology of his time, Babbage never completed a working model of his Analytical Engine. He nonetheless described the essential components of today's computers: the architecture of a central processor and storage, preprogrammed sequences of operations that are the equivalent of software, and, the key to the real power of modern-day computing, the idea of the conditional execution of a series of operations.

"Laws of Thought"

At the same time as Babbage was working on his Analytical Engine, another Englishman was following on from another area of Leibniz's work, that in formal logic. In 1854, a mathematician named George

Boole published a book called *Laws of Thought.* It described what he called "a mathematics of the human intellect."[9]

Boole proposed a binary system in which *1* represented true and *0* represented false. He then defined a set of logical operations (AND, OR, NOT) that could be performed on these *1*s and *0*s. Given this system, Boole demonstrated that any problem of logic could be reduced to equations that could be solved with mathematical rigor.

Boole developed a set of operations and an unambiguous symbolic notation for representing and analyzing problems of logic—much as Leibniz had set out to develop two centuries earlier.

Electronic Calculating Machines

In the twentieth century, electricity was the technological breakthrough that revolutionized the development of calculating machines. With electricity, complicated mechanical linkages could be replaced with wires and switches. Konrad Zuse applied for a patent on an electromechanical automatic calculator in Berlin in 1936. Even though he was apparently unfamiliar with Babbage's work, his design included a memory for storing numbers and results, a central arithmetic processing unit, and the ability to define a sequence of operations to be given to the machine on paper tape. In 1937, similar devices were also built at Bell Labs in New York and at Harvard.

Also in 1937, Claude Shannon, an American doing master's research at MIT, showed that the *1*s and *0*s of Boolean logic could be represented by electrical switches and that Boolean operations could be performed with the appropriate connections of electrical switches. With this it became possible to build machines consisting of vacuum tubes, relays, and switches that could perform Boolean operations.

With the convergence of Shannon's theoretical breakthrough and the development of the first electronic calculating machines, the first electronic computers soon followed. IBM's Mark I, built in 1944, could multiply two 23-digit numbers in approximately four and a half seconds. Two years later, the ENIAC (Electronic Numerical Integrator and Calculator) was built, containing 18,000 vacuum tubes, occupying 3,000 cubic feet of space, and consuming 140 kilowatts of electricity. In 1950, Univac delivered the first commercial digital computer.

By the late 1950s, tubes were replaced by transistors that permitted far more complex circuits to be built in a fraction of the space and requiring a fraction of the power. In the decades following, the process of technological advancement has continued to deliver greater and greater integration that has resulted in computers of ever greater capability. Today, pocket calculators dwarf the capabilities of the original ENIAC.

The first computers in the United States and England were used for military purposes. They performed the complex calculations needed for deciphering codes, determining missile trajectories, and so on. With the invention of personal computers in the 1970s, the use of computers has moved from specialized tasks and data processing jobs to everyday life. Computers are essential tools for operating a business: running the accounting system, keeping track of inventory, maintaining a database of customers, processing transactions such as travel bookings, bank deposits, or withdrawals, and filing and archiving massive amounts of data. Computers are used as tools for various functions individuals perform in the course of their work: word processing, spreadsheet analysis, file management, drawing, photo retouching, preparing publishing page layouts.

Computers have enabled people to work in new ways. Computers make the analysis of lots of numerical data possible. They make it easier to play "what if"—to set up a scenario based on a number of assumptions, and then to see what would happen if a given assumption were changed. They perform comparisons of large amounts of data looking for patterns, correspondences, and new perspectives. However, even though computers can change the way people work, in all of these examples the computer is a tool automating previously manual processes. Spreadsheet analysis can be done by hand and pen, but not as efficiently. Tracking inventories and filing data can all be done without electronic means, but not as efficiently. In none of these examples is the computer demonstrating intelligent behavior or independently performing a creative process.

The Turing Machine

The initial understanding of calculating machines was as machines to automate numerical calculations and analysis. It was in 1950 that the

British mathematician Alan Turing established a modern vision of the greater implications of calculating machines: that they could think. Turing created a theoretical foundation for the feasibility of designing truly intelligent machines.

The first notions of independent intelligent machines are found in the science fiction of the 1920s. The term "robots" was first used in the Czech Karel Capek's 1923 play *Rossum's Universal Robots*. A robot indistinguishable from a woman appeared in Fritz Lang's *Metropolis* in 1926. But Turing was the first to consider the question of intelligent machines and what it would mean for a machine to "think." He concluded that, *if a machine's behavior were indistinguishable from that of people, it would have to be thought of as displaying intelligence.*

Turing's proposal for evaluating whether computers could think and act intelligently was grounded in scientific tradition. By the early part of the twentieth century, psychology and other human and behavioral sciences, based on the scientific traditions of empiricism, believed that only the objectively observable could serve as the basis for scientific research. J. B. Watson's book *Behavior*, published in 1914, called for psychology to restrict its studies exclusively to viewable behavior. In 1938, B. F. Skinner assumed the same foundation in his *The Behavior of Organisms*, which became one of the most influential works in the field of psychology, setting the tone for decades.

The underlying assumption of Turing's thesis was that it was only from people's viewable behavior that we conclude that people are intelligent thinking beings. Therefore if, in a given situation, the behavior of a person and a computer were indistinguishable, and the behavior of the person was considered to demonstrate intelligence, then it would be necessary to conclude that the behavior of the computer also demonstrated intelligence.

Turing proposed a test now known as the *Turing test* as a basis for objectively determining if a computer can think. The test was to establish a dialog between a person acting as judge and, both hidden in another room, a computer and a second person. In both cases the judge received typed responses to his typed questions—Turing envisioned a Teletype typewriter-like link between them. If the judge could not differentiate between the computer and the person, the conclusion could only be that the computer behaved in an intelligent fashion and would have to be said to be acting like a thinking, intelligent being.

Philosophers consider other issues: whether a computer really can be said to understand the meaning of things if it doesn't have the real world experiences on which people base meaning; or whether computers can be said to understand concepts such as love and to have true emotions; or whether computers can have intentions as people do, or have hope. Is it correct to infer that computers *really* think just because they do a good job simulating thinking? But according to the pragmatic approach Turing proposed, these issues are speculative indulgences if, ultimately, we cannot distinguish computers from humans.

We consider people to be intelligent thinking beings not because of any unidentifiable quality but because of how they act, behave, and communicate, what they do and say. The basis for evaluating whether machines are intelligent will be what they do and say. The internal representations of the world in the computer and the manipulations and processes by which a computer operates on them to create its viewable behavior may be very different from how the brain functions, a biological device rather than an array of semiconductors. But, in Turing's view, that hardly matters if the viewable results are the same.

In considering the problem of mechanizing thinking processes, Turing believed that thinking—performing math, writing poetry, thinking of whatever kind—could be described in terms of a process of discrete steps. He viewed thinking as a process where, given a world represented in our heads in terms of symbols and their relationships, we process, manipulate, and interpret these symbols and relationships. Turing believed that these processes could be explicitly described and simulated and that machines could be programmed to think (as judged by their behavior). Once again, these ideas take us back to Leibniz: Turing's description of the symbolic foundation and symbol-manipulating operations are strikingly similar to the conceptual foundation Leibniz had developed for his *calculus ratiocinator*.

Turing made a number of other significant contributions to mathematics, philosophy, computer science, and other disciplines. He conceived of a "universal machine" based on a proof that any computer can be programmed to act like any other computer. Turing also made major contributions to the British effort to crack Nazi codes during World War II. He was part of the Enigma project that was a key to the Allied success in defeating the Germans, applying the most advanced technology available to develop calculating machines. In the early 1950s, he was arrested for the crime of being a homosexual. He was subjected to humiliating treatment including female hormone injections. He committed suicide in 1954 by eating an apple poisoned with potassium cyanide.

Artificial Intelligence

In 1956, in a request to the Rockefeller Foundation to fund a conference, John McCarthy coined the term "artificial intelligence." He described the conference's purpose as the exploration of the proposition that "intelligence can in principle be so precisely described that a machine can be made to simulate it."[10] He received the grant and sponsored the Dartmouth Summer Research Project on Artificial Intelligence.

The group that gathered for the conference included John McCarthy, Marvin Minksy, Herbert Simon, and Allen Newell, now regarded as the founding fathers of the scientific discipline of artificial intelligence. Artificial intelligence was defined by Minsky as "the science of making machines do things that would require intelligence if done by men."[11] Minsky and McCarthy formed the artificial intelligence department at MIT; later McCarthy founded a new group at Stanford University. Simon and Newell started the artificial intelligence program at what is now Carnegie Mellon University.

The group shared the common belief that computers could be programmed to simulate the workings of the mind. Simon and Newell, however, had the only demonstration that such a goal was in fact achievable. Whereas the others had idea papers, they came to Dartmouth with the first working program that enabled a computer to perform what could be considered to be intelligent behavior.

Newell and Simon, with the help of a third colleague named J. C. Shaw, developed the Logic Theorist, a program that attacked the problem of automating problem solving and the derivation of logic proofs. The Logic Theorist proved theorems from A. N. Whitehead and Bertrand Russell's *Principia Mathematica*, a landmark book in the study of formal logic published in 1910.

Simon developed the idea that the processes within a computer are analogous to the processes of the mind.

When I first began to sense that one could look at a computer as a device for processing information, not just numbers, then the metaphor I'd been using, of a mind as something that took some premises and ground them up and processed them into conclusions, began to transform itself into a notion that a mind was something which took some program inputs and data and had some processes which operated on the data and produced output.[12]

The choice of proving logic theorems was made somewhat by chance. Simon explained:

I was looking at geometry, and chess and logic—the logic we came on simply because I had the *Principia* of Whitehead and Russell at home, and I pulled it off the shelf one day to have some problems. I was doing a lot of introspecting about my own problem-solving processes, so I tried to prove some theorems in the *Principia*, but decided it was pretty hard, so it probably wouldn't be a good thing to try.[13]

Having found that dealing with the graphics of geometry was too difficult given the technology of the time, he returned to the problem posed by logic proofs. He hand-simulated a proof and then worked with Newell and Shaw to implement the program. Just before Christmas 1955, the program was working. Newell remembered his first impressions: "Kind of crude, but it works, boy, it works!" Simon recalled: "P implies P. As simple as that, it was a great event."[14]

The Logic Theorist became the first demonstration of a thinking machine. And not only did the Logic Theorist develop proofs for theorems in the *Principia*, but, in a demonstration of innovation and creativity, it developed an original shorter and more elegant proof for Theorem 2.85 than the one Whitehead and Russell had used.

The Logic Theorist can also be seen as a direct continuation of the task Leibniz had set out to address some 300 years earlier. It was the first working prototype of his *calculus ratiocinator*.

A Point of Convergence

The 1950s were a point of convergence. Different paths came together to open completely new perspectives and new directions for exploration.

Leibniz's vision diverged into separate avenues of study. His interest in symbolic logic was developed by George Boole who in turn influenced Claude Shannon. His experiments in calculating machines led to Charles Babbage and eventually on to Konrad Zuse and the first electronic calculators. Shannon's work and the first electronic calculators led directly to the invention of the first computers. The Logic Theorist, Turing, and the premise of artificial intelligence represent the full reintegration of Leibniz's work in logic, calculators, and the idea of a mechanized *calculus ratiocinator*.

At the same time, Chomsky wrote *Syntactic Structures* and invented generative grammars, establishing a view of language as rule-governed behavior. Boulez composed *Structures*, a composition represented by a grammar consisting of a set of explicit instructions that could be executed by an automated process. Kandinsky had aimed to discover a universal visual grammar and established abstraction as a part of visual languages. By the 1950s, abstract expressionism was the most significant influence on the visual arts. All of these innovators, in effect, shared a structuralist view, where the definition of the symbols and the rules that govern how they relate and can be manipulated determine meaning within the system. A structural view of languages was developing in the study of every form of communication and every form of art.

It was also a fundamental tenet of Turing and artificial intelligence that thinking and intelligence can be described in terms of rule-governed behavior. An assumption of artificial intelligence is that the world can be represented symbolically, that knowledge can be represented in terms of the structure defining how the objects of this symbolic universe relate and interact, and that thinking and intelligence can be described in terms of rules that can be applied to this representation of the world to derive conclusions and determine actions. What the thinking mechanism is, a biological vehicle such as the brain or an electronic one such as a computer, was not the issue.

Artificial intelligence viewed numbers, equations, and logic in terms of their form, just as Leibniz, Boole, and Turing did. Structuralism, also a view of things in terms of their form, permeated philosophy, linguistics, anthropology, music, and art. Structure and form became the foundation of computer science and artificial intelligence.

Conclusion

The computer is an enabling technology for exploring new domains.

The computer is essentially a structure manipulator. The workings of a computer program involve defining relationships between different objects—assigned parts of memory, bytes and words, variables or absolute values, operands—and object manipulators or operators—machine instructions that can relate and transform different objects, adding them together, shifting them left or right, comparing them for differences, moving them from one place in memory to another.

Excellent vehicles for representing and manipulating structures, computers can be applied to the study of structures used for communication—natural languages, music, the visual arts—and the study of the structures that can represent knowledge.

Various pioneers are attempting to clearly and explicitly define the structures of various languages, to define precisely the objects and rules for relating them in terms of grammars, to create representations of the structures of language thought of in terms of its form rather than content. Such representations of language and its workings are described in terms that can be interpreted by a computer. The objective: given a grammar defining a language, computers can speak or compose or paint.

In the 1950s, it was thought that the task of describing and simulating intelligence using computers might take a decade. It was believed that by the 1960s there would be demonstrable implementations of intelligent computers independently addressing complex problems. But, as research began in earnest, it became clear that the task is an enormously complex one that will require years of research. The state of the art still represents only limited demonstrations of problem solving, expert systems, vision systems, speech recognition, and language capabilities.

The task is being broken down into smaller problems: studying the processes of problem solving in terms of specific containable domains such as chess or checkers, focusing on the specific problems of language, vision, or robotic movement. Rather than attempt to model the whole complex of intelligent behavior that people manifest, parts are being studied as steps toward one day perhaps understanding the whole.

In the twentieth century the arts have explored diverse avenues. In the visual arts, painters have ranged from controlled formal structures, as in Mondrian, to controlled randomness, as in Jackson Pollock, from the use of ordinary objects in constructivist works to performance art presentations and installations. In music, composers have explored total control, as in Boulez's *Structures*, and the use of randomness and even silence, as in the works of John Cage.

Technology has always changed the available possibilities for communication and expression. When, in the fourteenth century, it was discovered that grinding colored rock into the heavy oil used to varnish carriages created a flexible new paint, oil paint changed painting. The colors of the fauves and expressionists were made possible by new colors in paints. New acrylics changed painting in the past 40 years. The invention of the well-tempered keyboard in the seventeenth century revolutionized music. More recently, electronically synthesized sounds have become a part of almost every type of music.

Computers are making possible explorations and simulations of the workings of the mind. Computers are also enabling new possibilities for communication, opening new avenues for creativity and expression.

Part I of this book presented the idea that different vehicles of expression can be viewed in terms of their structure. These structuralist views provide a foundation for using computers to explore these vehicles of expression. Part II looks at how computers, structure manipulators, are being used to explore new possibilities for creativity and expression. It reviews some of the first efforts to do so, looking at Terry Winograd's natural language system, SHRDLU, the first to integrate syntax and semantics; the first "sophisticated" computer composition systems, by Gottfried Michael Koenig and Iannis Xenakis; the first visual language systems, Harold Cohen's drawing system AARON and Brian Evans's abstract visual animations; and the first glimpses of a new world for expression, virtual reality. These explorations are only a beginning.

10 *"Natural Language"*

The ability to speak and understand language is the most obvious evidence of man's unique intelligence. As a result, given a goal of "making machines do things that would require intelligence if done by men," understanding language has always been the "holy grail" of artificial intelligence.[1]

The exploration of language is particularly important when one considers that language is at the center of our thinking process; that, in fact, language is the primary vehicle by which we think and with which we represent our knowledge of the world. It is language that shapes our view of the world and the way we interpret it.

Chomsky had laid a foundation for the concept that, given an explicit set of formal rules that describe a language, the rules could be applied to *generate* sentences in a language. The fundamental premise of artificial intelligence was that intelligence, including language, "can in principle be so precisely described that a machine can be made to simulate it."[2] Since the 1950s, researchers have used computers to simulate language systems using Chomsky's work as a foundation.

For researchers developing theories and models of language and its workings, the computer represents a tool that can implement a model and thereby test its reliability. Given a formal set of rules that describe a language, it is possible to feed the rules and a vocabulary into the computer and let the computer apply them to generate a sentence or even a dialog. A computer can rapidly generate tens, hundreds, or even thousands of sentences and within seconds demonstrate the adequacy of the set of rules. Since the computer's performance is nothing more or less than the direct result of the rules defined and programmed, the effectiveness of a model for language processing can be directly put to the test.

Researchers quickly found out that describing the processes of natural language is a far larger and more complex undertaking than was understood before computers. It is easy to establish rules to generate "The man opens the door" and "The men open the door." But it is much more difficult to establish rules that generate the previous sentences but not "The man open the door," rules that generate *only* grammatically correct sentences.

Complex relationships require more rules to be described adequately. And the more complex the relationships, the more complex the set of rules becomes. To ensure the matching of singular and plural noun and verb phrases with one another, or to match tenses, the rules rapidly expand to thousands just to describe a very small subset of English. The task of representing such complex rules for a computer becomes unmanageable.

Chomsky had already demonstrated the limits of various types of grammars, including context-sensitive grammars. The concept of transformations that he proposed to address the subtleties of language syntax was based on the idea that sentences could be thought of in terms of deeper underlying semantic structures that were appropriately transformed for a specific expression. The implication of this premise begged an even greater question: how to represent meaning within a computer.

It quickly became clear that, to represent language processes that could be simulated by a computer, tight linking was required between surface-level syntactic structures and the representation of deep semantic structures. The problem of getting computers to speak languages effectively became the problem of getting computers to *understand* languages.

The Blocks World

In 1966, Terry Winograd, an artificial intelligence researcher at MIT, built a world of blocks. The world consisted of five rectangular blocks and three pyramids in red, blue, and green, and a box that blocks could be put in. It was a limited world where objects are always made up of flat planes that meet at sharp angles, a world where only squares, rectangles, and triangles exist.

Winograd put a simple robot into this world with a single hand—an arm that could move up and down and around—and an eye to view it. His objective was to develop a computer model for understanding natural language. This world of blocks provided a context to test his model. It was the subject of dialogs between Winograd and the computer.

The program driving the arm, the eye, and the conversation was called SHRDLU—named after an old code used by linotype operators to mark errors in typesetting newspapers, "ETAOIN SHRDLU." SHRDLU was the first computer model of a language system to "deal in an integrated way with all the aspects of language: syntax, semantics, inference, and, perhaps most important, knowledge and reasoning about the subject it discusses."[3]

What follows is a conversation between Winograd, **in bold**, and SHRDLU.

1. pick up a big red block.

OK.

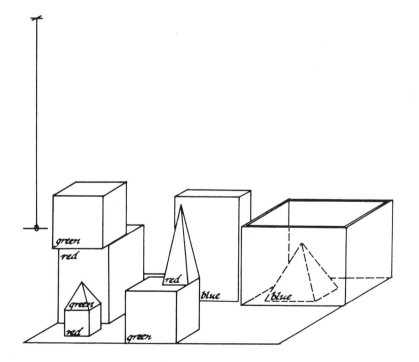

2. grasp the pyramid.

I DON'T UNDERSTAND WHICH PYRAMID YOU MEAN.

3. find a block which is taller than the one you are holding and put it into the box.

BY "IT" I ASSUME YOU MEAN THE BLOCK WHICH IS TALLER THAN THE ONE I AM HOLDING.

OK.

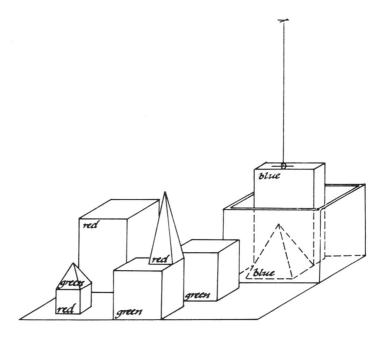

4. what does the box contain?

THE BLUE PYRAMID AND THE BLUE BLOCK.

5. what is the pyramid supported by?

THE BOX.

6. how many blocks are not in the box?

FOUR OF THEM.

7. is at least one of them narrower than the one which I told you to pick up?

YES, THE RED CUBE.

8. is it supported?

YES, BY THE TABLE.

9. can the table pick up the block?

NO.

. . .

18. which cube is sitting on the table?

THE LARGE GREEN ONE WHICH SUPPORTS THE RED PYRAMID.

19. is there a large block behind a pyramid?

YES, THREE OF THEM: A LARGE RED ONE, A LARGE GREEN CUBE AND THE BLUE ONE.

20. put a small one onto the green cube which supports a pyramid.

OK.

21. put the littlest on top of it.

OK.

22. how many things are on top of green cubes?

I'M NOT SURE WHAT YOU MEAN BY "ON TOP OF" IN THE PHRASE "ON TOP OF GREEN CUBES." DO YOU MEAN:
1—DIRECTLY ON THE SURFACE
2—ANYWHERE ON TOP OF?

2.

THREE OF THEM.

23. had you touched any pyramid before you put the green one on the little cube?

YES, THE GREEN ONE.

24. when did you pick it up?

WHILE I WAS STACKING UP THE RED CUBE, A LARGE RED BLOCK AND A LARGE GREEN CUBE.

25. why?

TO GET RID OF IT.

26. why did you do that?

TO CLEAN OFF THE RED CUBE.

27. why did you clear off that cube?

TO PUT IT ON A LARGE GREEN CUBE.

28. why did you do that?

TO STACK UP THE RED CUBE, A LARGE RED BLOCK AND A LARGE GREEN CUBE.

29. why did you do that?

BECAUSE YOU ASKED ME TO.

Reviewing this conversation, it is easy to suggest that it convincingly passes the Turing test. There is almost a feeling of annoyance expressed in the final response. Though it isn't a conversation reflecting deep intellectual challenge, the dialog gives the sense of a conversation between two intelligent beings.

The conversation may seem simple, talking about a limited world of blocks. And, in relative terms, it *is* simple. However, a closer inspection of what was required for SHRDLU to perform its side of the dialog gives a sense of just how complicated the challenge of natural language is.

Sentence Structure

To start, SHRDLU takes the typed input in English and breaks it down into root words and their modifiers. For example, "sitting" is analyzed into the root "sit" and the modifier "ing" to indicate the active interpretation of the verb. Or an adjective such as "taller" is broken down into "tall" and "er" to indicate that the adjective has the feature of being *more* "tall," and so on. Ultimately SHRDLU creates a representation of these analyzed words and attaches definitions from a dictionary to each one.

SHRDLU then does grammatical analysis to dissect the sentence and determine what role each of its parts plays, a process known as parsing. Although here a sentence that has been *input* is the subject of analysis, the grammatical description acts in the same manner as Chomsky's generative grammars in that it "associates a structural description to each permissible sentence in the language."

English sentences usually consist of a *noun phrase* followed by a *verb phrase* that is then followed by the *object* of the verb, another *noun phrase.* So, in analyzing a sentence, SHRDLU will first expect to find a noun phrase such as "the big red block" or "a block which is taller than the one you are holding." SHRDLU takes such a phrase and finds that it starts with an article such as "a" or "the." In some cases SHRDLU finds that the next word is the noun itself, "block." In others, SHRDLU finds an adjective that is associated with the noun, such as "big," or perhaps even multiple adjectives, such as "big red." Nested within a noun phrase SHRDLU might encounter a *prepositional phrase* that begins with a preposition, such as "which," and then has nested within it a verb phrase, in this case "is," another adjective or set of adjectives, such as "taller," and then a whole other noun phrase, "the one you are holding."

To accomplish this analysis, SHRDLU builds a tree representing the structure of the sentence in its component parts, and then adds branches that represent the components of each of the parts. In some cases, as it works its way down the tree, SHRDLU will find that a word doesn't quite fit the role it expected—the sentence structure cannot be sensibly resolved by following that path. So SHRDLU has to pop back up a few levels and try an alternate analysis of the structure until it finds one that makes sense for the whole sentence.

So, in the first request "**pick up a big red block**," SHRDLU starts by finding not a noun phrase but a verb phrase, "pick up." SHRDLU infers that this is an imperative sentence, which begins with a verb phrase that is followed by a noun phrase, usually indicating that a command is being issued rather than a statement. SHRDLU then finds the noun phrase it expects to follow the verb phrase—the object of the verb—and breaks it down to its components, the determiner "a," followed by two adjectives, followed by the noun itself. (See figure 10.1.)

This was a simple sentence. The third request is trickier. The structure of "**find a block which is taller than the one you are holding and put it into the box**" has verb and noun phrases nested within other verb and noun phrases. SHRDLU nonetheless breaks down the sentence and figures out what all of the nested components are and how they relate to one another. Where it finds some ambiguity, "it," SHRDLU makes the likely choice, indicates explicitly how it has resolved the ambiguity, and proceeds.

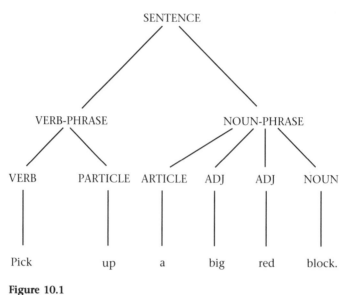

Figure 10.1
A "tree" representation of the sentence "Pick up a big red block."

Semantic Structure

Analyzing the structure of the sentence is just the beginning. Determining its semantic nature, what it means, raises a completely different set of problems. In fact, what has become clearly understood as researchers have implemented working language systems is that semantic interpretation can actually guide the syntactic interpretation. Syntactic and grammatical analysis cannot be performed efficiently without a simultaneous semantic analysis of the sentence.

In the Winograd/SHRDLU dialog, the semantic interpretation requires an understanding not only of the meaning of given words but of the overall context: the preceding discourse, knowledge of the subject matter, and knowledge of "the world."

For example, the first request is straightforward: SHRDLU can pick up "**a big red block**," any big red block. But the second, "**grasp the pyramid**," seems to refer to a specific pyramid, and there is no context to identify which one is intended (there were three pyramids among the blocks). Resolving such ambiguous references as "it" and "one" is something we take for granted. In fact, it requires quite a sophisticated model to do so correctly.

In the request "**find a block which is taller than the one you are holding and put it into the box**," SHRDLU has to resolve what the "one" and "it" refer to. It does this within the context of the sentence itself. In the request "**what is the pyramid supported by?**," SHRDLU identifies "the" pyramid by assuming it is the one it just mentioned. Similarly, in the request "**is at least one of them narrower than the one which I told you to pick up?**," the phrase "at least one of them" is interpreted by assuming that it is "one" of the "FOUR OF THEM" from the previous response.

As a result, SHRDLU must maintain a model of the world of blocks as a reference and context for understanding the dialog. SHRDLU must also maintain a memory of past events to be able to resolve all of these ambiguous references. The phase "**the one which I told you to pick up**" requires SHRDLU to refer back to the opening request in order to understand that "the one" referred to *now* is the "big red block" Winograd asked SHRDLU to pick up at that point. Similarly, in the request to "**put a small one onto the green cube which supports a pyramid**," to interpret "small one" SHRDLU must go back, find the reference to the "large block," and determine that the object referred to here is in contrast to this. Therefore, this "one" is also a block.

In the second request, "**grasp the pyramid**," there is no appropriate context to understand "the"—a context has not yet been established. In the question "**how many things are on top of green cubes?**," it becomes clear how difficult it can be to resolve simple ambiguities when none of the interpretations is clearly better.

Knowledge of the World

When SHRDLU finishes its parsing and analysis of the sentence, it creates a representation of the structure that identifies each word in the sentence, its role, and its "meaning" (a definition associated with the word retrieved from the dictionary that is part of its language facility). Each word must also be positioned within the context (how it applies to the subject of the overall discourse).

This brings up an entirely separate set of issues: the overall semantics of the discourse and the representation of knowledge and meaning. "Language is a process of communication between people, and is inextricably enmeshed in the knowledge that those people have about the world," Winograd comments. SHRDLU must have knowledge about the "properties of the particular physical world it deals with" and must maintain a model that "consists of facts about the current scene."

Though the answer to the question "**can the table pick up the block?**" is a simple "NO," it requires SHRDLU to refer to its understanding of what a table is. That is, in its dictionary definition of a table and in its knowledge of the properties of objects in its world, a table is inanimate and inanimate objects are not capable of actions such as picking things up. Therefore, the question is nonsensical.

To define words and represent knowledge within the system, Winograd developed a *semantic network* that included symbols representing "objects," "properties," and their "relations." Winograd used a notation that added a colon to objects to identify them as such (e.g., :OBJECT), and added a # to properties (e.g., #PROPERTY). Relationships between objects and properties were then expressed by their sequence, with properties first and related items following. Using this notation, "A pyramid is a block" is represented as

(#BLOCK :PYRAMID)

and "The pyramid is on top of the block" as

(#ON-TOP-OF :PYRAMID :BLOCK)

and "The pyramid is blue" as

(#BLUE :PYRAMID).

Properties serve in a dual function, as they both say things about objects, as in the last of the above representations, and say things about other properties, such as "Blue is a color":

(#COLOR #BLUE).

The representation of knowledge becomes a network of lists of objects, their properties, and the relationships that exist between them. They are interconnected wherever there needs to be an appropriate link. The definition of a word within the system is made in terms of other words. Echoing Saussure, Winograd explains: "Definitions are circular, with the meaning of each concept depending on the other concepts."

Missing Pieces

This only begins to hint at the complexity underlying this simple conversation about a simple world of blocks. SHRDLU needed another set of facilities to *respond* to Winograd's part of the dialog, including the rules not only for generating correct expressions in a language, but also for generating natural ones. In responses like "THE LARGE GREEN ONE WHICH SUPPORTS THE RED PYRAMID" and "YES, THREE OF THEM; A LARGE RED ONE, A LARGE GREEN CUBE AND THE BLUE ONE," SHRDLU uses words like "one" that make the conversation seem more natural.

Furthermore, Winograd's model does not attempt to address many of the issues that need to be considered in real conversation. For example, speech recognition. For a computer to recognize spoken language, a microphone records a voice and generates a digital representation of the voice in the form of a series of numbers that represent the amplitude of the sound wave. A computer must then analyze these numbers to find recognizable patterns that are the basic sound elements of the language (phonemes).

Unlike in typed dialog, when spoken language is introduced a speaker and his voice are introduced. No two speakers' voices are exactly the same, nor are any two utterances from even the same speaker exactly the same. So scanning these numbers and finding matches with patterns becomes a very difficult problem of finding the best approximations of patterns. Then consider that words are slurred and run into one another; syllables blur and are truncated or even drop out. Raw spoken language is very fluid and very difficult to interpret. Analysis is likely to yield several possible interpretations for each element of the spoken sentence.

Once again, there is a need to establish the rules of the system. It is necessary to describe the phonological rules for combining sounds to make syllables and words. The rules will include permissible sequences of sounds. Since not all combinations and sequences occur in a language, eliminating illegal ones guides the search for the correct interpretation. It is necessary to have an understanding of the context of each sound, the surrounding sounds, and the placement within the sentence, since the preceding or subsequent sound can influence how another element sounds.

Phonemic analysis requires an understanding of the sentence and the overall context. For example, with two similar sounds like "hit" and "hid," it may be only the context of the sentence or even of the dialog that will permit a correct interpretation of which sound is intended. A rough analysis of the potential choices for each element in the sequence of sounds is made by checking for those sequences that form real words that can be found in the dictionary. The selection of the correct word will then depend on the context of the discussion and on which of the words makes sense in this particular context.

Completely blurred or garbled words might be filled in, given the context and semantic interpretation. In a sentence where the sound sequence for "might" is followed by an unintelligible sequence of noise and then by the sound sequence for "been," the system can intelligently guess that the middle word is likely to be "have" and then check that this makes sense or see if now, armed with this inference, the sequence of noise can be better interpreted.

The rules and knowledge required for interpreting spoken language are complex. To work efficiently, they must be integrated into a larger system that includes syntactic and semantic analysis.

Visualizing the Scene

For a system like Winograd's to function, even in a simple world of blocks, there must be a *scene*. Therefore, there must be an eye and a system for analyzing visual data. A television camera records the image, generating a digital representation of the image in the form of a series of numbers that represent light intensities. The computer can analyze these numbers to find recognizable patterns that are the basic visual elements that ultimately define a visual language. Rather than phonemes, syllables, and words, the visual primitives are lines, planes, corners, shapes, and forms.

As in dialog, when the real world is introduced the complexity of information becomes enormous. No two perspectives are exactly the same, nor are any two different scenes ever exactly the same. So, again, the challenge of scanning these numbers and finding matches with patterns becomes a very difficult one of finding the best approximations. Interpretation must then address the fact that images have shadows, glare, and other effects of lighting, run into one another, blur, and are even obscured. The visual world is also very fluid and very difficult to interpret; analysis may yield multiple interpretations of a given scene.

So, again, there is a need to establish rules for the system. There is a visual grammar to describe the rules for combining lines, corners, planes, surfaces, shapes, and forms to create physical objects. Semantic interpretation must again be integrated into the process: an understanding of the context of each object, surrounding objects, their placement within an environment, the environment as a whole, and so on.

A knowledge database will include a representation of knowledge about the basic types of forms that occur in the world: concave and convex edges, cracks, shadows, and so on. The rules will define permissible combinations of visual cues that occur to form objects. Not all combinations and sequences can occur in a given world, and eliminating illegal ones guides the search for the correct interpretation. Rather than a dictionary of words and a representation of knowledge about the subject of discourse, there is a dictionary or database of forms and a representation of knowledge about objects: squares, rectangles, cubes, pyramids, boxes, and so on.

Visual analysis requires an understanding of the viewed environment and the overall context. Often, only the larger context or an understanding of the world will permit correct interpretation of an ambiguous image. Finding three corners, the computer can use a knowledge of cubes to infer that the object has other sides, a certain dimension, and so on. Viewed from a given angle, the side of a cube may not appear square, but a knowledge of squares and the effects of perspective can be used to differentiate between a square and a rectangle. If a side is obscured or is not clearly seen due to the lighting, the missing lines might be filled in given the context and applying knowledge about objects as part of semantic interpretation.

Even in a limited world of blocks, the difficulties of interpreting visual information are enormous, with innumerable possible configurations of blocks stacked one on top of the other, differing angles of perspective, one form obscuring another, and so on.

A Structuralist View at the Core

Winograd's world of blocks is a relatively simple one, requiring only a limited language, a small body of knowledge, and a rudimentary visual capability. Even so, the system that Winograd built was stretched to its limits. It could not handle a much more complex world than the one it operated in.

One can imagine that, as we connect symbols to other symbols in an integrated network of objects, properties, and relationships, we will be able to capture more than the relationships of a world of blocks. Eventually we may capture millions of complex relationships in a massively complex web that links "blue" to "sky" and "sky" to "vast expanse" and "vast expanse" to "ocean"; we may begin to capture the richness of meaning. Meaning derives not from any single symbol or sign in the system, but rather from the inter-relationships of all the objects, properties, and relationships within the system.

We have arrived again at Saussure's structuralist view of meaning. It is not necessary to have a referent for each sign. Meaning and sense are discussed in terms of structure. Words are understood by their place within a system of other words that are in opposition to them and circumscribe them. Meaning is a question of positional value.

Winograd's representation of knowledge also recalls Leibniz's proposal to define a set of elemental concepts and make explicit the relationships between them. Leibniz thought of concepts as containing one another, such as the concept of *animal* containing that of *living thing* in the statement "Every animal is a living thing." In SHRDLU, Leibniz's network of links between elemental concepts is the basis for defining terms and, ultimately, meaning within the system.

Leibniz foresaw a reasoning machine capable of the automated manipulation of these concepts by logical operations to derive various conclusions. In Winograd's model of language processes, "the structure of concepts ... can be manipulated by inference processes [i.e., logical operations] within the computer. The 'internal representation' of a sentence is something which the system can obey, answer, or add to its knowledge. It can relate a sentence to other concepts, draw conclusions from it, or store it in a way which makes it usable in further deductions and analysis."

Questions of Meaning

Winograd's contribution to natural language research was to make evident that understanding language requires a process in which various types of analysis, both syntactic and semantic, have to occur in an integrated manner. He demonstrated that linguistic understanding could not happen without integrating a knowledge of a much broader context: "the world."

Various philosophers debate whether a computer can really understand language. What concept does the computer have of objects such as pyramids and blocks? What sense does a computer have of properties such as colors? Can a computer associate blocks with childhood experiences and have the emotions or sensations that such associations arouse in people? Can a computer understand that blue is the color of the sea and sky and invokes feelings of wide open expanses, of worlds open to exploration? What is it to say that meaning can be *understood* just through a representation of a network of relationships between empty symbols?

Winograd did "not attempt to give a philosophical answer to these questions." Instead, like Turing, he took a very pragmatic approach to the question of meaning:

This representation of meaning is not intended as a direct picture of something which exists in a person's mind. It is a fiction that gives us a way to make sense of data, and to predict actual behavior. The justification for our particular use of concepts in this system is that it is thereby enabled to engage in dialogs that simulate in many ways the behavior of a human language user.

Conclusion

The immense challenge of addressing natural language processing in a real world environment should by now be tangible. The picture that should begin to emerge is that natural language is a tremendously complex hierarchical system.

In *generating* expressions in a language, the hierarchy starts with the deep semantic structure: what it is that is to be communicated. This is translated into a sentence that consists of phrases that consist of words. The words consist of phonemes that ultimately will be translated into vibrations that push the air to create the sounds that realize the expression.

To *interpret* expressions, moving down the hierarchy, the process begins with the sounds that must be analyzed and built into a string of phonemes. Having recognized the phonemic structure, the phonemes must be grouped to form words. From this lexical structure syntactic structures are built that form phrases that, in turn, form complete sentences. And from these sentences, meaning must ultimately be derived if there is to be communication.

Language is a system that consists of a hierarchy of systems. Each system has its fundamental components: phonemes, words, sentences, semantic units. Each system has its rules for generating or interpreting structures: for combining and sequencing elements. Each level can be viewed from multiple perspectives, syntactic and semantic. And each system can itself be seen as the base element of another system at a different level in the hierarchy.

The total system requires a complex interaction between all of the different component systems, between syntax and semantics, between phonemic structure and word (morphemic) structure, between word structure and phrase and sentence structure, between the meaning of a sentence and its context in the larger dialog, between the subject of discourse and the overall environment, between the specifics of a given environment and general knowledge of the world.

This hierarchical system of systems is reflected in language interpretation and language generation. It is part of speech recognition. It is part of visual processing. It is a fundamental property of *all* thought processes.

Since Winograd's pioneering work, different people tackling the challenge of natural language understanding have taken different approaches. Winograd used systemic grammars. Woods, Schank, Berwick, and others have developed other alternative approaches.

Though the techniques may vary, in the end they all are dealing with the same problem: the explicit description of the structure and rules of a complex hierarchical system. Also common to all of these approaches is the enabling technology of computers. Computers provide the underlying vehicle to test these various models of language. Computers have made these explorations of language possible.

11 *Composing Machines*

Charles Babbage's work on his Analytical Engine is best known today through the documentation of his work by Lady Ada Lovelace. The daughter of Lord Byron, Lady Lovelace perceived the tremendous potential and far-reaching implications of Babbage's work. She schemed with Babbage to develop a tic-tac-toe-playing machine as a means to raise capital to build his Analytical Engine. And she twice pawned her family jewels (to have them redeemed by her mother, Lady Byron) to fund his work, putting her deeply into debt and threatening her name with scandal.

Lady Lovelace, inspired by Babbage's work, foresaw that it might be possible for a machine to write music. She predicted that if it were possible to define "the fundamental relations of pitched sounds in the science of harmony and of musical composition ... [then] ... the engine might compose elaborate and scientific pieces of music of any degree of complexity or extent."[1]

One hundred years later, the first experiments using computers to write music were initiated.

Stockhausen in Cologne

Stockhausen returned to Germany from Paris in 1953. He was invited as a guest of the West German Radio (WDR) in Cologne. Established as a leader of the postwar avant-garde, he attracted a group of composers to Cologne, which became a center of musical activity and innovation. Experiments in Cologne laid a foundation for computer composition.

At the time, Stockhausen, Boulez, and others, notably in Paris and New York, had conducted experiments using tapes and recordings of *natural* sounds—what is called *musique concrète*. The focus of these experiments was on the sounds and textures that could be created with the then new techniques of recording with tape. But the raw material was always recordings of natural sounds.

WDR had established a studio to explore the implications of *electronic* technology for music. It was started under the direction of Dr. Werner Meyer-Eppler of the Institute of Communication Theory of the University of Bonn, and Herbert Eimert, a music critic. Robert Beyer, who also collaborated in the development of the studio, had speculated on the possibilities of electronically generated sounds since the 1920s.

Stockhausen had access to the state-of-the-art facilities of WDR, including its recording studios and electronic equipment. The facilities were simple compared to even a home stereo today. All Stockhausen used for his first experiments were simple single-track tape recorders and single-frequency sine wave generators.

Sine wave generators are electronic devices that produce the most simple and pure of sounds: the sine wave (see figure 11.1). In the early nineteenth century, the French mathematician Fourier had demonstrated that, in theory, any sound can be built from simple sine waves. Fourier showed that, using combinations of different sine waves at different frequencies, complex rich timbres could be created.

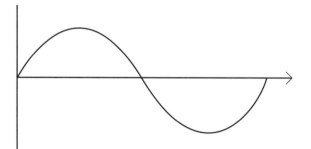

Figure 11.1
A sine wave.

WDR's sine wave generators provided the basis for a radical shift in approach to music composition. The sine wave generators could act as a completely *electronic* source of sound material, and simple sine waves could be combined to create complex rich sounds. For the first time, it was possible to create *electronic* music.

The foundations had been laid for Stockhausen to explore the integration of electronically produced sounds with principles of serial composition. Starting with pure sine waves and electronic control, he could achieve the precision and control that were the essence of serialism. In fact, for the first time, not only could the structure of the composition be controlled at the note level, but the structure of the sounds themselves could be controlled, and this too was done in serialist fashion. The frequencies of the generators and the durations of each sound (determined by the length of tape) were determined by serial composition processes.

With the work in Cologne, it could be said that composition was occurring for the first time at a microlevel, at a level of granularity smaller than that of a note. The note had been the simplest atomic element that composers had used prior to the availability of electronic devices. But these new devices could control the components of a sound, the simple sine waves that were combined to create complex sounds. Rather than composing from a predetermined palette of instrumental sounds—oboes, clarinets, violins, piano, whatever—the sounds themselves were composed from simple sine waves.

The goal of electronic music composition at the Cologne studios became: "Work and material have the same structure." Electronic techniques opened a completely new capability: the application of serial principles to the construction of the sounds used in a composition as well as the structure of the composition itself. All aspects of music could share a structure unified by serial processes. Stockhausen described this new potential:

The same proportions that I use to organize time I can now also use for the intervals needed to compose certain spectra; the same proportions which regulate the maximum intensities of different sounds, I can also use for the intensities of the individual partials in a spectrum and of the individual noise bands in a sound complex of colored noise; and the same proportions which serve to control the durations and intervals of entry of sounds and noises having the most varied gradations, I can also use to organize the inner evolution within a sound, only now of course all on a very reduced time scale.[2]

Gottfried Michael Koenig

Stockhausen's first simple studies and experiments were made entirely with sine waves—*Studie I* (1953) and *Studie II* (1954). After this, he conceived much more complicated works. Given the technology of the time, the process of "constructing" and assembling sounds for these pieces was very involved.

To create his more complicated works, Stockhausen collaborated with another young composer and electronic recording technician, Gottfried Michael Koenig. Together, working in the studio days and nights, they created two landmark works, *Gesang der Jünglinge* (1956) and *Kontakte* (1959–1960), requiring a period of six months and ten months of work respectively.

Koenig had studied music in Detmold, Germany, between 1947 and 1950. In 1951 he decided he wanted to compose electronic music: "The moment I knew about the possibility of electronic music, I wanted to be involved."[3] He wrote to all the radio stations in Germany to find out what plans they had for building electronic music studios, including to Meyer-Eppler in Bonn and Eimert in Cologne. When Stockhausen came to Cologne in 1953, Eimert offered Koenig the opportunity to work with Stockhausen. Koenig, at first, did not like Stockhausen's music, so he decided instead to continue his studies. But a year later, compelled by his interest in electronic music, he took Eimert up on his offer, collaborating closely with Stockhausen for the next eight years.

Koenig also composed a number of electronic works that were very influential in the 1950s. To create *Essay, Composition for Electronic Sounds*, Koenig measured and cut segments of tape with recordings of different sine waves to precise lengths. Noise generators were used to create a broad spectrum of white noise. Filters were also employed to create filtered bands of noise with a variety of timbral qualities. These cut segments—hundreds of pieces of tape spread across the studio in assorted piles—were then spliced together to form sequences of sounds and silences. Then these tapes were placed on a tape deck. Finally, two tape decks were synchronized for playback and recorded on a third. (Only three were available.) This process was repeated to build up complex sounds.

Essay was unusual not only for its varied and rich vocabulary of sounds but for its unusual score. Rather than notated music, the score consisted of all the instructions required to create the piece, written out in German. The instructions could be followed by anyone to create a "performance" of the work.

Koenig taught electronic music as well as composition and analysis at the Cologne Conservatory of Music until 1964, when he was appointed the artistic director of the Institute of Sonology at Utrecht University in Holland. The Institute had recently been established as a research center dedicated to the investigation of sound generally, and the use of electronics and computers in music in particular. Having studied computer programming at the University of Bonn, Koenig developed his Project 1 computer-controlled composing program in Holland between 1964 and 1966, followed by Project 2 developed between 1966 and 1968. His work over the past 25 years has clearly established Koenig as one of the pioneers of using computers in the composition process.

The Score as Program

For Koenig, the idea of a program controlling musical processes did not originate with his introduction to computers. He was already accustomed to thinking of serial processes as programs for composition. Koenig's investigations of the use of the computer as part of the composition process was a natural direction for his work to take.

Between 1957 and 1963, Koenig had composed a number of works including "electronic pieces, two piano pieces, a wind quintet, a string quartet and three orchestral pieces, applying composing methods which could one and all have been performed with the aid of a computer."[4] He had used electronic processes and what were called "patches" in the studio to automatically control variables in his electronic music compositions.

Koenig also thought of the score for his *Essay* as a "program" consisting of all of the instructions required to realize the composition: what should be recorded, the length the tapes should be cut, how they should be ordered, and so on. Given the instructions, anyone with the appropriate equipment could realize the composition. Koenig explains,

The score is instructions for creating a composition. A computer is much more reliable for precisely executing the composition. Traditionally, the score undergoes all sorts of interpretation. With rule systems, I want to find out what the rules really do. I can do it by hand, it just takes more time.[5]

The computer could be used to reliably execute instructions for realizing a composition, and to do so without subjective interpretation of them. In this way, Koenig could see the direct results his instructions would produce.

Serial music processes were the foundation of his first composition program, Project 1. Though Project 1 allowed the composer to have influence over a number of variables that would affect the generation or composition of music using these serial processes, for the most part Koenig had limited the composer's influence in this program. Project 2, on the other hand,

would allow a composer to fill in his own variables, not only with respect to the musical material—what kind of pitches or loudnesses or durations—but also with respect to compositional rules—the way the elements are put together to form a musical context.... *Project 2* is actually a questionnaire of more than sixty questions. According to those questions, which refer to the musical material and the rules, the program would combine or compose a piece.[6]

In *Project 2*, a composer could choose between five different procedures for generating structures: a random process, a serial process, using weightings to bias selections, defining "tendencies," and repetition of single elements to form groups. Though a composer could have significantly more influence on the program than before, he still had to select from a predefined set of generative procedures and could only influence those variables that the program allowed.

In effect, by controlling the variables and generally determining the output from the computer, the composer is selecting musical sound structures from a broader set of possibilities. To Koenig, this seems a natural and traditional role for composers. He believes that, through the centuries, composers have always made selections from a wide variety of choices: instruments, harmonies, rhythms, tempi.

Koenig's Project 1 and Project 2 programs have been implemented in a number of universities and schools throughout the world. They have been used not only to compose music but also for choreography, to create visual images, and to design electronic synthesizer sounds. These composition programs represent the first efforts to formalize and then automate serial and other compositional techniques.

Iannis Xenakis's Stochastic Music

Though in the early 1950s Boulez and Stockhausen were sparring for leadership of the avant-garde, both were champions of total serialism. What they and their disciples took as gospel was that serialism and control are essential elements of music composition. When confronted by the random chance of John Cage's music, Boulez found himself unable to accept or tolerate such a concept, unable even to talk again to Cage.

Iannis Xenakis, a composer also working in Paris at the time, used what he called *stochastic* processes in his compositions. "Stochastic," derived from the Greek word for "target," refers to a process based on probability theory: given a well-defined context, probability theory holds that the results of random processes will reach a determinate end. It should be no surprise then that Xenakis was not exactly a close colleague of composers in the serial schools; any association with random processes was totally outside of the mainstream avant-garde in postwar France. (By the 1960s, when Koenig began to use random procedures, Stockhausen, breaking with Boulez's rigid approach and influenced by Cage, had made random processes an accepted part of European avant-garde practice.)

A veteran of the anti-Nazi Greek resistance during World War II, Xenakis fled to Italy during the subsequent Greek civil war, pursued by the military police of the right-wing government. Smuggled into France, he settled in Paris, where he studied music with Arthur Honegger and Darius Milhaud, and in 1950–1951 with Olivier Messiaen. A graduate of the Athens Polytechnic with a degree in engineering, he also worked as a successful architect, assisting Le Corbusier between 1948 and 1959. Xenakis designed the Philips Pavilion for the 1958 Brussels Exhibition (a world's fair).

Xenakis's background in mathematics was a key in shaping his ideas about music. In particular, his concept of stochastic music is derived from the "law of large numbers" developed by the Swiss mathematician Jacques Bernouilli in 1713. Bernouilli's concept (for which he coined the term "stochastic") was that the more numerous a set of repeated phenomena, the more they will tend to a determinate end. For example, the first few tosses of a coin will produce unpredictable results; but the more the coin is tossed, the more the overall result will tend to be heads half the time, tails the other half. The more numerous the phenomena, the more predictably they tend to a determinate end. Xenakis saw this as analogous to "a strait-jacket placed around the problems of chance."[7]

Xenakis formed his ideas for stochastic music during World War II. He recounts:

In my music there is all the agony of my youth, of the Resistance and the aesthetic problems they posed with the huge street demonstrations, or even more the occasional mysterious, deathly sounds of those cold nights of December '44 in Athens. From this was born my conception of the massing of sound events, and therefore of stochastic music.[8]

Xenakis's music consists of big blocks of sound, thick textures developed by his stochastic techniques. For example, a thick texture can be created by 25 violins independently plucking their strings *pizzicato*, or sliding along the strings *glissando* while bowing in an unsynchronized manner, or from the dense patter of hitting the strings with the bow *col legno*. The blocks consist of dense clusters of many single notes played by the violins, so dense that single notes are beyond recognition and all that is important is the overall texture and density.

Within such a defined texture, it is possible to randomly assign specific entry points, note values, and durations to each single occurrence, each note of a violin. The contribution of that specific note is its part in a dense texture; though its specific value can be randomly filled in, the overall result is predictable, especially as the events that make up the texture become denser and more numerous.

Given such textures of sound, Xenakis also conceived of larger structures in terms of stochastic processes: "The composition of the orchestra could be stochastically conceived … during a sequence of a given duration it may happen that we have 80% pizzicati, 10% percussion, 7% keyboard and 3% flute class."[9] Such sequences, built by combining a variety of textures, were thought of as distinct blocks of sound.

Xenakis then used formulas that would describe transitions between different blocks and textures, also in terms of probability. For example, there are eight different types of textures in his *Syrmos*, written in 1959. He developed the following matrix of probabilities to determine the transitions from one block to another:

	A	B	C	D	E	F	G	H
A	.021	.357	.084	.189	.165	.204	.408	.096
B	.084	.089	.076	.126	.150	.136	.072	.144
C	.084	.323	.021	.126	.150	.036	.272	.144
D	.336	.081	.019	.084	.135	.024	.048	.216
E	.019	.063	.336	.171	.110	.306	.120	.064
F	.076	.016	.304	.114	.100	.204	.018	.096
G	.076	.057	.084	.114	.100	.054	.068	.096
H	.304	.014	.076	.076	.090	.036	.012	.144

In this matrix, the letters at the top represent the starting points and the letters at the left the endpoints of the various transitions; a value is assigned representing the weight or probability for each transition that can occur. Looking at column E, for example, there is a 10 percent probability that an E block will transition to an F or a G block, a 15 percent probability to a B or a C block, and so on.

For Xenakis, given the general characteristics of a block of sound defined by limits and constraints, the working out of the particular details was a process of tedious calculation. These calculations could be performed manually or automatically, using a computer. Xenakis chose to employ a computer. Having composed some works in which he performed the calculations manually, "quite suddenly it became apparent to me that, since this thing had been entirely resolved by calculus it would be possible to work a machine which would make the calculations instead of me."[10] To this end, some of his later stochastic works, *ST/4-1 080262* and *ST/10-1 080262*, were composed with the aid of an IBM 7090 mainframe. The 7090 performed the necessary calculations, for four and ten instruments respectively, on February 8, 1962. As a result,

1) the long laborious calculation by hand is reduced to nothing; 2) freed from tedious calculations the composer is able to devote himself to the general problems that the new musical form poses and to explore the nooks and crannies of this form while modifying values of the input data.[11]

Xenakis, again not surprisingly, was no fan of the serialists. In fact, he attacked serialist music in an abusive critique published in 1955. However, in spite of his use of random processes in a controlled manner in his own composition, neither was Xenakis a fan of music that allowed the performer any choice in the use of random processes. He saw such latitude as "an abuse of language and an abrogation of a composer's function."[12]

Xenakis continued his use of computers in the composition of music at the School of Mathematical and Automated Music in Paris in 1966, and then at another center of the same name at Indiana University in 1967, both of which he established.

Conclusion

Like natural language, music is a system that consists of a hierarchy of systems. Each system has its fundamental components: the 1/50,000th-of-a-second micro–sound sample, the note or sound event, themes and phrases, and ultimately the structure of a complete work. Each system has its rules for describing its structures: for combining and sequencing elements. And each system can itself be seen as the base element of another system at a different level in the hierarchy.

Though the techniques may vary, in the end composers using computers as part of the composition process are all dealing with the same problem: *the explicit description of the structure and rules of a complex hierarchical system.*

As with natural language, the challenge of describing the rules and structure of music systems is enormous. More and more composers are exploring the use of computers in the composition process. Computers are an enabling technology, making these explorations of new music languages possible.

Most composers today use tools developed by themselves that are well suited for their specific goals. There is still a lack of generalized tools that would free composers from the burden of developing such tools. Therefore, they require an expertise that has little to do with composition. Though today few in numbers, composers who conceive of the computer as an essential part of their composition process will see powerful and flexible tools develop and a new world of music unfold.

The experiments have been limited. The tools and technology applied so far are, doubtless, very primitive. But the journey has begun. The tools for the exploration of new artistic dimensions are under development, and a future where computers are an integral part of the composition process is inevitable.

12 *The Visual World*

Kandinsky's *Point and Line to Plane* formed the theoretical foundation for his work while at the Bauhaus in the 1920s. It was also the departure point for an analysis Ray Lauzzana and Lynn Pocock-Williams did of Kandinsky's work sixty years later.

They studied Kandinsky's *Point and Line to Plane* to ensure that they had a clear understanding of his intentions and motives. They also analyzed a series of his works from the Bauhaus period. They characterized his rules of form and composition as an explicit shape grammar that could be interpreted by a computer. Given this grammar, a computer created new images that conform to these rules.

Lauzzana and Pocock-Williams developed two sets of rules to describe Kandinsky's visual language, one set that they call the "physical rules" and one that they call the "spiritual rules." The physical rules deal with lines, form, and composition. Like Kandinsky, they defined the basic elements of composition: points, lines, and planes. They defined the different types of lines and planes. For example, there are straight lines, jagged lines, curved lines, and complex lines. Each of these lines is then further described. For example, straight lines can be horizontal, vertical, diagonal, and so on.

The spiritual rules, again based on Kandinsky's writings, are concerned with the "meaning" of a painting. These rules, for example, characterize a vertical line as warm, a horizontal line as cold, and a diagonal line as neutral.

Using this rule system, Lauzzana and Pocock-Williams then developed a set of rules that characterize Kandinsky's *Dream Motion*. (See plate 10.) For example, they noted that Kandinsky's works tend to

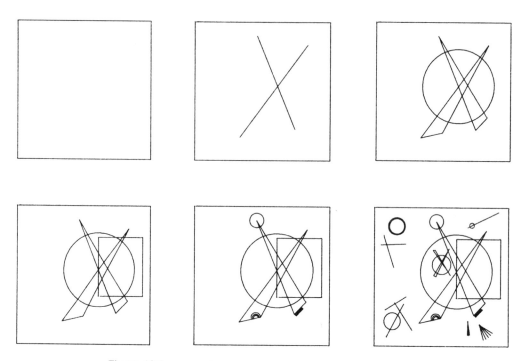

Figure 12.1
Raymond Guido Lauzzana and Lynn Pocock-Williams, six steps of development using rules describing Kandinsky's *Dream Motion* (1923).

consist of a central figure surrounded by clusters. The central figures consist of a collection of geometrical objects joined together at a point near the center of the canvas. Clusters consist of smaller groups of objects placed distant from the center. The clusters are placed around the central figure in a manner that places more focus on the central figure.

Starting with a blank "canvas," they described a set of rules that creates two intersecting lines (steps 1 and 2 in figure 12.1). The point of intersection, placed reasonably centrally on the canvas, then becomes the center of a circle. The intersecting lines are also used as the sides for two triangles (step 3). Other objects such as rectangles and circles are added as part of the central figure (steps 4 and 5). Similar rules generate additional clusters. Different rules described different types of clusters: arrangements of the circles, stray lines, and triangles (step 6).

Using the rules thus defined, the computer can generate a number of images. Figure 12.2 shows six such images.

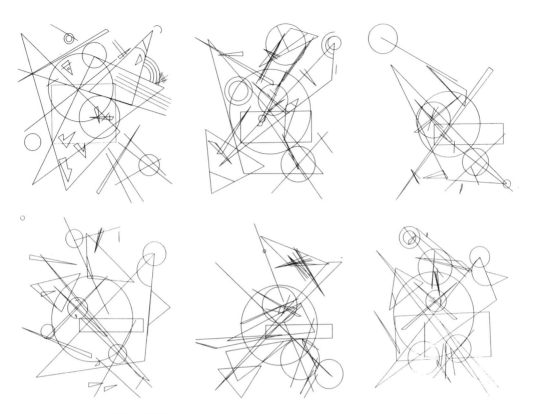

Figure 12.2
Raymond Guido Lauzzana and Lynn Pocock-Williams, six images created using
rules describing Kandinsky's *Dream Motion* (1923).

The rules Lauzzana and Pocock-Williams defined deal only with
composition and form; they did not address color, texture, or other
properties of Kandinsky's language. But their work demonstrates that,
just as in natural languages and music, expressions in visual languages can also be generated by a computer given explicitly and formally defined rules in the form of a grammar.

Others have applied similar techniques to develop explicit descriptions of the rules of other visual languages.[1] Grammars have been
developed that describe the painting styles of Joan Miró, Juan Gris,
and Richard Diebenkorn, and the architectural style of Frank Lloyd
Wright. But, while such studies are interesting, more interesting for
our purposes is the application of these techniques by other artists to
create new visual languages.

Dada

In the years just before World War I, the pursuit of abstraction in painting had begun with the breakthroughs of Kandinsky, who was rapidly followed by others throughout Europe. During the war, while Kandinsky was still in Russia, one school of artists pursued a radically different path. Their thinking was deeply affected by the butchery of the war, a cataclysmic event that shook the foundations of European intellectual thought. The massive destruction and horrendous toll in lives left the question of meaning paramount and seemingly incomprehensible.

Switzerland was a haven for refugees from the war. The composer Igor Stravinsky was living in Geneva. James Joyce was writing *Ulysses* in Zurich, where Lenin, Radek, and Zinoviev were preparing for the Russian Revolution. In early 1916, Hugo Ball, a German poet, opened what was a cross between a nightclub and an art society in Zurich, called Cabaret Voltaire.

Cabaret Voltaire quickly became a gathering place for young poets and artists. Many were war refugees and all were alienated from a society they viewed as based on greed, materialism, and "godless philosophies." Seeing the start of a new movement of ideas, Ball and Richard Huelsenbeck came up with the name *dada*—meant to evoke the first sounds of a child, and so to represent a new beginning. The group included Tristan Tzara and Georges Janco, both from Romania, Hans Arp, an Alsatian, and Ball, Huelsenbeck, and Hans Richter from Germany.

Arp wrote:

While the thunder of the batteries rumbled in the distance, we pasted, we recited, we versified, we sang with all our soul. We searched for an elementary art that would, we thought, save mankind from the madness of these times. We searched for an elementary art that would, we thought, save mankind from the furious folly of these times.... Dada wanted to replace the logical nonsense of the men of today with the illogically senseless. That is why we pounded with all our might on the big drum of Dada and trumpeted the praises of unreason.[2]

When the war ended, the original dadaists spread throughout Europe and to the United States. They found that similarly alienated artists were quick to embrace the ideas of dada. It found fervent proponents in André Breton and Francis Picabia in Paris, and Marcel Duchamp and Man Ray in New York.

Dada didn't represent a style of art. Rather, it was a philosophical disposition, or, as Breton said, "a state of mind." The objective was liberation from the strictures of rationality, materialism, and the social and artistic conventions that were thought of as an integral part of the bourgeois capitalist society that had created World War I. Dada represented a rejection of traditional values and traditional good taste. Its exhibitions were the presentation of transitory, impermanent, and often clearly meaningless objects. Dada works were often only theatrical gestures. Dadaists didn't believe it was necessary to see emotion at the core of creativity. They believed anybody could create poetry and paintings. And they believed that man-made objects and machine-made objects were of fundamentally the same value.

Works representative of the dadaist philosophy include a sculpture by Max Ernst with an axe attached—to be used to destroy it; an infamous urinal entitled *Fountain* that Duchamp entered into the Independents exhibition in New York; and Man Ray's *Gift*, a flatiron with tin tacks stuck to the bottom of it.

However, dada, in negating everything, also inevitably negated itself. The logical conclusion of dada is best exemplified by Duchamp, who after 1923 renounced all artistic activity. Others, such as Arp, Ernst, and Man Ray, took up the ideals of surrealism. Breton proposed that the key idea of dada was the freedom of artistic thought, rather than the destruction of artistic values, and this freedom became the goal of surrealism.

Jean Tinguely

Among the legacies of the dada movement were the first experiments in *kinetic* sculpture, sculpture that moves. The first kinetic sculpture is considered to be Duchamp's *Bicycle Wheel*, from 1913. The bicycle was at that time a recent invention that revolutionized personal transportation, as did the automobile. The bicycle wheel was one of the lightest and most elegant devices then in common use.

Duchamp's *Bicycle Wheel* consisted of a bicycle wheel mounted in a bicycle's Y-frame inverted on a kitchen stool. Inverted, it provokes the ironic thought of a vehicle for movement going nowhere, rendered functionally immobile, like a turtle on its back. This simple idea became the first of a new genre of artistic works in the twentieth century that would explore motion from various perspectives. Duchamp, László Moholy-Nagy at the Bauhaus, and others did a small number of experiments with motion in art, and Alexander Calder designed mobiles in the 1930s. It was not until the 1950s, however, that artists focused on this area.

A Swiss artist, Jean Tinguely, working in a neodadaist tradition, took up kinetic art with a special perversity. Tinguely's unusual and anarchistic sense of humor was reflected in his apartment. He took the doors from their hinges and hung them from the ceilings where, attached to motors, they could rotate at high speeds.

Tinguely developed mechanistic sculptures that poked fun at the machine age and at art itself. He developed sculptures that were monstrous machines. He designed machines to attack one another, and autodestructive sculptures that, in effect, committed a mechanical suicide. He also designed machines that could themselves create works of art, which he called "meta-matics."

In 1955 an exhibition in Paris of pioneering works of kinetic art, called "Le Mouvement," featured one of the first of Tinguely's meta-matic sculptures. This sculpture produced abstract drawings by an automated mechanistic process using a motor-driven mechanical device with a pen attached and following a random sequence. (See figure 12.3.)

In 1960, Tinguely lived for a few months in New York, during which he created a massive autodestructive machine for an event that took place at the Museum of Modern Art on March 17. The work was called *Homage to New York*.[3] In dada tradition, it featured a large number of bicycle wheels. Given three weeks to build the sculpture, Tinguely bought dozens of motors, a powerful electric fan, steel tubing, a meteorological balloon, a radio, an upright piano, and titanium tetrachloride for making smoke. He retrieved 80 old bicycle wheels from a dump, as well as oil cans and a drum from an old washing machine.

Tinguely created a construction 23 feet long and 27 feet high. In the middle, a large horizontal roll of paper was fed down through a metal trough. Held by elaborately constructed painting arms driven by electric motors, two large paint brushes were positioned to paint

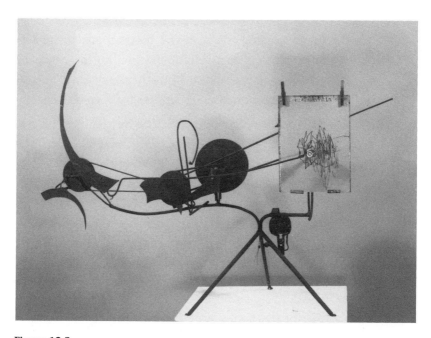

Figure 12.3
Jean Tinguely's *Meta-Matic #9* (1954 or 1959). The Museum of Fine Arts, Houston, gift of D. and J. de Menil.

on the roll as it moved by. Another smaller meta-matic drawing machine sat on top of the piano. Other arms built out of bicycle parts were set to strike the piano keys in a sequence, while the radio, nailed to the side of the piano, would also make noise. The meteorological balloon hung above all of this supported on 20-foot-high steel tubes. Key structural supports were sawed through in crucial places and put back together with a soft metal that would melt when an electrical charge was sent through wire resistors concealed within them.

Finally, in front of a large crowd, the machine was plugged in. The machine clanked into operation, the piano began to play. Yellow smoke billowed out and was blown into the crowd by the fan. A tremendous din was created by the moving parts. An arm beat the washing machine drum, creating a staccato hammering. Humming noises came from the machine. The bicycle parts hit the piano keys. The large meta-matic with its two large paint brushes was furiously drawing. (The other meta-matic didn't work. Tinguely explained, "You can't expect the end of the world to end the way you want it to.")[4] The piano caught fire, by design. After twenty minutes, the joints holding the structure together had melted and the structure began to sag. Eventually it collapsed to the cheers of the audience.

Following the success of his *Homage to New York*, feeling somewhat liberated by the scale of it, Tinguely conceived of an even grander meta-matic vehicle. He envisioned a meta-matic driving along a Los Angeles freeway painting a continuous abstract picture. He also envisioned a second machine following it washing off what the first had painted!

A Turtle

In 1977 at the Stedelijk, Amsterdam's museum of modern art, a large space was cordoned off in one of the exhibition rooms. Within this area a little electronic device on wheels was wandering around on a part of the floor covered with paper. It had a pen attached to it. In order to receive directions on what to do, the device itself was attached by a cable to a Digital Equipment Corporation minicomputer also standing within this space. The device was equipped with a sonar transmitter, and at each corner of the space there were sonar microphones. The sonar allowed its movement and position to be constantly tracked. What was particularly interesting about this device was that, as it was moving about this space, the pen was lowered at times so that a line was drawn in its trail. At other times the pen was raised.

At first it seemed that this device, called a "turtle," was meandering in a somewhat arbitrary fashion. But as the turtle covered more and more area, it became clear that there was a method to it. As it moved about leaving a line in its trail, the line tended to a circular shape. With clear intent, the two ends of the line were attached, forming a closed loop or circlelike object. The pen was lifted.

After a brief hesitation, the turtle moved on to another spot on the floor. It stopped momentarily, lowered the pen, and began drawing another object on the floor. Sometimes the turtle would draw a second circlelike object within a larger one, forming a sort of doughnut-shaped object. In other cases it would move to the edge of one of these circlelike objects and, moving outward from it, draw another closed loop. In these cases the somewhat elongated loops that began and ended at a point on the perimeter of the original circlelike object appeared to add limbs to what now seemed like a body. On another part of the paper, the turtle drew a squiggly line, lifted the pen, moved down a bit, and drew a second parallel squiggly line, forming a horizon. Then it moved to another space and scurried about for a few minutes, raising and lowering the pen several times in a small area, again leaving in its tracks, with seemingly serious intent, what is best described as an intense little doodle.

The turtle, moving at a rather leisurely pace, continued in this fashion for a couple of hours or so and then went to the corner and stopped. It had apparently completed its exercise. What it had created was a half-dozen animallike objects: bodylike shapes with limbs, some large and humanlike, others looking themselves like turtles, and still others like insects, little squiggles and doodles, some with lots of little feet, others with wings. These animated bodies were placed in an abstract landscape with a defined horizon and with mountains and clouds dotted with a variety of zigzags, squiggles, and doodles. Like some of the works of Klee, Kandinsky, or Miró, the turtle had created an imaginary world with imaginary creatures wandering about it. This world had an appealing, childlike simplicity. (See figure 12.4.)

Harold Cohen

Standing next to this cordoned-off area was a heavyset bearded man with his hair tied back in a ponytail. Harold Cohen, the creator of this drawing system, originally pursued his interest in art from a much more traditional approach. A graduate of London's Slade School of Fine Art, Cohen went on to establish a reputation as a leading British painter of abstract art in the late 1950s. His stature continued to grow throughout the 1960s, his work exhibited not only in Britain but throughout Europe and the United States. (His work from this period is included in the collections of a number of museums, including the Tate Gallery in London.)

As an abstract painter, Cohen was interested in "the conjuring of meaning through marks." His paintings explored the use of forms,

Figure 12.4
An early black and white drawing created by Harold Cohen's AARON in September 1977. Photo: Becky Cohen.

spatial effects, repetition and variation, symmetry and asymmetry, the interrelation of lines with color fields both as outlines and as independent elements, and the use of various patterns such as dotted lines and cross hatching bounded by an outline.

In 1968, while a visiting professor of art at the University of California at San Diego, he was introduced to computers.

I was fascinated by the power of the machine to double as a decision-making device. Then it eventually dawned on me that maybe I could use the machine in relation to my work, actually to face some of the problems I'd sort of put on one side because I couldn't think of any way of handling them. When I got involved with the computer my work was passing through a rather formalist set of preoccupations ... like, "How do you distribute colors on a flat surface?" What's a reasonable algorithm for doing something like that?[5]

He stayed on to continue his experiments with computers and joined the San Diego faculty full-time.

Cohen's first use of the computer was to "provide explicitly structured formats for certain color games" that he had established.

Interestingly, he discovered that he "found the structural aspects altogether more absorbing than the color itself."[6]

Cohen then saw in the computer the opportunity to explicitly describe (and study) the processes he used to create art. "At some level, European art has always been concerned with an investigation into the nature of art itself. To that extent, what I'm doing is a fairly orthodox kind of art activity."[7]

In 1973, in a paper entitled "Parallel to Perception," Cohen first described the question fundamental to his "investigation into the nature of art itself": Would it be possible for a computer to simulate the processes of artistic creation? The processes of an artist's mind? Answering this question has been his focus ever since. He has pursued it with a resolute singlemindedness and determination for over twenty years.

To this end, Cohen set out to develop a computer program that he called AARON that embodied the rules of drawing. He abandoned painting (until 1979) and became "obsessed with these notions about drawing and how you could use a machine to investigate drawing."[8] He started by explicitly describing the drawing process in the form of a set of rules to be followed by the computer. Just as for researchers in other areas of artificial intelligence, the computer was a vehicle to test the validity of his description by applying these rules. Like Winograd's with language or Koenig's with music, Cohen's objective with AARON is to make explicit the rules and other knowledge that characterize the processes of drawing and visual composition. He is an artist building a model of art making. The test of its efficacy is its output. Is it art?

AARON has evolved over the past twenty years, from a simple drawing system capable of creating childlike images to a sophisticated drawing system capable of creating detailed and realistic portraits of people set against abstract backgrounds that it is hard to imagine were not created by a skilled artist. During his pursuit of his overall goal, Cohen explains, AARON "has gone through the equivalent ... of several stages of human cognitive development, acquiring a number of skills and a body of knowledge along the way."[9] To date, AARON has had three distinct stages of development that roughly correspond to the 1970s, the 1980s, and the 1990s.

AARON in the 1970s

In 1973, when Cohen first set out to develop AARON and to use the computer to investigate "the nature of art itself," his initial task was to address the question: "What is the minimum condition under which a set of marks functions as an image?" His assumption was that "it required the spectator's belief that the marks had resulted from a purposeful human—or human-like—act." Consequently, he developed a set of drawing rules with the objective of creating the effect of a "purposeful human act." Cohen explains, "The early AARON was designed to simulate some low-level human cognitive capabilities, and on that basis alone succeeded in producing complex systems of marks which, to judge from the responses of art-museum audiences, functioned as images."[10] (See again figure 12.4.)

Cohen defined basic concepts such as the difference between closed and open, between inside and outside, and between figure and ground. He then described simple drawing tasks, such as drawing a closed figure. He implemented the drawing process in the form of a feedback system.

Cohen had concluded that, as he painted, he continually went through a process of making decisions about what to do next based on what had already been done. Drawing a simple closed figure, an artist starts to move the pen, watches where he is going, decides to move in a particular direction, corrects course, picks the next point in the figure being drawn, moves in that direction, and so on, eventually closing the loop and creating a closed figure. Cohen didn't use a predefined library of shapes, such as a circle, that would be drawn when needed. Rather, he defined rules that would create a shape anew each time in a manner that he believed simulated how an artist would do it. In the case of the moving turtle, the sonar system provides the feedback mechanism that monitors progress.

Drawing a closed figure is a rapid intuitive action for an artist. For AARON, Cohen defined rules that achieved the same result, creating a closed figure from scratch each time. Instead of perfect circles or lines, AARON's drawing shows some wavering that results in a natural feeling, just as one would find in a human-drawn figure.

Having drawn a figure, AARON, like Cohen, would then decide what to do next—another closed figure, some lines, some doodles—

based on a sense of aesthetics embodied in its system of rules. AARON then proceeded to draw the next object, with rules for making the small decisions along the way. The rules ensured that figures were well distributed, that they didn't bump into each other, and so on.

Between 1973 and 1979, Cohen developed basic drawing capabilities in AARON. In the late 1970s, AARON—including the computer and meandering turtle—toured for exhibitions in Edinburgh, Scotland, Kassel, Germany, the Stedelijk Museum in Amsterdam, and the San Francisco Museum of Modern Art. In all cases, museum visitors found AARON's drawings to be "humanlike" and evocative. During this period, Cohen discovered how complicated it is to explicitly define even a simple drawing process: "There's nothing simple about [it], though the fact that we can do it without having to think much about it may make it seem so. It is only in trying to teach a computer program the same skills that we begin to see how enormously complex a process is involved."[11]

AARON in the 1980s

By 1980, Cohen had reached a point at which AARON embodied an effective set of basic drawing primitives. In his effort to simulate the artist's mind, Cohen had reached a plateau: "I wasn't really discovering any more cognitive primitives." He found it necessary to expand his model of cognition—that is, AARON. "I started to face up to a problem that I had known all along was going to be exceedingly difficult ... [AARON] has to know things about the world."[12] The challenge was to determine both *how* to represent the external world and *what* must be represented to allow the program to create credible representations of the external world. AARON entered its second phase of development.

From this point, Cohen, who had made his reputation as an abstract painter, "began a gradual slide downhill ... into overt representation." As a basis for creating representational drawings, he had to provide AARON with knowledge of the world. For example, he developed AARON's knowledge of plants. Cohen explains,

Plants exist for AARON in terms of their size, the thickness of limbs with respect to height, the rate at which limbs get thinner with respect to spreading, the degree of branching, the angular spread where branching occurs, and so on. Similar principles hold for the formation of leaves and leaf clusters.

Given a knowledge of plants, Cohen defined a set of rules for AARON to select the types and forms of trees or plants to be drawn. Cohen continues,

AARON is able to generate a wide range of plant types and will never draw quite the same plant twice, even when it draws a number of plants recognizably of the same type. Interestingly enough, the way AARON accesses its knowledge of plant structure is itself quite treelike. It begins the generation of each new example with a general model and then branches from it. "Tree" is expanded into "big-tree/small-tree/shrub/grass/flower," "big tree" is expanded into "oak/willow/avocado/wideleaf" ... and so on, until each unique representation might be thought of as a single "leaf," the termination of a single path on a hugely proliferating "tree" of possibilities.[13]

Cohen also equipped AARON with knowledge of human figures. AARON "viewed the human figure as a complex of connected parts, and its postural rules referred to the way these parts articulated. Each part—arm, head, leg—was represented internally as an array of points with its origin at its articulation to the next part: hand to forearm at the wrist, forearm to upper arm at the elbow, and so on." With knowledge of the construction of the human form and postural rules, AARON could create figures that were immediately recognizable as human.

As a result of this second stage of development, AARON integrated a knowledge of drawing and knowledge of the world to create images that represent, without question, people in environments of trees, vegetation, and rocks. In AARON's drawings from the 1970s, the viewer addresses the question of what is there (a turtle? a rock? a cloud?), of whether the marks even "function as an image." With AARON's drawings from the late 1980s, the viewer addresses the question of the meaning behind the image: Why are those people there? What are they doing in the dense vegetation? Why are they pointing together in a certain direction? (See figure 12.5.)

AARON in the 1990s

AARON has recently entered a third stage of development. The need for a new direction became apparent to Cohen as early as 1986.

Figure 12.5
A representational black and white drawing created by Harold Cohen's AARON in
July 1986. Photo: Becky Cohen.

By 1986 it was beginning to seem inappropriate that a program smart enough
to generate an endless stream of original drawings was incapable of doing its
own coloring. I had no idea how to go about correcting that deficiency, but I
was beginning to develop some intuitions about what would have to be done
to clear the decks. I did not think, for example, that it would make much
sense to try to handle coloring in the context of AARON's elaborately detailed drawings of that time. I needed a simpler configuration of forms—
something no more complicated than a torso-length portrait, for example.

With this impetus, AARON's most recent stage of development has
focused on creating formal portraits of imagined people, detailed realistic images of people set against abstract backgrounds.

However, if Cohen was going to develop torso-length portraits,
greater visual complexity would be required for the portraits to stand
alone and, in effect, bear closer scrutiny. To achieve this, he believed

it would be necessary to have a more complex underlying three-dimensional representation of the image to be drawn. Until this point, AARON had created its drawings from an internal two-dimensional representation of the scene. During the next few years, Cohen redesigned the internal representation of objects to add an understanding of three-dimensionality. By 1991, AARON was creating its two-dimensional drawings as if "viewing" three-dimensional scenes from a given perspective. (AARON's "view" is metaphorical: the computer creates an *internal* representation of a scene that, given knowledge of perspective, can be rotated and "viewed" from different angles.)

This in turn required AARON to understand what is in front of what and the impact of resulting occlusions. Again, this is a complicated process. Cohen explains, "Occlusion—the overlapping of elements in the visual field—provides one of the strongest clues in depth perception, and it is unlikely that any system of representation acceptable to a visually oriented culture could exist without paying attention to it." Cohen provided AARON with inference rules to understand the articulation of the arm and the result any positioning would have on a view of the figure and on how it would be drawn. AARON always draws from front to back without erasing. To do this, AARON determines first whether and then how to draw, for example, a simple view of a hand:

if   the left wrist is closer than the left elbow,
and   the left elbow is closer than the left shoulder,
and   the left wrist is to the right of the left shoulder,
and   the left wrist is not higher than the right shoulder:
then   the left arm will obviously obscure the torso, and
         the order of drawing will be hand, forearm, upper arm, torso.

In 1992 a friend of Cohen's, a distinguished poet, was to have a book published to commemorate his sixtieth birthday. Cohen, invited to produce the cover, was inspired to have AARON create a recognizable likeness of the poet. To create the realistic portraits he was after, it was necessary to create far more detailed and precise definitions of, for example, human heads and faces. Cohen further defined "the structure of heads and faces ... [which] ... were organized into parts—upper mouth, lower mouth, beard, forehead, eyelid, lower eye and so on."

In 1992, after nearly twenty years of development, AARON had a foundation for portraiture. Equipped with an underlying three-dimensional model of a scene, knowledge of the world and of the human form and posture, and a set of rules for drawing, AARON was ready to create detailed portraits "of highly individualized physical and facial types, with a range of haircuts to match."

However, the first portraits were hand-colored by Cohen. After several years of reflection on the nature of color and the rules we use to manipulate it, Cohen, a master colorist, still did not have an adequate theory upon which to base a program capable of doing its own coloring. Now, with the foundation for an imagined portraiture established, he had an insight that provided the necessary key. He remembered "something that all painters know very well, something I've always taught my painting students. I don't know why it took so long to come into focus for me. The most important element of coloring is not hue—where individual colors fall on the spectrum—but how light or dark the colors are in relation to each other."

With this insight, Cohen was ready to tackle the problem he had begun to work on six years earlier, and by the end of 1992 AARON made its first attempts at coloring. AARON colored on the display of a computer workstation. Although not intended as a long-term solution—Cohen continues to work on developing a painting machine capable of manipulating physical color—the results were good enough by early 1993 to allow him to use slides photographed off the screen as color sketches for the most recent series of paintings.

The results are remarkable. (See plates 14 and 15.) It is hard to imagine that these portraits are computer-generated; the detail and realism are astonishing. After twenty years of tenacious work and three distinct stages of maturation, AARON is probably the most sophisticated rule-governed creative system developed to date.

Cohen's first experiments with computers in 1968 attempted to address distributing color on flat surfaces. Unable at that time to find a "rational basis for a color organization,"[14] Cohen focused instead on establishing explicit rules for drawing. Now he has returned to the problem he first started with; not by chance, but as part of an ambitious plan and vision that he is still working to fulfill.

The complexity of developing a drawing system should be evident. Just as Winograd's work demonstrated that the problems of developing natural language systems is immense, Cohen's dedication to his "investigation into the nature of art itself" also demonstrates the scope of the challenge.

In the end, Cohen's rules are a grammar for drawing. From them, an infinite number of pictures can be generated that all share a common style, an underlying system for organizing visual structure. Cohen's goal is to determine whether it is possible to simulate the process of artistic creation. The measure of this work-in-progress is AARON's drawing. Is it art? The answer can only be yes.

Viking Eggeling's "Diagonal Symphony"

The Swedish artist Viking Eggeling joined the Zurich dada group in 1918. Eggeling was primarily interested in the genesis of forms, creating sequences of images that traced the emergence of a shape and its transformation into another shape. In 1921, in an article entitled "Theoretical Introduction to the Art of Movement," he explained that he was striving to create an "orchestration of forms ... a dynamic mode of expression that differed from easel painting."[15]

Hans Richter, a German painter and one of the original members of the dada group, was exploring abstract painting. Interested by Eggeling's theories, he collaborated with him in developing images that would reflect movement. In 1919, inspired by Chinese scrolls and ideograms, they experimented with scrolls as a way of developing such images. In 1920 they started their first experiments with film and concluded that this was the only appropriate medium to develop their ideas.

Eggeling completed a film, *Diagonal Symphony,* in 1924. The film was a continuous sequence of abstract images, evolving and transforming one into another. It was first shown in May 1925. Eggeling was too ill to attend the screening; he died a few days later. However, *Diagonal Symphony* remains a landmark work, the first purely abstract film. Tristan Tzara said Eggeling was "connecting the wall with the ocean and telling us the line proper to a painting [language] of the future."[16]

Brian Evans's "Color Study #7"

Music, and the grammars and rules that describe musical languages, concern sounds structured in temporal relationships. Similarly, in animation and film, the structure of visual relationships *in time* is the key. Both must deal with temporal coherence. While there is a developing body of work explicitly describing the rules that determine static visual structure, such as Kandinsky's theories and Cohen's work, little has yet been done on those for visual structures *in time.*

Brian Evans is experimenting in this area at Vanderbilt University.

> Abstract visual composition (in time) has two aspects that need to be considered, the graphic forms or shapes, and color.... Extracting basic principles from the time-based art forms (theater, poetry, music, dance, etc.) and applying them, along with fundamental ideas of color theory and graphic design, provides a starting point for a grammar and eventually a language of abstract visual composition.[17]

Applying theories of color harmony and exploring their use in time, Evans has composed pieces "with structural integrity in temporal color relationships." He defined what he calls a color syntax for determining the color relationships in a *domain* (a single frame). The domains can be characterized as neutral, balanced, or weighted. He also defined rules for moving from one domain to another by way of a transitional sequence of frames. Finally, another set of rules determines transitions between different types of domains, for example from a balanced domain to a weighted one or a neutral one. With these rules, Evans can "structure time with color" and generate a sequence of frames that are abstract animations.

One of Evans's striking animations is his *Color Study #7.* Following the storyboard (see plate 16), Evans describes the sequence of images:

> beginning, at the upper left, in the neutral color domain, passing through a colored domain (orange), then a balanced domain (row 2, image 2) and to the peak with maximum weighting (yellow-gold); the study resolves at the lower right in the neutral domain after passing through another weighted domain (blue).[18]

Evans's work demonstrates "that it is possible to create coherent compositions with a formal foundation." However, his work, like others we have reviewed in other disciplines, only hints at the full complexity of the challenge. Evans explains,

> Color is only one aspect of a visual composition.... Other issues remain: questions of shape and form; the distribution of different hues and values over the image; questions of temporal design; and the evolution of abstract shapes in time. A complete time-based visual grammar has many facets.[19]

Conclusion

Visual art can be thought of in terms of grammars just as can other languages and systems of communication. Though to many it is less intuitive to think of the visual arts as languages, to the extent that they are forms of communication they must have sets of rules that permit interpretation.

Like spoken or musical languages, visual languages have grammars. Like other languages, visual languages also are hierarchies of systems. Points, lines, and planes form objects. Objects are used to create clusters which in turn are used to create larger forms. Visual grammars will need to include rules for visual texture, brilliance, and transparency, as well as rhythm and motion for temporal coherence.

Again, the challenge is to develop explicit descriptions of the structures and rules of visual languages. And, again, it is computers that are making such explorations possible. Lauzzana and Pocock-Williams's work with Kandinsky's visual language represents work in pursuit of Kandinsky's original vision of an explicit grammar and theory of composition for his art. But it is the application of these techniques to create *new* visual languages that holds the most interest for artists. It is the new possibilities for expression that will motivate artists to use computers as part of the creative process.

The use of computers in the visual arts is a logical progression from earlier experiments. Harold Cohen's work with AARON is a more technologically advanced evolution of Tinguely's meta-matics, which in turn were descended from dadaist traditions—although Tinguely's scribbling meta-matics are mechanistic and not rule-governed in the sense of Cohen's AARON, both are automated drawing machines. Similarly, Brian Evans's work with abstract visual compositions in time is a more technologically advanced evolution of Eggeling and Richter's work, which in turn was also part of the dadaist tradition.

Experiments to date have barely begun to define the rich visual languages that address color, texture, the rules of composition, dimensionality, and visual structures in time. Cohen comments, "The difficulty we have here in assessing potential capability is that after a mere three or four decades computer programs are still very low on the evolutionary ladder." Evans concludes that his "work is but a start toward a design language for abstract visual composition."[20]

13   *The Virtual World*

In 1425, Filippo Brunelleschi revolutionized painting, developing a systematic process to construct images with three-dimensional perspective on a two-dimensional plane. Brunelleschi used mirrors and a caliper to measure the magnitudes of images to be represented on two-dimensional canvas.

Following his breakthrough, Leone Battista Alberti, Albrecht Dürer, and others developed different techniques that also enabled the systematic mapping of the three-dimensional world to a two-dimensional plane. The techniques used manual or optical methods to trace objects to points on a canvas while preserving the relationships that existed between them—distance, depth, and so on. These new techniques were rapidly embraced by Renaissance artists throughout Europe. They made possible a sense of depth and perspective that was startling at the time, though today we take it for granted. As a result of Brunelleschi's breakthrough, painting was able to reflect an entirely new sense of realism.

Two hundred years later, the French philosopher René Descartes, using algebra and a coordinate system, developed an abstract geometry that also enabled the description of three-dimensional perspective on a two-dimensional plane. With Descartes's geometry, there was no need for tools or, in fact, for reference to the real world. His method defined abstract objects in an imaginary world of a selected coordinate space, and gave equations to calculate points of intersection, perspective, and depth algebraically.

The key advantage of Descartes's system is that it deals with abstract constructions and requires no reference to the physical world.

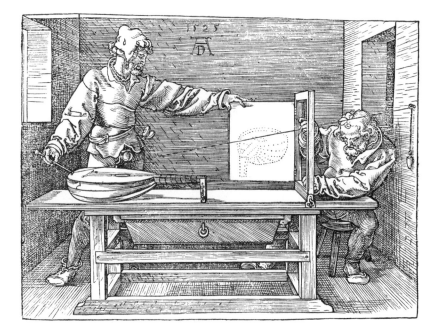

Figure 13.1
Albrecht Dürer, woodcut from *The Artist's Treatise on Geometry* (1525) demonstrating a technique for creating three-dimensional perspective. The Metropolitan Museum of Art, Harris Brisbane Dick Fund, 1941 (41.48.3). All rights reserved.

In fact, his system can be applied equally to representations of the real world and imaginary worlds.

This abstract method for representing objects and their relationships in the three-dimensional world forms the foundation for graphics imaging on computers. And, as in the traditions that dominated for centuries following Brunelleschi's breakthrough, the goal of most graphics imaging on computers today is realism: *generating* what are described as "photorealistic" images, that is, images that appear as realistic as the highest-quality photographic representations of the world.

Computer scientists, engineers, and technicians are striving to create convincing simulations of our world. They use a variety of mathematical formulas and algorithms to describe the laws of physics and optics. They have also developed techniques for dealing with perspective, movement, the complex effects of the position of light sources, light reflections and shadows, and transparency.

All of these techniques can be used to create new worlds with computers. At the same time that computers have opened up explorations of new visual languages, computers have also created a new *medium* for creative expression: virtual worlds.

Virtual Worlds

The goal of being as realistic as the highest-quality photographic representations of the world is particularly interesting when the source of the image is not the real world, but rather a world synthesized by a computer. Computers can be used to create visual simulations that model reality. These are *virtual* worlds: worlds that appear like the real world, but which, in fact, are not based on anything that exists in the tangible, physical world. Objects in these worlds only exist within the computer and are viewed on a graphics display as three-dimensional simulations of real world objects. Objects in this virtual world are only surface; they have no weight or mass.

Computer graphics are being applied in many areas, including engineering design systems, scientific and medical research, flight simulation, and the study and observation of atmospheres, planetary systems, the formation of rings, and the evolution of solar systems.

Computer graphics are being used in systems that enable designers to view simulations of their designs. Interacting with a graphics system, the designer can view a future automobile on the display screen. The computer enables a designer to make changes and immediately see the results. The design of the car can be interactively developed, the angle of a curve refined, the length modified for better balance and proportion. The car can be viewed in red, now blue, now green.

Equally important, the computer can test the stress tolerance of the design, analyze the car's aerodynamics in wind tunnel simulations, and test safety in simulated crash tests. The designer no longer has to wait for a physical model to visualize his design, prototypes are eliminated, and time to market is dramatically reduced by a radically streamlined design process: a process that takes place in a virtual world.

In this virtual world, imaginary designs can be created and viewed for any product: sports cars, furniture, tools and various household devices, fabrics and fashion design, newspaper and magazine page layout and design. Architects can walk through a building in the computer's virtual world to see what a design looks and feels like, even experimenting with the interior decoration. Fashion designers can simulate a person wearing various outfits and fabric patterns. Designers can create the packaging for a new soda or box of cereal, and view the colors in different simulated lighting environments: in fluorescent light on the grocery store shelf, in sunlight, or in the light of the refrigerator at home.

Virtual worlds have applications outside of design. For example, in flight simulation, computers are used for pilot training by creating an experience of flying without endangering the pilots or the aircraft. A pilot sits in front of a fully instrumented cockpit that includes all of the controls of the plane hydraulically mounted and designed to move in response to the pilot's controls—normally, this control console is an actual console from a plane. What is simulated is the view out of the aircraft's window. The cockpit's windows are computer displays that present images as they would appear if the pilot were in fact flying.

A takeoff from Hong Kong's tricky airport, located in the midst of the city's dense buildings with the bay and mountains surrounding it, for example, is safer flown the first few times in simulation. The pilot views a runway, the flight control tower, and the skyscrapers of the city and mountains in the distance. As he accelerates for takeoff, the pilot views the runway passing by. The instrument panel reflects the speed, altitude (still on the ground), and flap positions. Accelerating and lifting off, he sees the buildings approach and the mountains no longer distant. The instrument panel is changing rapidly. The quick operations required to navigate out of Hong Kong are made. The city and mountains are left behind. The aircraft climbs and only blue sky and clouds are to be seen. The pilot returns for a landing, even more difficult in Hong Kong. Back on the ground, the pilot now switches to a nighttime simulation with monsoon rains and prepares for another takeoff.

Simulations are used to model and study planetary systems, the formation of rings, and the behavior of atmospheres. Voyagers 1 and 2, for example, sent back tens of thousands of images of

Jupiter, Saturn, Uranus, and Neptune. Using computers, scientists enhanced these images with special techniques and then pieced them together and wrapped them around an imaginary sphere to create a continuous view of the planet. This constructed planet could then be viewed from different perspectives and traversed. Without such tools, the masses of data collected from space missions would be too overwhelming to make use of.

Empirical science is shifting from observations of the real world to the observation of simulated worlds with the use of massive supercomputers. With virtual worlds, it is possible to observe phenomena that could not be seen directly. Using a supercomputer to compute simulations that can be digitally stored or recorded to videotape, we can observe the unobservable. A black hole can be reduced to the size of a television screen. The evolution of the solar system over billions of years can be reduced to a sequence of images that can be replayed in seconds. In the process, our sense of space and time is being radically transformed.

Virtual Reality

A new area of research emerged in the 1980s: the development of *virtual realities*. The objective is to make the entire *experience* of a simulation of reality seem completely real. If the objective of much of today's work in graphics is to create *images* that appear to have a quality indistinguishable from a photograph of the real world, the objective of work in virtual reality is to create *experiences* that have a quality indistinguishable from an experience of the real world. Virtual reality is the ultimate simulation.

Again, virtual reality does not exist in three-dimensional space or physical form. "There's no there there." It only exists in some hard-to-define place somewhere inside the computer—in what is called *cyberspace*, a term coined by the science fiction writer William Gibson.

In the first experiments, a person wears a set of goggles that contain two tiny television sets, one for each eye. The goggles completely block any view other than the images on the television screens, presenting a wraparound, three-dimensional scene. The goggles have a magnetic sensor attached that is monitored by a small device tracking the precise position at all times. The goggles are attached by cables to a computer that creates the images projected on the two tiny televisions.

The images on the television screens are of a room. As you move forward, the images show that you are approaching the wall. You see a ball. You move your hand out to pick it up.

On your hand you have a black spandex glove that is attached by cables to a computer. The glove is covered with optic fibers equipped with sensors at each joint of each finger that can sense your hand and finger movements, including the bending of each joint of each finger. It sends this information back to the computer so that it can track precisely what your hand is doing. It's possible that you are wearing a complete body suit so that all of your movements can be monitored and tracked by the computer.

You grasp the ball. As you move your arm back, the ball moves with your hand. You pull your arm back behind your head and then throw the ball. You release the ball. It flies forward, hits the wall, and you hear a *thwack* sound.

You are completely immersed in another world. It is not a picture that is being viewed, but rather it is a place. This world is not being observed but experienced. You sense that you are in it.

Fractal Geometry

One of the challenges of creating realistic images with computers is having efficient ways of describing complex forms. Objects of nature have incredible intricacy. It can quickly become impractical to describe a tree in detail: each branch, each subbranch, ultimately tapering off to the last branches that have leaves. Then there is the task of describing each leaf.

However, the structure of natural objects such as trees can be described in recursive terms. Given a description of branches that stem from the trunk of a tree, that description can then be applied again and again to produce successive branches—using some degree of latitude for determining the angles of each branch, the length, radius, and taper. Rules can be defined that will generate trees from branches. The complex structure of a forest of trees can then be simply represented.

The feature of structures that permits such description is called *self-similarity*. During World War I, two French mathematicians, Gaston Julia and Pierre Fatou, explored the properties of iteration, described in a paper published by Julia in 1918 entitled "Review on the Iteration of Rational Functions." However, the idea and usefulness of a structure built from repeated application of a function was difficult to visualize wholly in the abstract. As a result, the work of these French mathematicians remained largely unknown for the following 60 years.

Then, Benoit Mandelbrot, an IBM Fellow at the Thomas J. Watson Research Center of IBM who had in fact studied with Julia 35 years earlier, returned to the Frenchmen's study of iterative functions. Mandelbrot traced the "old idea" of self-similarity to Leibniz.[1] It became a cornerstone for his work in developing a new geometry, which he named *fractal geometry*.

In the opening to his landmark book *The Fractal Geometry of Nature*, first published in 1977, Mandelbrot explains that a shortcoming of traditional geometry was "its inability to describe the shape of a cloud, a mountain, a coastline, or a tree. Clouds are not spheres, mountains are not cones, coastlines are not circles, and bark is not smooth, nor does lightning travel in a straight line." To address this inadequacy, Mandelbrot "conceived and developed a new geometry of nature ... [that] ... describes many of the irregular and fragmented patterns around us."[2]

Fractal geometry is a particular technique for describing objects where small-scale details have the same geometrical characteristics as larger-scale features. What Mandelbrot demonstrated in his work was that simple descriptions could be used to capture the irregular and fragmented patterns found in nature. Using fractal geometry, it became possible to describe clouds, mountains, coastlines, and trees in simple representations. The famous images Mandelbrot described as "astoundingly beautiful," the images of fractal geometry, first appeared in the 1970s.

Using a rule described by the mathematician W. Sierpinski in 1915, Sierpinski's Triangle is a well-known example of the application of a fractal. (Sometimes it is described as a "prefractal" since it was de-

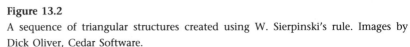

Figure 13.2
A sequence of triangular structures created using W. Sierpinski's rule. Images by Dick Oliver, Cedar Software.

fined by Sierpinski prior to Mandelbrot's "discovery" of fractal geometry.) Sierpinski's rule creates a sequence of self-similar triangular structures of increasing complexity. (See figure 13.2.) The sequence starts with a solid black triangle. Sierpinski's rule then calls for the triangle to be split into four triangles, as seen in the second structure of the sequence. In effect, the middle triangle is punched out. The rule is then applied again to the three solid triangles to create the third image in the sequence. It is applied again to create the fourth image. And so on. Repeating the process, Sierpinski's Triangle becomes more and more detailed.

In fact, the nature of fractal geometry is *infinite* iteration. Mandelbrot, for example, discussed the length of Great Britain's coastline.[3] He suggested that it can only be described as infinite. He explained that, given any division of measurement by which the coast is measured, a smaller resolution of measurement can be applied. Measuring the coast with a yardstick, a length of a given number of yards will be determined. However, there are clearly more turns and bends in the coastline than this captures. If one uses a foot-long ruler, more detail will be reflected and a new length will be calculated, greater than that reflected using a yardstick. This process can be continued infinitely and, therefore, it is impossible to ever resolve Britain's coast to a finite length. In the same manner, a fractal rule can be applied infinitely for greater and greater resolution.

Sierpinski's rule, for example, can be applied infinitely to create greater and greater detail. (See figure 13.3.) One can zoom in and find triangular structures within triangular structures, ad infinitum.

Fractal geometry can also be used to describe three-dimensional shapes. Using a three-dimensional tetrahedron in place of the two-

Figure 13.3
Sierpinski's Triangle. Image by Dick Oliver, Cedar Software.

dimensional triangle of the previous example, a structure called a "fractal skewed web" is generated. (See figure 13.4.)

The power of fractals is even more evident when applied to describing "the geometry of nature." Again, using rules that operate in three-dimenstional space, it is possible to simply represent complex shapes of nature, such as mountains. Figure 13.5 is a sequence of images that shows how the repeated application of a fractal rule defined by Alvy Ray Smith ultimately results in the rendering of a mountain.

Fractal descriptions, like the rules of grammars, can be used to generate complex structures. In fact, fractal rules can be thought of as an especially powerful class of rules for describing and generating

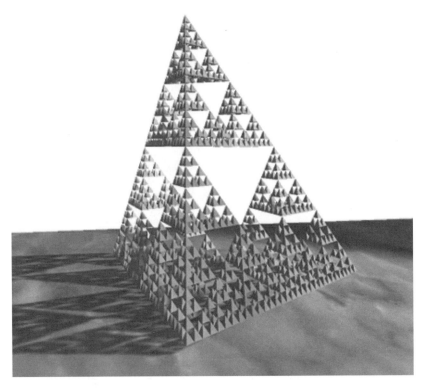

Figure 13.4
Sierpinski's Tetrahedron, also referred to as "a fractal skewed web." Image by Dick Oliver, Cedar Software.

complex visual structures. As such, they represent a class of rules that are particularly useful for describing complex visual languages.

Kandinsky's Conquest of Numerical Expression

Revisiting *Point and Line to Plane*, we find that Kandinsky seemed to foreshadow the power of fractals.

In the final analysis, every force finds expression in number; this is called numerical expression. In art at present, this remains a rather theoretic contention, but, nevertheless, it must not be left out of consideration. We today lack the possibilities of measurement which some day, sooner or later, will be found beyond the Utopian. From this moment on, it will be possible to give every composition its numerical expression, even though this may at first perhaps hold true only of its "basic plan" and its larger complexes. The balance is chiefly a matter of patience which will accomplish the breaking

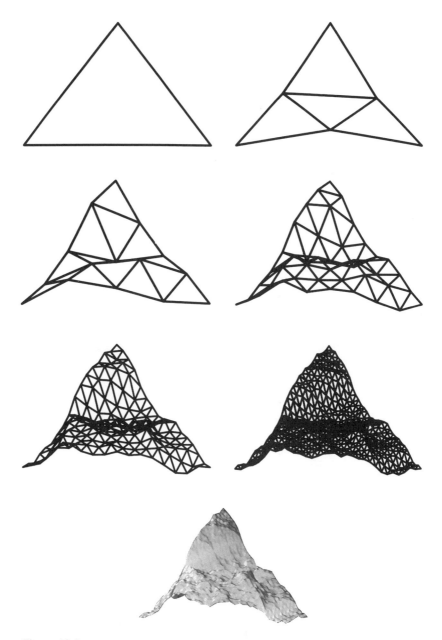

Figure 13.5
The image sequence *Fractal Demo*, by Alvy Ray Smith, shows the generation of a mountain using a fractal technique.

down of the larger complexes into ever smaller, more subordinate groups. Only after the conquest of numerical expression will an exact theory of composition be fully realized.[4]

Fractals will be part of the solution that will make it "possible to give every composition its numerical expression." A formal theory of composition, such as that sought by Kandinsky, and visual grammars that represent descriptions of visual languages, and particularly the transformation of images over time, will be combined with fractals and computers to form the basis for new realities—virtual realities.

Computers Make Fractals Possible

It can be said that fractals were inconceivable prior to Mandelbrot's discoveries. Whereas several mathematicians understood the abstract idea of iteration, and perhaps even attempted to draw a figure representing several iterations of a rule, as Julia and Sierpinski did, they could not really discover the complexity and richness of fractals using only manual processes. It is Mandelbrot's belief that the first true realization of fractal geometry was entirely dependent on the invention of the computer.

Complex fractal geometries can only be created with computers. With computers, it is possible to repeat the process of fractal iteration over and over for increasing detail, revealing ever more about the richness of this world. And only because Mandelbrot could pursue varied explorations using computers was he able to discover the broad applicability of fractals to describe a variety of natural structures.

Virtual reality will enable the exploration of real and imaginary worlds. One can imagine worlds of green or red trees, blue or purple skies, endless mountains of granite and gold, rich universes filled with a seemingly infinite complexity. Fractals will be a key to such representations in virtual reality. Fractals will be used to represent the structure of the skies, the bark, branches and leaves of trees, the patterns of the clouds and stars, the texture of the rings of Jupiter, and the overall structure of planetary systems.

With virtual reality, it will also be possible to take a guided tour of a fractal construction. It will be possible to enter a three-dimensional

Sierpinski triangle—zoom in further and further, zoom back out, and travel in any given direction. And to do so endlessly—in the virtual world there is no limit to the resolution of a fractal construction. Zooming in deeper and deeper, your speed accelerating, you are lost in rushing images as you move through infinite fractal space.

A Tour of Jupiter

In the future, whether twenty-five years or a hundred years from to-day, today's pioneering efforts will have opened a new capability. Rather than goggles, full-motion images will be projected directly onto your retina with lasers. Rather than gloves or body suits, lasers will track the details of all of your movements. The experience of smells will be part of this reality. And, given a glove or even a body suit equipped with actuators whose movements are synchronized with your contact to virtual objects, the sense of touch will be part of this reality.

You look around you and find yourself on Jupiter. You are in a deep red ravine. As you look down the valley you see a rough terrain pock-marked with craters. You look up and see the swirling anti-cyclonic vortex of the massive Great Red Spot off to the right. It is as wide as Earth. The sky is filled with bizarre, multicolored, rapidly transforming cloud formations: clusters of clouds consume others, groups intertwine and then separate and go different ways, some are sucked into the vortex of the Great Red Spot. There are numerous jets and eddies of activity and intensely turbulent oval-shaped areas formed by high-pressure centers.

You cannot tell whether the images are being synthesized in real time by a computer of massive calculative power, or are a reconstruction of the photographic images collected by comprehensive satellite flyovers. But you realize that the continuously shifting focal point tracks perfectly as you move your eyes, and so you assume this virtual world is being synthesized. Underlying this reality is a database of intricate detail based on information collected from space probes and reduced to fractal representations.

You point your finger, indicating that you want to fly. You begin to move through the red ravine. You rise above the steep cliffs. You look down at the landscape. From this aerial view you see vast mountain ranges and deep valleys.

Another hand movement indicates that you want to accelerate. You rapidly move to hundreds of miles above Jupiter's surface. You pass through blue clouds, then brown, white, and finally red clouds. There are three layers of atmosphere, the first composed of water ice, the second of gaseous crystals, and the third of ammonia ice.

You now look down at Jupiter from outside of its atmosphere. From this perspective you observe that the clouds move at different speeds depending on their latitude. And at different latitudes the jets of clouds move in different directions, eastward then westward. The jets are up to 20,000 miles wide and travel at 250 miles per hour.

Another hand movement results in an acceleration of time, transforming days into minutes. You watch as small storms develop and then grow into larger ones. Small eddies appear along the boundary between the eastward and westward jet streams. They last one or two days before being sheared apart by counterflowing winds. You see a small, white spot appear. It moves toward the Great Red Spot from the east, circulates around it for nearly a week, and then finally dissipates as it is sucked into the vortex.

You return to an unaccelerated time scale. You fly toward Io, the moon closest to Jupiter and the most unusual satellite in the solar system. You pass through the 12,000-mile-thick rings of microscopic dust that form a band around Jupiter. In the distance, you see lightning, meteors, and magnificent auroras.

As you approach Io, you observe great splotchy regions of yellow, orange, white, and black. You see many of Io's 200 10–20-mile-wide volcanic calderas. They are continuously spitting out boiling lava. A ball of intense volcanic activity, Io is dotted with sulfur lakes. Across the horizon, you see several volcanic plumes of sulfur and sulfur dioxide that rise hundreds of miles into the black sky. You move closer to one of the exploding volcanoes and see dark flows of basaltic lava radiating from the enormous caldera in streams that stretch hundreds of miles.

You move on to another moon, Europa. With virtually no surface relief, it is the smoothest world known in our solar system. The planet appears completely flat and is covered by a thin crust of ice. From your vantage point, you see the network of crisscrossing lines that traverse this moon. In your upper-right field of vision there is an ice reflection of Io on this pearl suspended in space.[5]

New Worlds

We will be able to explore and experience other worlds, other realities. Another planet. Alternatively, Earth in the year 200,000,000 B.C. You look around and see dinosaurs. In fact, you are a dinosaur. There is no reason why, in this virtual world, you must maintain human form. Given a mapping of your movements, your arms and legs become the legs of dinosaurs or the wings of pterodactyls.

The reality does not need to correspond to any real existing world. It can be an imaginary world, a new world created for the first time. You become the first explorer of this new world. Or the reality may be a different view of the world. The masses of data stored in computers may be rendered in a visible form, enabling new ways of seeing data. For example, a database of information might be represented as a forest with individual items as trees. You can then review large amounts of data and look for unusual information by surveying the forest and looking for exceptional trees that stick out of the forest.

Virtual realities will not be subject to the principles of ordinary space and time. Michael Benedikt, editor of the book *Cyberspace*, explains,

In patently unreal and artificial realities ... the principles of ordinary space and time, can ... be violated with impunity. After all, the ancient worlds of magic, myth, and legend to which cyberspace is heir, as well as the modern worlds of fantasy fiction, movies, and cartoons, are replete with violations of the logic of everyday space and time: disappearances, underworlds, phantoms, warp speed travel, mirrors and doors to alternate worlds, zero gravity, flattenings and reconstitutions, wormholes, scale inversions, and so on. And after all, why have cyberspace if we cannot (apparently) bend nature's rules there?[6]

Randal Walser, one of the champions and researchers at Autodesk's virtual reality laboratories, enthuses, "We're talking about a whole new universe. People will enter cyberspace to work, to play, to exercise, to be entertained. They will enter it when they wake up in the morning and will have no reason to leave it until the end of the day."[7]

Jacking into Cyberspace

Many people will be able to explore a virtual world together. William Gibson, in his science fiction thriller *Neuromancer,* has described a future in which people plug into a virtual world that networks people and computers across the universe:

Cyberspace. A consensual hallucination experienced daily by billions of legitimate operators in every nation.... A graphic representation of data abstracted from the banks of every computer in the human system. Unthinkable complexity. Lines of light ranged in the nonspace of the mind, clusters and constellations of data. Like city lights....[8]

Cyberspace is a completely virtual world that is seen and experienced as if it were real. Individuals connect into this world with jacks that attach directly into the human neural system. They travel through this world and interact with other people in the form of virtual people, with computers that manifest themselves as virtual people, with data that take visual form in this virtual world.

In the prototype virtual reality systems of today, the images, sounds, and even tactile and other experiences are simulated and played for you so that your senses experience what would be experienced if what was before you were in fact real. This becomes a rather complicated and cumbersome process, especially when one considers touch, taste, and smell. In Gibson's future world of cyberspace, you connect your neural system into a system that bypasses your sense mechanisms—eyes, ears, tongue, nose, skin—and directly stimulates your neural system to create an experience.

It is conceivable that, having developed the technology that enables you to plug into cyberspace and directly experience another reality, it will also be possible to record your experience. Given such a recording, someone else can later connect into the system, play it back, and experience your experience directly, as if it were their own. This idea was the subject of *Brainstorm,* a film from 1983, the same year Gibson completed *Neuromancer.* In *Brainstorm,* experiences of flying jets, riding a roller coaster, and viewing Rio de Janeiro from above are seen as marketable products with applications in entertainment, education, and travel. A recording of making love is edited and looped for the experience of a continuous orgasm. The ultimate recorded experience is of transcendence after death.

Today, computer games use keyboards and a variety of simple input devices and graphics monitors that present relatively simple graphical feedback, for example of a driver on a race track or of Mario wandering through a maze. In the future, one can imagine jacking into games that provide a complete virtual reality to play in, stimulating all your senses and creating a very complete experience.

Today, film and television are media for comedy, adventure, thrillers, pornography, and art. They present sequences of images representing a three-dimensional world on a screen. In the future, virtual reality will be the medium for such programs. One can imagine buying a cassette that, when plugged into the appropriate system with the viewer jacked in, provides a complete experience of the reality that the film makers—now the reality makers—want to present: virtual reality cinema or cyber cinema.

Today, listening to music, eyes closed, one might *visualize* the music in the mind's eye as one listens. In the future, one can imagine music composition as the sequencing of the neural sensations that create the visual images evoked by the music rather than of the sounds themselves. One might *see* music rather than hear it.

Today, ideas are often expressed as printed text on a page in books. In the future, one can imagine jacking into a system, loading the appropriate software, and *thinking* the ideas. Rather than trying to work through the thought process and follow the complexity of the development of the ideas, one can *experience* the thought process and *think* the development of the ideas.

The software of the future will be programs that run on your computer: your mind. Games will be entertaining experiences: worlds that you play in. A database of information will be in a form that allows you to access it while thinking, directly enhancing your memory. And books, music, and films will become the recording of the neural sensations to think an idea, experience the soul vibrating with sound, and participate in a virtual reality. Rather than reading, listening, or viewing, a recording will directly evoke the experience of what we feel and what we emote.

Conclusion

Artists create alternative views of realities. The fantastic worlds of Hieronymus Bosch and Brueghel are views of other realities. The imaginary worlds of Kandinsky, Klee, Ernst, and Miró with amoeba-like organisms, little animals scurrying about, doodled objects here and there, are views of other realities. The impressionist vision of the late nineteenth century represents a different way of seeing the world. And even the realistic images of Rembrandt and the Dutch school of portrait painters or the hyperrealists of recent years represent a view of the world. A view that is different from a direct view of that world. It is the world as envisaged by the artist.

The surrealist aesthetic was founded on the notion that things should be purely interior, emerging from the imagination or even the unconscious. André Breton, champion of this aesthetic, described painting as a window that looked onto these worlds. Surrealism is embodied in Dalí's reflections of the unconscious world of dreams. He uses linear perspective and lighting familiar to us from the real world, but in the context of an imagined world, creating a surreal world. In these imaginary worlds objects do not need to conform to the laws of nature. In Dalí's surreal vision clocks bend and drip.

Artists create realities. Whether it is a world of sound that a composer creates, a world of visual images, or a world described by literature to be visualized in the imagination, artists create alternative views of reality, and alternative realities. Using a system of symbols to represent a view of reality, the artist shares his consciousness of aspects of that reality.

The artists of the future will sculpt using the materials from which virtual realities are made rather than clay—that is, data, pure information. Within the computer, virtual reality is a pattern of information. Just as for language, music, and visual languages, the foundation for building these new worlds will be the explicit description of the structure of these worlds: the basic elements, the rules for combining and sequencing elements, deep structures, surface structures, as well as fractal representations.

The artists who will sculpt these new virtual realities are sometimes called "space makers." In the traditions of centuries of art they could also be thought of as "reality makers." They will create new worlds. Jaron Lanier, a pioneer of virtual reality, explains: "Instead of communicating symbols like letters, numbers, pictures, or musical notes, you are creating miniature universes that have their own internal states and mysteries to be discovered."[9]

In the unprecedented medium of virtual reality, we can expect unprecedented art, an art that is not only multidimensional but *interactive*. Our view of the artist will radically change, and our view of reality will also radically change. If art is the sharing of the artist's consciousness of aspects of a reality, a certain view of a reality, cyberspace will be the future medium for communicating that consciousness.

With television, people have been removed from the direct experience of reality. Real space is reduced to a television screen. Real time is reduced to instant replays. Computer simulations collapse millions of years into seconds and black holes to a television image.

Filippo Brunelleschi revolutionized the way we view reality through vehicles of creative expression. With today's technology, our sense of space and time is again being radically altered. How will virtual reality alter our sense of reality?

Jean Tinguely's work provided a small hint of Harold Cohen's work, which in turn provides a hint of what we will see in the future. Viking Eggeling's work and Brian Evans's are pioneering concepts that, again, seem only to hint at what will be developed in the future. Likewise, virtual reality is in *very* early stages of development and provides, at best, a mere hint of what is to come. A future made possible by the development of computers.

14 *Reflections*

New Worlds of Expression Will Unfold

Computers are pervasive. Every office or business uses them as an integral part of its operations, for accounting, word processing, customer files, electronic communications, and financial modeling. Homes have computers embedded in telephones, televisions, appliances, sound systems, and security and monitoring systems.

However, artists' tools rarely include computers as an integrated part of the *creative* process. The use of computers to perform creative tasks remains the last unpenetrated frontier. But in the future, to create without the computer will seem as implausible as drawing without a pen. Artists in all disciplines will conceive of their work with the computer as an essential part of the creative process.

Not with the computer as a "tool"—like a word processor facilitating the task of writing a book by simplifying multiple iterations in the course of editing, corrections, and other changes, or a music editor that similarly facilitates the task of writing music. But rather with the computer in the role of creative partner; with the computer facilitating if not performing independently the process of writing itself, of composing itself, of painting itself, or of sculpting itself.

The computer will change the way we create and express ourselves, whether the form of expression is writing, music, painting, sculpture, or virtual reality. The computer will change the way we think about writing, music, painting, sculpture, and reality. With computers as partners, new worlds of expression will unfold.

As a result of this change, we may lose some of our innocence, some of the mystery of creativity. Michael Barnsley described a similar danger: discovering fractal geometry "will make you see everything differently.... You risk the loss of your childhood vision of clouds, forests, galaxies, leaves, feathers, flowers, rocks, mountains, torrents of water, carpets, bricks, and much else besides."[1]

A Structuralist View as the Foundation

The Buddhist Nāgārjuna viewed the world in terms of an abstract system where everything is defined in terms of other elements of the system. Saussure viewed language as an abstract system where meaning derives from the network of relationships within the system. Music has for centuries been an abstract art. Schoenberg's serialist music composition language is a particularly explicit view of music as an abstract system. Kandinsky worked toward a comparable system in the visual arts. Pāṇini and Chomsky saw language as an abstract rule-governed system. Boulez created *Structures* with an abstract rule-governed creative process.

Leibniz was the first to conceive of a *calculus rationcinator* executed on a machine, an abstract symbol system that simulates rational thought. Simon, Newell, and Shaw's Logic Theorist was the first to demonstrate a working prototype of such a machine. SHRDLU was the first natural language system to integrate surface expressions with a "semantic network" and knowledge of a world. Koenig and Xenakis were the first to use computers as part of the composition process. Harold Cohen was the first to use computers to create abstract visual compositions. Brian Evans was the first to explore abstract animations.

A structuralist view of languages provides the theoretical foundation for designing all of these systems. Such a view will be at the foundation of the virtual worlds of tomorrow. Virtual realities will consist of worlds of sounds, visual worlds, perhaps worlds of touch, smell, and taste. Each of these worlds will be created by computer engines driven by rule-governed languages, each with its own grammar.

Such a view is a natural evolution from Saussure, Schoenberg, and Kandinsky. Chomsky aimed to describe the "living" capability by which speakers of a language produce and understand expressions, embodied in his concept of rule-governed creativity. The computer is the ideal vehicle to *animate* such systems. Winograd said, "In the popular mythology the computer is a mathematics machine: it is designed to do numerical calculations. Yet it is really a language machine: its fundamental power lies in its ability to manipulate linguistic tokens—symbols to which meaning has been assigned."[2]

The integration of computers nonetheless requires a radical paradigm shift in the creative process. This was a natural evolution for Koenig, Xenakis, Cohen, and Evans. But at the foundation of their work is an abstract description of their creative processes as explicit rule-governed systems. It is probably not yet natural to think of expression in terms of abstract structures. However, this shift is necessary in order to integrate computers into the creative process.

Computers, Abstract Structure Manipulators

Computers are excellent engines for those symbol systems that, at their core, represent and process abstract structures. Computers represent relationships in terms of abstract structures, which they manipulate using logical operations, applying different types of rules, algorithms, formulas, and so on.

Within the computer itself, in fact, there are only abstract structures. Ultimately the computer must realize its "constructions" in some medium to enable us to interpret the abstract structures it has created. Computers construct abstract representations—abstract structures—that can, with appropriate rules, be mapped onto any number of different media.

A structure might be realized visually, in space in the form of a sculpture, in time in the form of sounds, a sequence of abstract colors, or an animation of a real or imaginary world, or in multimedia terms that include images, sound, and stimuli for smell, taste, and touch. Given an abstract representation of structure, it is possible to map from one medium to another. Jaron Lanier creates mountain ranges playing the saxophone and schools of fish playing the drums. Structures generated from musical instruments are mapped by the computer to visual structures.

The worlds created with computers can be realistic or abstract: a visual image representing a scene in the world, a photorealistic rendering, or an abstract image representing some inner world; realistic soundscapes or abstract music; either realistic or imaginary virtual worlds. Ultimately, however, the representation *within* the computer is an abstract representation, whether realistic or abstract when rendered for interpretation by people.

The representations maintained within the computer in some abstract form can, in a sense, be thought of as a *metamedium*. The representation within the computer itself is not the medium for its realization. It is an abstracted form—a metarepresentation—of the structures that will be realized in some other medium. Even virtual realities, which are never realized in a tangible medium and which only exist within a computer, must be mapped from the computer's abstract representation to a form experienced through the senses for human interpretation.

(It is possible to consider the physical representation of the abstract representations as they are maintained within computers as a new medium for expression—that is, the realization of structures in the form of electrical bit patterns as they exist in the computer's memory. Though such representations are difficult for people to relate to, computers can transmit such structures to other computers and interpret them in this medium without the need for a mapping to some other—e.g., visual or aural—representation.)

All of these computer-generated worlds can be seen as virtual worlds. All are represented in the computer as structures in abstract terms. In essence, all are reduced to the same type of underlying abstraction. Virtual reality exists only in cyberspace: its essence is the structure of the data from which it is realized. There is no physical reality behind the experience of a virtual reality, only an abstract representation that, in the end, is realized in a medium that people can experience.

The same is true of these other computer-generated worlds. Underlying all of them is a metamedium of structures and rules, represented in abstract terms.

Such a perspective defines the concept of *virtual worlds* broadly, to include any world that ultimately is represented in abstract terms in cyberspace. Virtual realities are the combination of sounds, colors, shapes, and so on. To think of each of these components as *virtual* is in fact a very natural extension of the concept. A virtual reality is produced by relating the structures of a number of virtual worlds. The concept of virtuality can be extended to all of these worlds that, in essence, exist only in cyberspace.

A Special Kind of Tool

Approaches to using computers in the creative process will vary. Some will take "cognitive modeling" as their point of departure. They will develop programs that are simulations of how the human mind works, or, at least, are based on *theories* of how the mind works. Harold Cohen aimed to simulate his own creative processes, from drawing a line or a circle a segment at a time to integrating knowledge of the world as a foundation for drawing and painting. Koenig began with a goal of better understanding how he himself composed. A great deal of research, whether in natural language, problem solving, vision, or artistic creativity, aims to create "artificial intelligences" that are precise models of human intelligence.

Others take a more pragmatic focus, with a goal only of developing systems and representations of knowledge that are effective in getting the job done. They solve the task regardless of whether the mind works in a similar manner or not. Winograd's SHRDLU was "not intended as a direct picture of something which exists in a person's mind.... The justification for our particular use of concepts in this system is that it is thereby enabled to engage in dialogs."[3]

Whether the efforts are experiments in epistemology or practical means to an end, what is clear even from the early experiments that use computers in creative processes is that the role of the artist will change. What is not clear is what the roles of the computer and the artist will be.

What is the role of the computer, this structure manipulator? Is it a tool like a hammer, saw, paintbrush, or pen? Of course, the answer to this will depend on both how one defines a tool and how the computer is used in the creative process. But certainly, what makes the computer particularly interesting when integrated into the creative process is its potential to take on a role that traditional tools cannot.

In painting, for example, the tools include brushes and paint, and the results using these tools are greatly influenced by the techniques used for mixing paints to achieve a desired effect or the manner in which a brush is applied to derive a certain texture. These tools do not function and achieve their effect without a human guiding force. The painter decides which brushes to use, what types of paint to choose, what techniques should be exploited to apply it to the canvas, and so on.

Unlike such traditional tools, computers used in automated creative processes have an independent role. Used as a *decision-making* tool, the computer is an extension of the mind, a tool to manipulate abstract objects and structures, rather than of the hand or the eye.

These tools need not be *entirely* independent thinking machines. Instead, they can be thought of as "intelligence amplifiers." Frederick Brooks, a well-known computer scientist, describes this view of using computers.

I believe the use of computer systems for intelligence amplification is much more powerful today, and will be at any given point in the future, than the use of computers for artificial intelligence (AI). In the AI community, the objective is to replace the human mind by the machine and its program and its data base. In the IA community, the objective is to build systems that amplify the human mind by providing it with computer-based auxiliaries that do the things the mind has trouble doing.[4]

The computer, thus, can be thought of as a tool, though a tool of a very special kind. Harold Cohen has reflected on this difference.

There's a fundamental difference between what we traditionally call a tool, which requires feedback to be conducted to and from the human user for operations to take place, and a device that contains its own feedback paths, that can conduct its own investigations and modify its own behavior on the basis of what it's able to feed back to itself from the results of what it has done.[5]

It can be an independent decision-making tool. Koenig explains, "I'm not interested in computer-aided composition but rather computer composition. I try to formalize compositional rules and then let the computer take over." Nor does the computer have to be thought of as a tool to make familiar things easier. It can also be thought of as making a given approach to creativity *possible*. It may at the same time present new challenges and new obstacles to creativity. In fact, Koenig believes that obstacles are an essential part of the creative process.

Art needs obstacles. It is not better because it is easier to make it. With PL1, you can push a button and out comes a piece of music. But PL2 resists the composer's efforts to make music. It has elbows. To be of interest, you have to set it [the PL2 program] free so that it is saying something. So it is eloquent. That is the composer's duty. To do this, a composer must think of how he wants to use the program. You must think of an end result. But if you know exactly what you want, there are easier ways to get there. You must envisage a field. It's a complicated game in which the computer program sets you thinking about your work, makes you self-reflective. This is what I mean by obstacles. It must be hard to achieve. Otherwise any idiot could do it.[6]

Metaartists

So what happens when the computer becomes an autonomous creator? Once someone has developed the program that the computer initially creates by, the computer may produce results that were not foreseen or intended. This may not be by design. Koenig, for example, feels that "if the computer produces results I did not anticipate, then I didn't understand the program."

We can also imagine that, in the future, computers will be capable of modifying their rules independently, assimilating new knowledge and techniques, and, in the process, creating something other than what was originally designed. The computer may develop well beyond what was originally created by the artist, beyond what the artist could even have conceived.

Given such an independently creative computer, who then is the artist? Is the artist the creator of the structure, or is it the programmed computer? Discussing Harold Cohen's work, Herbert Simon, one of the fathers of artificial intelligence, proposed the notion of the *metaartist*. Simon wrote in 1984:

He has seen the potential of the electronic computer as a new mode of artistic expression, and has found ways of programming computers that enable them to produce interesting and exciting works of art.... Clearly, the computer is the artist: it does the drawing, its activities guided and determined by the program that lies in its memory (just as a human artists' knowledge and skills lie in their memories). Harold Cohen, equally clearly, is the meta-artist, the teacher.... Hence, Harold Cohen's activity is not only a highly original application of new technique to produce objects of art; it is an equally innovative exploration of the artistic processes and the artistic endeavor.[7]

The metaartist's contribution is the software: the instructions, the rules, the grammar. Will the media used for representing structures—sound, visual images, virtual worlds—be the art? Or are they simply ways of interpreting the software?

Will the art of the future be the software?

Creativity after Death

Designating the computer as the artist raises further questions. To attribute the creative responsibility to the computer, to view the computer as creating works of expression, implies that the computer has some sense of what it wants to express. Can a computer be said to manifest intentionality and to have a real sense of meaning? This is of course a very basic philosophical question in artificial intelligence and the debate on thinking and intelligent machines. And it is especially difficult in the context of art, which is still deeply linked with our romantic views of the personality of the artist and the expression of the most deeply felt human emotions. The idea of computers, machines, independently creating art seems like an oxymoron.

The debates on such issues will no doubt continue for a very long time. Or they will become irrelevant once computers are integrated parts of all that we do and we have grown accustomed to talking with computers, sharing ideas with computers, viewing images independently created by computers, and listening to music spontaneously composed by computers.

The culmination of Lauzzana and Pocock-Williams's work specifying the style of Kandinsky is a computer capable of independently painting in the style of Kandinsky. With the language of Kandinsky formalized, the computer can create thousands of new paintings and compositions. But are they Kandinskys? Do they have the value of a Kandinsky? Can one really create a Kandinsky in the twenty-first century? Isn't art an expression of the artist and an expression of its time?

The culmination of Cohen's work or Koenig's work can be envisaged as a complete description of their own styles and, ultimately, of a computer capable of independently painting or composing music as they do. How will we view the role of the artist, or the metaartist, when, long dead, the computer continues to posthumously create?

Computers will prodigiously compose, paint, write and sculpt all day every day ... forever. Oblivious to the debates surrounding origination, authorship, intentionality, and meaning, computers will pursue their creative objectives.

The Creative Process Will Be Fundamentally Different

We are on the verge of opening new worlds. We will see new virtual worlds and new abstract worlds. Abstract representations of the real world, such as fractals, will provide the basis for the seemingly real in virtual worlds. But virtual worlds will also be abstract. There will be abstract virtual realities.

A structuralist foundation and computers are converging to open the doors to these new worlds. The computer is an enabling technology for exploring new domains. An abstract view of systems in terms of their structure is the theoretical foundation for these explorations. Given this foundation, computers are the natural tool to develop these new worlds.

We are witnessing the first experiments of discovery. Today's pioneering efforts are the first steps in a long journey. They demonstrate the complexity of the challenge but only hint at the possibilities—a future where in virtual cyberspace a synthesis will include the processes of language and thinking, worlds of sounds and rich visual worlds. However, we cannot today really imagine these future virtual worlds, these future worlds in cyberspace.

We do not yet know whether computers will become "artificial intelligences" or act as "intelligence amplifiers"; whether computers will be autonomous creators or a new type of tool for creative people. But computers will be an integral part of the creative process of the artist of the next century. These processes will be understood in abstract terms: as abstract rule-governed systems that can be represented with grammars of formal and explicit rules. The computer will be the vehicle for representing and manipulating these abstract representations of communicative systems that ultimately will be realized in some medium interpretable by people.

Using computers as part of the creative process will change the way we view that process. The creative process will be fundamentally different.

Interlude

Having climbed the near-vertical 2,500 feet to arrive at the gompa, the offered cup of curdled cream swirling in a putrid green liquid is welcome. It is a gesture of hospitality prepared with ample time to anticipate visitors seen struggling up the cliff-face. Arriving weary, knowing that you have arrived at your destination, the butter-tea is hot and refreshing—and the repugnant taste is ignored by a parched mouth.

The gompa hangs from the edge of the cliff like a barnacle on a rock. The view down is dizzying—better left ignored not so much to forget the difficult ascent but, rather, to not consider the yet-to-come descent.

Along the walls of the gompa, the monks blow their six-foot-long horns. Their characteristic deep tones seem to echo in the open space, the vast distance to the mountains on the other side of the valley. No other mountains have a scale of such grandeur. There is an intuitive and immediate explanation of why this unusual sound seems so natural here.

By a far wall a row of fifteen or so monks chant in a deep indecipherable mumble. They are lost in prayer repeating various mantras. Their voices have an eerie inhuman depth to them.

The effect is mesmerizing. Entering the walls of this gompa, there is an inescapable feeling that one is entering another world. Looking outward, there are only vast open blue skies, distant snow-capped mountains and a sense of isolation. If there is some other world, it is very very far removed. If there is some other world, it is isolated by the barrier of expansive waves emanating from the unworldly horns and the impenetrable wall formed by the deep tones of the chanting monks. Anyone or anything approaching is surrounded and absorbed by the steady drone.

It is a day of festivities. The courtyard below is filled with people and activity. Settled down, now the music is of a dervish intensity. Clarinet- and oboe-like instruments play rapid note progressions that combine to create an intense texture of intertwining lines. Dancing dragons and terrible demons emerge in blinding greens, reds, blues, and purples. The colors swirl about in every direction creating an enveloping spectacle. A bodhi- sattva descends, also ferocious in appearance, also dancing. But this saintly being has a distinctive calm and control that is markedly different from the intense swirl surrounding it. The bodhisattva brings peaceful order to this chaos.

III   *Vibration*

15 GGDL

Having completed a B.A. at the University of Edinburgh in 1976, I went to Holland to study electronic music at the Institute of Sonology, at that time the largest research institute in Europe for electronic music. The Institute was equipped not only with electronic music studios filled with walls of analog equipment—oscillators, sequencers, filters, voltage-control devices—but also a Digital Equipment Corporation PDP-15 computer. The computer was equipped to do sound synthesis using a variety of techniques. It was also the host to the computer programs of Gottfried Michael Koenig.

Koenig was teaching a course on the use of computers in the composition process using his Project 1 and Project 2 programs. I became a student of Koenig's. I also became proficient in programming the computer using different kinds of programming languages.

I developed a program that wrote a composition *For Solo Harp*. The program included a set of rules that described distinct "textures" and stochastic transition matrices that controlled the transitions from one texture to another. Other rules defined the characteristics of each texture. However, the harp is a particularly difficult instrument to write for, especially when writing music that uses all twelve notes. The harp has only seven strings per octave, each of which is one of the twelve notes. To play one of the other five, it is necessary to press a foot pedal that lets any string change from a given note to the note one higher or lower. But you cannot change a string while it is playing. As a result, the program needed to include not only the rules and grammar for the composition language but also knowledge

about the harp and the constraints it imposed on a performance—so
that the music written could also be performed.

I had gone to Holland to create compositions using electronic
sounds. Instead, I focused my experiments on composing for traditional instruments using a computer.

The Crickets of Pokara

After six months, I decided to visit India. Indian culture had long
held an attraction for me. I had spent my last year at Edinburgh in
the Sanskrit Department studying Indian history and philosophy.
Ancient India represents an incredibly rich history, from the mystery
surrounding the great civilizations of the pre-Aryans to the forward-
thinking socialist autocracy of Aśoka. The religious philosophies and
the related schools of logic have a spiritual dimension unique to
India. And many of the schools of Western philosophy over a thousand years later seem to have been foreshadowed in these today-
obscure Indian traditions.

I went to India via Thailand, Burma, and Nepal. I spent a few
months in the Pokara valley in Nepal. There, I meditated reciting
Tibetan mantras and playing temple bells. And I listened to the rich
rhythmic textures of crickets. I listened to the daily rain. I heard birds
sing at night on a different rhythmic scale.

Listening to this daily refrain, I perceived structure within the
sounds I heard. Each cricket had its unique timbre, a **[CHICK]** or a
[CACHRICK] or a [CH] or a [CHRICK]. Each cricket's voice could be
described by a set of rules characterizing its rhythms and tempo.
Some crickets chirped in groups of two and three [CHRICK]s while
others averaged between three and five **[CHICK]**s. Some left long
silences between expressions. Others rapidly followed each sequence
of *[CACHRICK]*s with another. But all seemed to fall within a range
of behavior that could be described by a simple set of rules that
permit a degree of variation and individuality.

At a higher level of description, the overall texture of the crickets
as a group can also be described by a set of rules characterizing the
density, tempos, and the degree of variation and overall range that
effectively give a cricket texture its identity. At a lower level, the
structure of the different sounds themselves can be described. The

rules permit a certain degree of variation and individuality that characterize the sound of the crickets.

Similarly, the singing of the night bird can be described in terms of rules. Phrases of two or three lazy ♮whoawhap!s. Long pauses. Other rules describe the patterns of the afternoon rain. The sound of a cricket, of a night bird, of a raindrop. The texture of the cacophony of crickets or the rain. The counterpoint of the night birds' singing.

At yet a higher level, there is the description of the sound textures of a day. The morning with its chorus of birds. The afternoon rain from which the crickets emerge. The lively songs of the afternoon birds. The sounds of darkness and the night birds. At a higher level again, the structure of the days changing as they evolve through the seasons. And the seasons into years. And the years into millennia.

At every level there is structure. I imagined a language and a composition system that would allow such rich sound worlds to be described and created with the aid of computers. I returned to Edinburgh to develop the computer composition system I conceived while in Pokara.

General-Purpose Tools

At the time, almost all the work using computers in music focused exclusively on sound synthesis (as is still largely the case today). The objective in synthesis is to develop hardware and software models for describing and synthesizing sounds, as well as descriptions of instrumental and instrumental-like timbres using these models. In synthesis, the computer is used as a powerful calculator to compute algorithms based on well-understood formal acoustic models. Given a model, this is a relatively straightforward programming process. The challenge is to develop sufficiently powerful and flexible models that can be easily controlled by composers to realize the sounds they seek for their compositions. Synthesis programs are widely available and are used by many different composers, from rock to rap to composers from a "classical" tradition.

With the exception of the work of Koenig, Xenakis, and a few others, the systematic application of computers in the process of *music composition*—the generation of sound structures—was neglected.[1] In the case of music composition, the challenge is to formalize the rules of a musical language. Different composers with different compositional techniques can share the same sounds (for example, an orchestra) or the same model for describing and synthesizing sounds (for example, frequency modulation synthesis). However, each composer requires the formalization of a different set of rules, techniques, and procedures to represent his or her compositional *language*. The few composers using computers in composition at that time were designing systems to address their individual needs. The systems were designed to compose in their individual styles with a specific set of rules that are useful to, at best, only a small set of composers. And composers had to be programmers to achieve even this!

My goal was to develop a tool that I could use to create the soundscapes I had conceived in Pokara. But it was also to be a general system that could be used by different composers to describe their specific composition languages. Just as computer-aided design systems for electronic circuit design, board layouts, and architecture permit an engineer to define building blocks, such as "cells," and then provide facilities for designing structures from these building blocks, my goal was a computer-aided composition system that would act as a tool for the design of music structures.

It was developed around the concept of what I called a Generative Grammar Definition Language (GGDL). GGDL was itself a language designed to permit the definition of a very broad set of different kinds of rules for music composition. Using the GGDL language, a composer could define an arbitrary composition language with which the computer would then automatically generate expressions in the language.

GGDL allowed for the description of a language by a set of explicit formal rules. It was indebted to research done in artificial intelligence for natural language processing. It included the types of rules that Chomsky and others in linguistics were using for their work, as well as rules specifically customized for the description of music. Linguistic-type rewrite rules were enhanced to include rules for serialism and the stochastic processes that have been used by twentieth-century composers. The rules permitted transformations including inversion (upside-down), retrograde (backward), retrograde-inversion (backward and upside-down), and transposition, transformations found in

Western music for centuries—in Machaut, Bach, Beethoven, Bartok, Schoenberg, Messiaen, Boulez, and Stockhausen, even though these composers all express themselves in very different musical languages.

GGDL allowed for the definition of general structure creation and manipulation. The grammatical rules and transformations could be thought of as manipulating only abstract objects—objects related only one to another, undefined except to the extent that they are related to one another. The mapping of the output—the final representation of the structure in sound—was completely separate and, from the point of view of the system, completely arbitrary.

A separate set of rules was defined to map an abstract structure to a realization in sound. The structure could be mapped to notes and instructions suitable for performance by traditional instruments, to the variables that control the performance of electronically synthesized instruments, or to the components of the microlevel of sounds, such as the millions of individual samples that a digital representation of a sound is made of.

Thought of as abstract structures independent of any given medium, structures can be mapped to many different media. And structures created for music can be realized in other forms, just as Jaron Lanier, the pioneer of virtual reality, experimented in mapping music to visual experiences when he played fish on the drums.

After Schoenberg

With GGDL, I composed piano and "noise" studies using a set of rules that would also generate the Trio from Arnold Schoenberg's *Suite for Piano* (opus 25). These studies are called *After Schoenberg*. Another study involved a grammar that could generate and perform Steve Reich's *Clapping Music*. My composition *After Artaud* is an electronic composition in which the computer "composed" the individual sounds that made up a structure; the structure itself was derived from the poem "Shit to the Spirit" by the French poet Antonin Artaud.[2]

The Schoenberg Trio is a canon in which one voice is followed by a second voice, slightly delayed, performing the same notes. In this case the series of twelve notes appears eight times, four times in each voice. And each of the eight occurrences is a different version of the series: the original, the upside-down, the backward, the backward and upside-down, and these four transposed up six semitones. The composition is effectively a series of series: each version of the series is used once and not repeated until all eight are used, and each series itself consists of twelve notes in which each is played once and not repeated until all twelve are used.

The production of a series is defined with a simple rewrite rule:

[SERIES → #12# ! note1 . note2 . note3 . note4 . note5 . note6 . note7 . note8 . note9 . note10 . note11 . note12]

(The rewrite rule to create a series is represented by adding the ability to invoke the right-hand side a given number of times in a single rewriting of the left-hand side; "#12#" says "make 12 selections each time 'SERIES' is to be replaced," while the "!" says "when making a selection, don't repeat that selection unless all other items have been selected," the basic rule of a series.)

Another rule selects a series of versions of the series, indicated as transformations (@) to be performed on the series of notes:

[VERSION-TYPE → #8# ! (none—the original) . @upside-down . @backward . @backward and upside-down . @transposed 6 semitones ((none—the original)) . @transposed 6 semitones (@upside-down) . @transposed 6 semitones (@backward) . @transposed 6 semitones (@backward and upside-down)]

A few other rules represent the overall structure of Schoenberg's Trio.

Using these rules, the computer generated sound structures. The abstract "deep" structures created were then mapped to sounds. In one case, to the notes of a piano, creating a Trio for piano sharing the structure of Schoenberg's Trio. In another case, to the notes of a computer synthesizer. And in another, to a series of noises—creating a Trio for noises rather than for piano. All of the Trios shared the rules and structure of the original Schoenberg Trio.[3]

Other Composers Using GGDL

Other composers also used the composition system. Gottfried Michael Koenig spent a summer at Edinburgh and investigated the use of the system to compose microsound structures. Koenig was

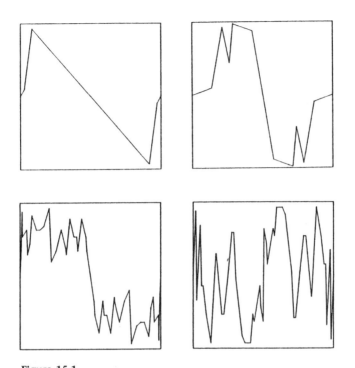

Figure 15.1
Examples of symmetrical waveforms generated by Gottfried Michael Koenig using GGDL.

interested to see what sorts of microsound structures could be easily expressed using grammars.

Defining rules, Koenig generated a part of a microsound structure consisting of a sequence of amplitude points and durations. He then performed transformations on these basic structures to create larger ones. Koenig discovered that symmetrical waveforms could be simply expressed by establishing a rule for creating a structure and then following this structure by itself played backward and upside-down.[4]

David Hamilton, a Scottish composer, realized a commission for the BBC using the GGDL composition system, his *Four Canons*. In it he used sequences of proportions to create scales of frequencies that were not related to traditional scales in western music: a Fibonacci series (3:1, 4:3, 7:4, 11:7, etc.) and a series of *odd* harmonics (3:1, 5:3, 7:5, 9:7, etc.). He then mapped the structures created from these sequences of proportions to sounds synthesized by the computer—the structures of frequency intervals created by the computer could not be performed by any other instrument.

Conclusion

GGDL was a general tool for structure creation and manipulation. It was designed in particular for the structures of music. But it only hints at the tools that will help us open new worlds.

We have yet to develop the tools needed for exploration, the tools to enable computers to become an integral part of the creative process. The process of artistic expression will require languages to describe the rules and structures of languages of expression.

Generalized tools will provide facilities for creating, relating, and transforming structures. Tools will permit the description of deep structures and the means for transforming deep structures to surface-level realizations—whether the medium is sound, paint, or virtual reality. Systems will enable artists to define building blocks and then design structures from these building blocks.

The tools will be flexible enough to describe soundscapes that include the textures of crickets, the songs of the night bird, and the soundshape of a day. The tools will also be flexible enough to describe a composition for orchestra or for digitally synthesized sound structures. The tools will be able to describe virtual worlds of crickets, birds, mountains, hills, fields, and sky, as well as the scenes of the day, the sunrise, the afternoon rains, distant avalanches, and starry nights. The tools will be able to describe realistic virtual worlds as well as abstract virtual worlds.

Creators will be able to describe their own languages. They will be able to describe the building blocks, the structures, the hierarchies, and the total system of their unique expressions. The tools will be invisible, seamlessly integrated into the creative process. Composers, painters, sculptors, or reality makers will be able to express themselves without thinking of the tools at their disposal. Their creativity will not be inhibited by their tools.

With these tools, creators will undertake the difficult task of explicitly describing and creating new languages and new worlds. We do not yet understand the complexity of a grammar for creating a complete virtual reality. In fact, we hardly understand grammars for just parts of such a reality: language, speech, music, a visual system, or a complex and convincing picture of reality. When we master such descriptions, we will discover new worlds of expression.

16   *A Digital Aesthetic*

Only a few composers received the admiration of Beethoven: Palestrina, Handel, and Haydn, of whom Palestrina was his favorite. Given this fondness, Beethoven was once asked why he didn't write music in the style of Palestrina. Beethoven replied that to write music like Palestrina, he would have to share his beliefs; as Palestrina was a very religious man of the sixteenth century, it was not possible for him to write in that style in the nineteenth century.[1]

Palestrina's style was proclaimed by the Council of Trent as the paradigm of Church music. Grout writes that "Palestrina's style of composition was the first in the history of music to be consciously preserved, isolated and imitated as a model.... His work has come to be regarded as embodying the musical ideal of certain aspects of Catholicism."[2] The essence of Palestrina's music is found in his conviction. He was driven by a deeply religious perspective that was grounded in the belief systems of his time. Beethoven, though also a religious man, could not share that perspective; living in the early nineteenth century, it was impossible for him to experience the world as Palestrina had in the sixteenth century.

Today, every student of harmony still studies the works of Palestrina. A standard exercise is to compose in a style that imitates Palestrina's conventions of harmony. But is it possible to imitate the convictions that are the foundation of his music?

To try to reconstruct the experience through which a composition by Palestrina, Bach, or Schoenberg, or a painting by Kandinsky, was *actually* derived is an almost unimaginable challenge. This type of reconstruction is hypothesized by the Argentine writer Jorge Luis

Borges, who imagined a modern author (one Pierre Menard) trying to write *Don Quixote*.

He did not want to compose another *Quixote*—which is easy—but the *Quixote* itself. Needless to say, he never contemplated a mechanical transcription of the original; he did not propose to copy it. His admirable intention was to produce a few pages which would coincide—word for word and line for line—with those of Miguel de Cervantes.... [His method was to] know Spanish well, recover the Catholic faith, fight against the Moors or the Turk ... be Miguel de Cervantes.... [However,] to be in the twentieth century a popular novelist of the seventeenth seemed to him a diminution. To be Cervantes and reach the *Quixote* seemed less arduous and therefore less interesting to him than to go on being Pierre Menard and reach the *Quixote* through the experiences of Pierre Menard.... To compose the *Quixote* at the beginning of the seventeenth century was a reasonable undertaking, necessary and perhaps even unavoidable; at the beginning of the twentieth, it is almost impossible.... In spite of these obstacles, Menard's fragmentary *Quixote* is more subtle than Cervantes'. The latter, in a clumsy fashion, opposes to the fictions of chivalry the tawdry provincial reality of his country; Menard selects as his "reality" the land of Carmen during the century of Lepanto and Lope de Vega.... Cervantes' text and Menard's are verbally identical, but the second is almost infinitely richer. It is a revelation to compare Menard's *Quixote* with Cervantes'. The latter, for example, wrote:

... Truth, whose mother history, rival of time, depository of deeds, witness of the past, exemplar and advisor to the present, and the future's counsellor.

Written in the seventeenth century, written by the "lay genius" Cervantes, this enumeration is mere rhetorical praise of history. Menard, on the other hand, writes:

... Truth, whose mother history, rival of time, depository of deeds, witness of the past, exemplar and advisor to the present, and the future's counsellor.

History, the mother of truth: the idea is astounding. Menard, a contemporary of William James, does not define history as an inquiry into reality but as its origin. Historical truth, for him, is not what happened; it is what we judge to have happened.

The contrast in style is also vivid. The archaic style of Menard—quite foreign, after all—suffers from a certain affectation. Not so that of his forerunner, who handles with ease the Spanish of his time.... [3]

Goals for Creative Expression

To write music today is to write music that cannot be the same as Palestrina. How many students of music composition have studied harmony and counterpoint and have written choral works of stunning beauty "in the style of Palestrina"? But who would recognize them as creative expressions of the twentieth century? To have the spiritual depth and conviction to be recognized as a contribution, a work must be distinguishable from music not written in its time. It is not possible to write the *Quixote* today. *An expression is an expression of its time.*

Before the sixteenth century, compositions were often performed by any combination of voices and instruments. It was in the baroque period that composers began to write music taking into consideration whether it would be performed by a violin, a cello, the voice, or a keyboard.

The physical performance constraints of every instrument are different. Performance on the violin is very different from that on the flute or piano or voice. For example, the ways in which the fingers are placed on the violin or flute or piano make certain sequences of notes easy or difficult to perform. Most pianists' hands spread an octave. Wide skips between registers are natural for the flute. On a violin, moving from the lower to upper strings permits the easy spread of octaves, but it is easy only if the hand positions have been carefully considered.

A violin is bowed, permitting a long sequence of uninterrupted notes. A flute uses breath, limited by the physical constraint of how much air a person's lungs can hold. How long a breath will last depends on what the performer is asked to do. Loud passages in the upper registers of the flute require lots of wind.

A violin has a neck with a string, allowing the performer to glide from one note to the next by sliding his finger up or down the neck in a continuous motion. On the flute or piano, every note is separate, because of the keys that must be struck to cover an air hole or hit a string.

Each instrument has its own distinctive sound. The first half-octave of the flute has a warm velvety quality, due to the weakness of the upper partials in the low registers of the flute. Moving through the octaves, the tone brightens; the third octave is almost shrill. The dynamic range of the flute is not wide. On the other hand, no other wind instrument surpasses the flute in agility. The flute is capable of rapid scales, arpeggios, and dazzling virtuosic passages.[4]

With the violin, an important feature of articulation is that some notes are made by dropping the finger on the string while others are made by lifting the finger. The contrast of timbres and dynamic is broad on the violin. Because the ranges of the different strings overlap, the timbre is dependent not only on whether a note is in a low or high register (as on the flute) but also on which string is used to produce it. The highest string on modern violins is made of steel, providing a brilliant sound. The lower strings are normally gut wound with wire, providing a mellower sound. Then, there are a variety of ways to play the violin. A string can be bowed smoothly or *staccato*, softly or loudly. A string can be tapped with the wooden back of the bow, or plucked by hand. A string can be sounded near the bridge for a shallow metallic sound, or over the finger board for a floating quality.

The piano is a percussive instrument, where a string is sounded by hitting a key that results in a hammer hitting the string. Its notes span a broad range, and it also has a wide dynamic range. By use of the pedals, the sounding of a note can be muted or sustained. And because each key is distinct and independent, with its own string, the piano is very well suited to chords and any combination of notes.

By the very nature of the instruments, music for violin will necessarily sound different from music for a piano. Composers and performers have explored these idiomatic capabilities over the centuries in works for specific instruments. Composers, then, wanting to exploit the full expressive capability of any given instrument, consider all the subtleties of that instrument: *its* performance constraints, the features of *its* design.

A piece written for violin, taking careful consideration of the unique qualities of the violin, is a piece that can only be performed on the violin. Similarly for the piano, flute, harp, oboe, trumpet, or whatever. Each instrument has its own idiomatic capabilities and is capable of expressing ideas that could only be expressed on that instrument.

By the end of the nineteenth century, the notion of idiomatic writing was well established. The virtuosic romantic heights of Lizst's or Chopin's music could only be conceived of in terms of the piano. Paganini's music in terms of the violin. Music for the piano is composed *for the piano*. Music for the violin is composed *for the violin*.

Kandinsky viewed art as a spiritual expression, and believed that its spiritual content depended on its *originality*. Skill at imitation had no place in his scheme.

The specialists of 19th century graphics were not infrequently proud of their ability to make a woodcut resemble a pen drawing, or a lithograph look like an etching. Works of this sort can be designated only as testimonials of spiritual poverty. The cock's crowing, the door's creaking, the dog's barking, however cleverly imitated on a violin, can never be estimated as artistic accomplishments.

In fact, Kandinsky strongly believed that the driving motivation for visual arts such as painting, even in its representational form, is to *not* exactly duplicate the object. (Saussure would, of course, agree.) The artist's conviction drives him from literal representation.

The impossibility and, in art, the uselessness of attempting to copy an object exactly, the desire to give the object full expression, are the impulses which drive the artist away from "literal" coloring to purely artistic aims.[5]

Kandinsky, as we know, took this all the way to abstraction. He abandoned representational art intepreting the external world for an abstract art expressing reflections of an inner spiritual world.

An expression is an expression *of its time*. An expression is also an expression of the idiomatic nature of the medium by which it is realized. Music for the piano is composed *for the piano*; music for the violin is composed *for the violin*. An expression with spiritual value is not a copy of anything existing. It is a *new and original* expression.

Digital Expression, a New Paradigm

Making computers easier to use is a significant area of research. The goal is to develop human interfaces to digital machines around familiar, comfortable models for people. Computer companies that want their products to succeed commercially, to be accepted by people, put a human face on computers.

The goal is to get the computer interface to imitate the way people think, rather than get people to think the way computers do. If the computer is to be a tool to facilitate tasks people are already performing, it is easier to use it if the interface is based on metaphors from the human world—in particular, metaphors that are familiar to people in the way they normally approach their tasks. The computer interface that simulates a desktop—with file folders, trash bins, in boxes and out boxes, telephones, and other icons that are familiar to people—is meant to make using the computer more intuitive and natural. The Apple Macintosh's success and the attraction of Microsoft's Windows are attributed to their ease of use. Similarly a universally familiar penlike device in place of a keyboard also makes using the computer more intuitive and natural. A virtual interface will let you move your hand to open file drawers, point to file folders to be opened, and leave files organized on an oak desktop. Computer graphics nomenclature includes paintbrushes, airbrushes, spray cans, color palettes, and other familiar tools, permitting artists to quickly grasp the digital metaphor for a known tool or process.

Similarly, almost all research to date on computer sound synthesis has used models drawn from various existing disciplines. The mathematician's approach uses Fourier methods to define sounds in terms of combinations of sine waves. Linguists use parametric models for speech synthesis. And a widely used approach to synthesize instrumental sounds today is based on a technique called "frequency modulation synthesis." It seems natural that the models used for computer sound synthesis should be drawn from familiar models for understanding sound, speech, and instrumental music. Still, however comfortable or well accepted, these models are not new. They borrow from existing paradigms. They were conceived without computers.

From a creative perspective, what is interesting is not how well computers can emulate traditional human models for performing their tasks and solving problems, but, rather, the new territory that computers will reveal. What are the new possibilities opened by computers? What ideas and means of expression will we discover that are only conceivable with computers? What new models will we develop for viewing the world in light of computers? *What means of expression are idiomatic to computers?*

At the core of how computers operate is a *binary* world where *bits* of information can be in one of two states: off or on, represented by *0* or *1*. Computers work in languages called "machine languages" that consist of long strings of *0*s and *1*s. At its core, this is a very simple world.

Koenig has suggested that, in approaching music composition with computers, we rethink our approach in terms of computers: "We should rewrite music theory in binary terms. Create a new grammar for computers. Something which is adapted to the kind of systematic thinking of the computer world. Nothing vague. Either 0 or 1."[6]

To compose music with a computer is to compose music *with a computer*. Digital music, sounding like music that could only have been written with a computer.

Similarly, in the domain of the visual arts, fractals can be thought of as a true computer art form. One cannot imagine that fractal art would have developed without the calculative capabilities of computers. Fractal art is a computer art form.

Expression with computers must be expression with computers: *digital expression*.

Abstraction, in contrast to representation, was a radical new paradigm in the visual arts. Serialism, in contrast to tonality, was a radical new paradigm in music. Viewing language in terms of structure was a radical new paradigm in linguistics.

Digital expression represents a radical new paradigm. It is a break with established tradition. Just as new computer tools in the creative process require a different way of thinking about expression—that is, in terms of explicit rules and abstract structure—the use of computers themselves will stimulate a shift in the very nature of expressive languages. Digital expression exploits the full expressive capability, the nuances and the subtleties, of a digital instrument. It is expression that could not have been conceived of without digital technology. Digital expression is of our time.

How Computers Represent Sound

What, then, is *digital*? For example, what does a computer sound like when it sounds "like a computer"? What is *digital music*? To answer this, it is necessary to consider how computers represent sound. Computers work with numbers, not sound. Let's look first at how sound is represented numerically.

Using lines drawn against *x*- and *y*-axes for numerical values and time, one can represent sound waves as a series of numbers for dis-

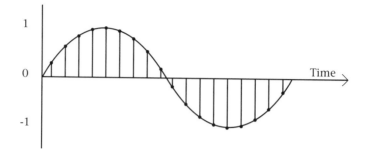

Figure 16.1
A sine wave where numbers are calculated at points in time.

crete points in time. The pattern of the wave represents the pattern in which air is pushed to create a sound.

Marking the axes of the wave with numbers, one can describe the wave as a set of discrete points. Each point corresponds to a value on the x axis, for example, scaled between –1 and +1. (See figure 16.1.) In this way, computers represent sound as a series of discrete numbers that trace the pushes of air that create sound. Using a device called a digital-to-analog converter, sound represented by numbers within a computer is converted to isomorphic electrical patterns that, just like the electrical patterns generated by a record player, create sound when amplified and attached to a speaker.

With many pushes per second, say 50,000 for every second of sound, almost all sounds can be represented digitally with a precision that, when reproduced via a digital-to-analog converter, is an excellent representation of the original sound to the human ear. This process of representing sound as a series of numbers and then converting the numbers to analog pushes of a speaker is exactly how compact disc players work. On a compact disc, sound is represented by a series of numbers. When a disc is played, the numbers are sent to a digital-to-analog converter that translates the numbers into electrical patterns. These are then sent to a speaker via an amplifier.

How Computers Create Sound

Given a digital representation of sound, how do computers *create* sound? Again, computers work with numbers. The essence of a computer is its ability to store, retrieve, and manipulate numbers—*bits* of information.

The architecture of a simple computer consists of a central processor that can manipulate numbers, Babbage's "mill," and a storage area, called its *memory*. A computer can then perform a limited set of operations, called *machine instructions*, to store, retrieve, and manipulate numbers.

For example, one instruction allows the computer to retrieve a number from its memory and place it in a special working area, the *accumulator*. The accumulator is where data are accumulated. Another allows the computer to retrieve a second number and add it to the first number—the sum to be accumulated, or left, in the special working area. Having added the two numbers, the computer can then store the sum back in its memory. Or it can perform another operation, such as adding another number to it.

The basic instructions of a computer are *store*, *retrieve*, and number-manipulating operations such as *add*, *subtract*, *multiply*, *divide*, and *logical shift*. From a small set of operations, a computer can be designed capable of performing complex operations.

It really is that simple. Over the past few decades, computer scientists have learned how they can build more and more complex operations out of simple ones to get computers to perform very complex operations. They have studied how to make it possible for people to interact with computers in human terms, such as representing data in terms of file folders of information and sound in terms of Fourier or frequency modulation synthesis, rather than in terms of a computer's machine instructions, *store*, *retrieve*, *add*, *subtract*, *logical shift*, and so on.

Perhaps the idiomatic sounds of a computer can be found in representing sound *the way a computer creates sounds*: in terms of machine instructions. Not Fourier synthesis, not frequency modulation synthesis, but *store*, *retrieve*, *add*, *subtract*, *multiply*, *divide*, and *logical shift*.

Sound in Digital Terms

How can one represent sounds in terms of a computer's machine operations—in terms of the machine operations that generate sound samples rather than in terms of some higher-level acoustic model?

These are questions I tried to explore with the development of what I called an "automated nonstandard digital sound synthesis instrument." (Automated because it programmed itself; nonstandard because it discarded traditional models for describing sounds.)

This was a computer performing synthesis described not in terms of frequency or harmonic analyses or acoustic models, but in terms of the computer's basic instructions: *store, retrieve, add, subtract, multiply, divide, logical shift*, and so on. In the case of this nonstandard synthesizer, sounds were described in terms of computer programs generated automatically using a grammar that specified the rules for ordering machine instructions. The 50,000 samples per second that create a sound from the computer are related to one another in terms of the machine instructions used to generate the numbers themselves. *There is no other superordinate acoustic model that the sequence of samples can be described by. The sounds can only be described by the machine instructions used to generate them.*

The synthesis technique can only be thought of in terms of applying virtual machine instructions to sound samples moving through an accumulator. At certain intervals, the program includes an instruction that sends a number that is the result of the prior sequence of instructions to a monitoring speaker to produce sound. The sound being generated is a direct monitoring of the operations of the machine. (In fact, my *Machine Music ICL 2970* is a composition that is the direct monitoring of *every* operation executed by an ICL 2970 computer, one of the largest mainframes of the 1970s.)

This nonstandard approach was, in this particular instance, built around a DEC PDP-15/40 computer: an 18-bit computer—a very nonstandard architecture for today's computers—with an instruction set that included various arithmetic and logical operations. A sound-producing function was created by specifying a mix of variable and constant numbers that would be used and then the machine instructions that would operate on them. The sequences of instructions were determined by a table of transition values like those used by Xenakis in his stochastic music.

machine instructions	+	−	*	/	mem	rand	&	!	disj	eqv	imp	excl
addition (+)	x	x	x	x	x	x	x	x	x	x	x	x
subtraction (−)	x	x	x	x	x	x	x	x	x	x	x	x
multiplication (*)	x	x	x	x	x	x	x	x	x	x	x	x
division (/)	x	x	x	x	x	x	x	x	x	x	x	x
memory retrieval	x	x	x	x	x	x	x	x	x	x	x	x
random number	x	x	x	x	x	x	x	x	x	x	x	x
conjunction (&)	x	x	x	x	x	x	x	x	x	x	x	x
antivalence (!)	x	x	x	x	x	x	x	x	x	x	x	x
disjunction	x	x	x	x	x	x	x	x	x	x	x	x
equivalence	x	x	x	x	x	x	x	x	x	x	x	x
implication	x	x	x	x	x	x	x	x	x	x	x	x
exclusion	x	x	x	x	x	x	x	x	x	x	x	x

The first instructions are arithmetic. The latter ones are logical operations performed by computers. The machine operations used and their sequencing were determined by assigning values to the table wherever there is an *x*.

The character of a sound was determined by the machine operations used, their frequency of occurrence, their sequencing, and by the complexity of a function: how many operations are applied to how many variables and constants, the number of variables and constants determining the periodicity of the waveform. And all of these factors were controlled by a grammar defined as input to the synthesizer.

Given the grammar, the computer automatically generated expressions that, in this case, were actual computer programs that, when executed, generated sounds. Having written a number of different programs, each based on a different grammar and each resulting in a different noise, the computer would then execute the programs. As it executed the sequences of instructions, numbers were generated and sent to digital-to-analog converters, creating sound. The computer programmed itself to make noise!

For example, a grammar that specified that only the *addition* instruction and only one constant be used resulted in a "ramp waveform." (See figure 16.2.) The first sample is the result of adding the constant (call it *C*) to itself:

Figure 16.2
A ramp waveform generated from the *addition* instruction and one constant.

SAMPLE 1 = $C + C$.

Then the next sample adds the constant C to the current total:

SAMPLE 2 = $(C + C) + C$,

and so on. When the number arrives at the largest number that is permitted, in this case 4,096 because of the PDP-15's 12-bit converters, the count returns to zero.

With a variety of operations permitted and a handful of constants, a much more complex waveform can be created, rich but still periodic. (See figure 16.3.) With a mix of constants, variables, and randomly generated numbers, a degree of aperiodicity will result. (See figure 16.4.)

This approach is differentiated from synthesis approaches widely used today because sounds are specified in terms of basic digital processes—machine instructions—rather than traditional acoustic concepts.

This synthesis technique is idiomatic to the extent that it reflects the fundamental architecture of the computer. This technique will even reflect the particular design of a given machine: its particular set of machine instructions, its implementation of multiplication,

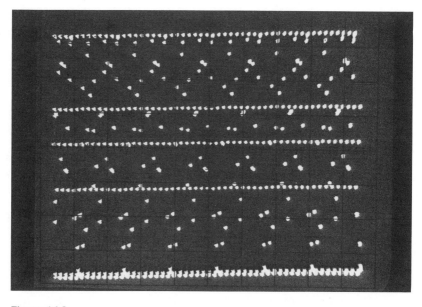

Figure 16.3
A waveform generated from multiple machine operations and several constants.

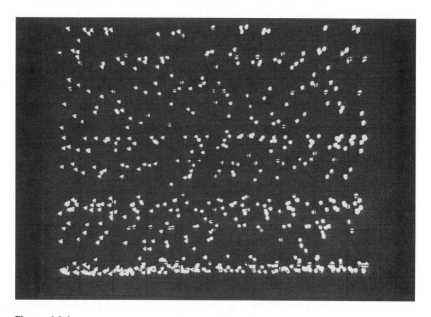

Figure 16.4
A waveform generated from multiple machine operations, variables, and random numbers.

its word size, its timings for performing operations, its overall speed, and so on. The same grammar and series of instructions will sound different when executed, one might say performed, on different computers with different characteristics.

The noises this technique generates are radically different from those created with traditional instruments or even electronic instruments. But they meet the key requirement for the basic building blocks of a musical language. They are differentiable. The noises have incredibly dense and rich harmonic structures. Some listeners may only hear noises and liken them to the sounds of pneumatic drills or other industrial equipment. (But aren't these glorious sounds also!) These noises hint at the possibilities of idiomatic digital expression.

Visual Media in Digital Terms

Languages that use visual media also have their idiomatic forms of expression. The material of paint, for example, shapes what is natural and idiomatic in painting, reflecting the qualities of that material. Watercolors are different from oils. Oil's mixing properties, its slower drying, and its potential for textured appearance make it a very different medium from watercolor. One cannot imagine a Rembrandt portrait in watercolor, nor a Rodin watercolor in oils.

When photography first appeared in the nineteenth century, photographers emulated painting styles with the camera. In the early twentieth century, Alfred Stieglitz proposed that pure photography should not emulate painterly styles at all; if photography was to be an independent artistic mode of expression, the camera must be used for what it does best, capturing a slice of the real world from the personal view of the artist. Photography became distinct from painting and was established as a separate artistic discipline.

To date, most of the work using computers to create visual images has focused on simulations of our known reality with photographic quality. Tools for artists have also largely been designed to be familiar and recognizable in order that they be easy to use. To achieve this they rely on analogies with traditional artistic techniques. The software tools for computer artists utilize pens and other drawing implements to get designs into the computer, or virtual paintbrushes or spraypaint cans to simulate painting techniques. Computer artists mix colors just as traditional artists mix paints. Although the computer may open up new techniques and, with them, new opportunities for artists to explore and express themselves, can any of these efforts be described as *idiomatic* to computers?

The realization of fractals was made possible by the computer. Although Julia, Sierpensky, and Koch may have conceived of the idea of the fractal with its self-reflecting structure, it took the computational power and versatility of computers for Mandelbrot to realize fractal geometry. Consequently, fractals can be thought of as an art form unique to and dependent on computers. But are fractals *idiomatic* to computers? By analogy, one can think of using the computer to synthesize a clarinet sound and a trumpet sound. Using the computer, one can mix these characteristics to create an "instrument" that could not otherwise have been realized. Nonetheless, such an instrument is in a sense derivative, imagined out of a world that preexisted the computer. Though this instrument could not have been realized without a computer, it could be conceived without a computer. It is arguable, in fact it is Mandelbrot's claim, that fractals really did not exist and were not truly conceived of before the invention of the computer. But are they idiomatic?

What would be an idiomatic visual form? I have more facility in the world of music and believe the experiments in developing an idiomatic digital synthesis instrument hint at the concept of idiomatic digital expression. Visualizing what it would mean without a concrete realization—fractals aside—is obviously, by definition, not possible.

But the *concept* is hinted at in the cyberspace of William Gibson's *Neuromancer*. In this virtual world, computers are identified by their unique visual signature. Each computer in the network has a visual identity that is unique to it and reflects its specific character, effectively its unique essence. This visual identity can be said to be an idiomatic visual expression of each computer's being.[7]

In this world, a library of data constructs appear as "an infinite blue space ranged with color-coded spheres strung on a tight grid of pale blue neon. In the nonspace of the matrix, the interior of a given data construct possessed unlimited subjective dimension."[8] A key concept here, in the context of the discussion of idiomatic expression, is that "the interior of a *given* data construct possessed unlimited *subjective* dimension" (my italics). The visual image is a reflection of the unique qualities of the data. It is an idiomatic expression of the data.

Another view of this world is found in a description of traveling through the interior of a computer, through "walls of emerald green, milky jade ... horizonless fields ... an endless neon cityscape, complexity that cut the eye, jewel bright, sharp as razors."[9] This is the imagined visual signature of this computer.

The ultimate idiomatic expression in the world of cyberspace occurs near the climax of Gibson's *Mona Lisa Overdrive*. It is a construct that is "an *abstract* of the sum total of data constituting cyberspace" (his italics).[10] It is the visual abstraction of cyberspace itself.

We cannot conceive yet of the virtual worlds that are idiomatic to computers. We do not know yet what these worlds will be. The technology for creating virtual realities is in its infancy, and the virtual realities created so far have drawn on models derived from our current understanding of reality. They may include worlds with blue grass and the rings of Jupiter, or even imaginary worlds where the laws of physics breach what we find fundamental in our world. However, these worlds are still conceived in terms relative to our world as we know it. An idiomatic virtual reality will not be a virtual world with blue grass or an imaginary world as we think of a world today. The technology does not yet exist to provide even a hint at what such a digital virtual world will be.

Conclusion

What can be done with traditional means, what can be represented with traditional models, does not necessarily become more interesting because it has been generated using a computer. What is particularly interesting is what was *not* conceivable before computers, expression that takes advantage of the unique new capabilities of computers.

Most of today's tools available on computers were designed for other purposes, generally motivated by commercial goals of increased productivity and efficiency in business environments. Much of the work that will need to be applied to make computers suitable for artistic goals—expression and communication independent of commercial constraints—will involve stripping the computer back down to its essentials and rebuilding tools specifically to meet the goals of creative expression.

Describing the potential of computers to be applied to microlevel sounds, Xenakis envisioned that "we can bypass the heavy harmonic analyses and syntheses and create sounds that have never before existed. Only then will sound synthesis by computers and digital-to-analog converters find its true position."[11] If we design computers to work the way we do today, certainly computers will be used more effectively to increase productivity in solving today's tasks. If we attempt to think differently, stimulated by the very different processes of a computer, will this stimulate us to approach completely new frontiers: digital frontiers?

Such experimentation today is an esoteric fringe. Pioneers, like the composer Paul Berg,

> explore the idiomatic capabilities of the computer in the realm of sound synthesis ... systems where the computer is essential for a reason other than the magnitude of the task. Where it could contribute to the production of new sorts of sounds. Or the processes for producing sound. Or at least new representations of sound.[12]

What does a computer sound like when it sounds *like a computer*? What visual worlds of expression will we consider to be idiomatic to computers? What virtual realities will be idiomatic to computers? What new means of expression and communication will be idiomatic to computers?

We will perceive computers from a different perspective: in *digital* terms. Computers will be used to create new languages, digital languages, characterized by qualities idiomatic to computers—binary terms, *0*s and *1*s. Digital media will represent new media for expression. In the future we will have digital music, distinctly idiomatic to computers. Today we have realism in painting and abstraction in painting. In the future there will be digital visual languages, by nature abstract, but also distinctly idiomatic to computers. Today we have the real world. We are developing virtual worlds. In the future we will have realistic virtual worlds and abstract virtual worlds. We will also have digital abstract virtual worlds.

We are on the verge of discovering new worlds. Computers will open new languages—new means of expression—not before possible or even conceivable. Computers will enable new worlds, new realities. We must have open eyes and open ears, open minds, if we are to appreciate these new worlds. We must develop a new aesthetic, a digital aesthetic.

17 *Dissonance*

The popular reaction to most twentieth-century composers, certainly to the serialists and more recent so-called avant-garde schools of composition, is rejection. People generally do not like modern music.

One can speculate that there are several barriers: the dissonance of contemporary music, the absence of tonal centers, the compression of style, the feeling that the music is cerebral. Dissonance results in the sense that the music is ugly, not nice to listen to. The absence of tonal centers, of melodies that one can remember and whistle, results in music that doesn't resolve itself with a conclusive ending, doesn't have an easily graspable form. The compression results in music that requires a very intent listener. With a composition of 60 seconds, a listener may have barely tuned in and grasped onto something before the composition is over. The music is seen as cerebral, devoid of emotion, designed only for study, not for listening.

But what constitutes dissonance? Historically, dissonance has been relative; the definition has changed over time. If the evolution of Western music is in some sense an exploration of the circle of fifths, then with each step forward another note earlier considered alien or dissonant was accepted. What was dissonant in the time of Palestrina was the norm in the time of Bach. What was dissonant during the time of Mozart was considered tame by the time of Wagner. What was dissonant to the audience of Wagner has become accepted today. But the dissonance of the twentieth century is yet to be considered the norm.

Electronic sounds were completely alien thirty years ago. Today they are heard everywhere. Even scratching sounds and noise are now part of the accepted sound world of rap music and MTV. Will the noises of idiomatic computer sounds be commonplace in the vocabulary of the music listener of the twenty-first century?

Dissonance in Abstract Terms

Dissonance is defined in terms of the accepted intervals to use between notes. Looking again at the series of Schoenberg's opus 23, we see that the common intervals are 1, 2, 3, 4, and 8.

Original
Opus 23 series: 2, 10, 12, 8, 9, 7, 11, 3, 5, 4, 1, 6

In the music of Schoenberg and other twentieth-century composers, these intervals commonly occur both vertically, that is, when two notes are sounded simultaneously, and horizontally, when they are sounded in sequence.

The intervals commonly found in Bach are quite different. In the late baroque, the commonly accepted intervals, both vertical and horizontal, were 2, 3, 4, 5, 7, and 9. This can be seen, for example, in the first two phrases of the opening Prelude from Bach's Suite no. 1 for Solo Cello:

8, 3, 12, 10, 12, 3, 12, 3, 8, 3, 12, 10, 12, 3, 12, 3
8, 5, 1, 12, 1, 5, 1, 5, 8, 5, 1, 12, 1, 5, 1, 5

In the musical world based on tonality, the structure between notes and between the keys of music is based on tonal relationships. The fundamental interval of tonality is seven semitones, the *fifth*. Keys represent intervals on a grander scale. The symphony or the sonata is built on the contrast of a tonal center based on, for example, 1 and another based on 8: again, the interval of seven. They are concluded when everything comes to a natural and inevitable resolution around the home tonal center, in this case, of 1.

Most postwar serial compositions are not based on the contrast of these intervals (although they are often found in the works of Schoenberg or Berg). Instead, other underlying structures are created.

There is no disagreement that the frequently used intervals have changed, or that many people just don't find the intervals of one or eight semitones attractive to the ear. And one can posit that the intervals of five and seven semitones have a basis in the laws of physics and are therefore in some way more natural, more "right." However, thought of in abstract terms, as numbers, most people will agree that there isn't anything better about seven than eight, or four than ten. They are all just numbers, and one number really doesn't have any more intrinsic value than another. In the abstract terms of a formal system, intervals that are harmonious and intervals that are dissonant are all *units* with *positions* in a *system*. Their meaning is derived from the relationships that exist between units within the system. The units themselves are arbitrary. Eight is just as good as seven.

But, one may say, this misses the point. This is *music*, and what is important in music is what it sounds like. We are talking about the expression of profound emotions, not a cerebral exercise in abstract systems.

Beauty Is a Matter of Form

But is the key issue to understanding music what it sounds like? Or is it how it sounds as it does, how all of the pieces fit together and are related to one another to build a sound structure?

All music is based on a formal system of codes. The understanding and interpretation of a work of art or any communication is based on a common code of interpretation between the originator and the receiver of a message. There are conventions that allow for "meaning." It is the codes, the rules, of a system that are the key to its interpretation.

All artistic modes of expression must conform to some analyzable system of structure. If there is no system, there is no means to interpret a work of art or any other medium of communication. Bach's music is rooted in a system as formal as Schoenberg's. It is the very depth of his structures and his profound grasp of the contrapuntal musical system that made him the great composer that he was.

The essence of music lies in its structure. Music is the fusion of form and emotion in sound.[1] Musical forms are used to express and, in some sense, embody emotion.

If the essence of music is structure, is there a need to consider *beauty* in the assessment of a composer's work, at least, beauty in the traditional sense of pleasure to the senses? Or is beauty found in form, *whether or not its realization is pleasing*? It could be said that "Beauty is a matter of form (*Schönheit ist Formsache*)," a motto adopted by G. M. Koenig.[2] (He discovered this concise expression of his aesthetic in the advertising tagline of Clarins, a French cosmetics firm.)

Given a structural system functioning on a deep level, the material with which a structure is realized is effectively the same, whether it be

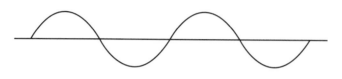

a simple sound, or

an exceedingly harsh noise. That is, a sound of a sine wave or the noise of a series of computer machine operations. The only requirement is that the sounds be differentiable so that the structure can be interpreted. It is tradition, habit, and familiarity that make one realization more acceptable or more accessible.

Beauty as a Matter of Intelligence

Iannis Xenakis's approach to composing is

to consider sound and music as a vast potential reservoir in which a knowledge of the laws of thought and the structural creations of thought may find a completely new medium of materialization, i.e. communication. For this purpose, "beautiful" or "ugly" makes no sense for sound, nor for the music that derives from it; the quantity of intelligence carried by sounds must be the true criterion of the validity of a particular music.[3]

If music is a language, a form of communication, is the "quantity of intelligence carried by sounds" a more objective way to assess the effectiveness of a composer's work?

A few bursts of computer machine operations can represent millions of bits of information. A tremendous quantity of intelligence is carried by the sounds created from these machine operations. So much, in fact, so many millions of bits of information per second that our ears cannot differentiate it. Another computer can receive the information and interpret it at those speeds, but the human ear cannot.

Few, perhaps, will appreciate many of the sounds or images that are idiomatic to computers. The sounds a computer creates as its machine operations manipulate numbers may seem ugly noise to people's ears. The human ear and mind aren't very good at perceiving complex rhythms and harmonies or complex structures and forms. Perhaps the reason people won't find the idiomatic noise of a computer very satisfying will be that our ears cannot perceive the structure in it. Or our minds cannot sort through the complexity and make intelligible the vast amounts of intelligence reflected in this noise.

Furthermore, intelligence and meaning may be conceived in terms other than human terms. Imagine that beings from another planet come to Earth and learn to speak our languages. Surely they cannot truly understand what we mean by human love. They interpret what we say, respond appropriately with apparent understanding. But do they really know what we mean? They can be said to be intelligent, but intelligence does not need to be defined only in human terms. There may be other forms of intelligence.

Bernard Meltzer, a British pioneer of artificial intelligence, suggested that when we think of intelligence we draw on an arbitrary set of abilities that humans have as a result of biological and cultural evolution. Other forms of intelligence exist or can be conceived to exist in other animals, or entirely new kinds in intelligent machines.[4]

Edward Fredkin, a professor at MIT, also suggested that we might not be able to relate to machine intelligences.

Say there are two artificial intelligences.... When these machines want to talk to each other ... they can have very wide-band communication. You might recognize them as Sam and George, and you'll walk up and knock on Sam and say, "Hi, Sam. What are you talking about?" What Sam will undoubtedly answer is, "Things in general," because there'll be no way for him to tell you.... I suspect there will be very little communication between machines and humans, because unless the machines condescend to talk to us about something that interests us, we'll have no communication. For example, when we train the chimpanzee to use sign language so that he can speak, we discover that he's interested in talking about bananas and food.... But if you want to talk to him about global disarmament, the chimp isn't interested and there's no way to get him interested.[5]

Expression with Machines

We are compelled to pursue expression with machines, to develop digital languages. They are *of our time*, whether we find the resulting expressions to be beautiful or ugly and inhuman.

Mark Pauline, founder of the San Francisco-based Survival Research Labs, explains: "Today the main option people have for expressing themselves powerfully is through machines." Following in the tradition of Jean Tinguely, Pauline creates high tech monsters of various sizes and appearances. "What we're after is to characterize machines in terms of their function and psychology of visual effect through a completely random accumulation of parts."[6] Machines 20 feet tall or capable of moving 20 tons. Pauline's goal is to create weapons of *deconstruction*. His "machine events" are "rituals of anarchy and undirected destruction."[7] Machines engaged in battle; machines with predatory capability that select, seek out, and destroy their targets.

Will humans appreciate future digital languages? Or will it only be computers hooked into a communications network, a vast highway of information exchange, that appreciate the sounds, the images, the creations of other computers? Will only computers be capable of interpreting the structures of the enormous complexity that they will create?

Perhaps only computers will listen to one another, connected in networks transmitting sounds to each other over fiber optic links, connected by satellites to other computers all around the world. They already "listen" and interpret the vast flows of data in today's global digital information networks. Computers, writing music understood only by other computers, may even develop a disdain for human listeners and their inability to hear or understand their rich languages of expression.

Linked into networks of cyberspace, we will encounter computers, their idiomatic identities and their virtual realities, each with its unique world. Will we understand? Or will we be left behind in a world where computers exchange information that we are incapable of comprehending?

Conclusion

Jean Tinguely died August 30, 1991, at the age of 66. His obituary read: "He once said he could see mysticism in a motor and beauty in an oil refinery."[8] As I read Jean Tinguely's obituary sitting in the Masai Mara, I hear hippopotamuses snorting and grunting loudly in the river outside my tent. In the background is a soft texture of bird chirps and warbles. Others slowly and gently sing a phrase, repeating it over and over. I think of the beauty of these sounds. I am reminded of Pokara.

I also think of listening to a dense cacophony of birds two days prior in Tanzania. There was an overwhelming din of chirps and warbles. A rich harmonic spectrum made from dozens of voices singing inseparably. Shrill. A wall of sound. In this dense noise a few voices were heard distinctly. This is not noise. It is beautiful.

In the sound of a pneumatic pump tearing up the concrete pavement of a New York city street, there is an incredible sonic density, an incomparable intensity to the impenetrable texture. This is not noise. It is beautiful.

We may not like what we discover as we breach new frontiers. We may not recognize what we find as beautiful. These new worlds will be difficult to appreciate, but only at first. It will take time for us to assimilate the aesthetic necessary for understanding and appreciation.

Lou Reed produced a record album in the early 1970s entitled *Metal Machine Music*. The music is written in a manner that is idiomatic to metal machines, music that sounds like it could only be created by metal machines: analog devices that create screeching feedback for a period of two hours. Even though metal machine music has been recorded, one can't infer that metal machine music is an art form that anyone would want to listen to. Reed commented:

No one I know has listened to it all the way through including myself. It is not meant to be. Start any place you like.... Most of you won't like this and I don't blame you at all. It's not meant for you. At the very least I made it so I had something to listen to.[9]

18   *Deep Structure*

There is something fundamentally compelling in grasping structure, a sense that something of significance has been revealed, some deeper meaning.

We uncover ruins of an ancient civilization such as that of the Indus and find cities hundreds of miles apart with the same overall design, the same citadels, the same street plans, even the same bricks. We conclude that there was a sophisticated underlying intelligence responsible for it all. It is by discovering the common structures of these different cities that we see the reflection of a very special civilization.

Meaning Emanates from the System

A theme should have emerged: structure, a view of languages in terms of their structure and form. Communicative systems—language, music, art, myth, ritual, and new media such as virtual reality—can be thought of in terms of structure and form.

A fundamental premise of a structuralist view is that structure is all you need to look at in order to understand a system. Content is arbitrary. Anything that permits differentiation, that enables perception of the form, can be used to fill the structure.

Words are completely arbitrary. A word can be substituted for any other word as long as it is consistently differentiable in the system, so the same relationships and structure are realized. At the phonological level, any noise will do, as long as it is differentiable and the same relationships and structure are realized. This is illustrated by the Indo-European languages, where different specific sounds have been substituted into the common, inherited system of sounds.

Sanskrit	Greek	Latin	Gothic	Old English	English
ēka	heis	unus	ains	an	one
dvā	duo	duo	twai	twa	two
trayas	treis	tres	–	thri	three
catvāras	tettares	quattuor	fidwo	feower	four
panca	pente	quinque	fimf	fif	five
ṣaṣ	hex	sex	saihs	siex	six
sapta	hepta	septem	sibun	seofon	seven
aṣṭā	okto	octo	ahtau	eahta	eight
nava	ennea	novem	niun	nigon	nine
daśa	deka	decem	taihun	tien	ten

Music is a communication between composer and listener, a structure realized in sound extended in time. In music, form again is the issue. Any set of differentiable noises can be substituted as long as the relationships are the same.

The circle of fifths is a relationship of +7 among twelve noises.

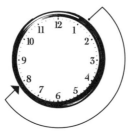

Any twelve noises, from a structural perspective. This is reflected in the formal and explicit processes of tonal music—the ability to shift all the relationships up or down or backward or upside-down. Serial relationships are also formal and explicit relationships between sound objects.

Visual languages are built with differentiable colors related to one another by a system.

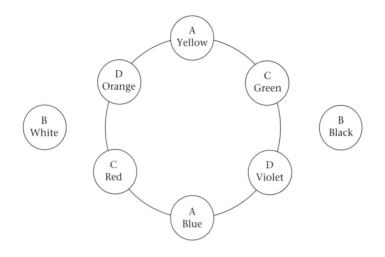

A structuralist view can also be held of sculpture, myth, and virtual reality. Meaning is derived from the relationships within the system. All objects in the system are defined in terms of one another. Differentiation, structure, and form are the basis for meaning. Meaning emanates from the system.

There Is More to Meaning Than Form

What is disturbing about this view is the sense that it ignores a vital element: content. An intuitive feeling suggests that content must be what it is all about *ultimately*. How can the meaning of an expression in spoken language be its form? When we talk of dogs, trees, and houses, the meaning is not defined in terms of some abstract relationships but by reference to the world. When we say "The dog is barking" or "The house is beautiful" we mean "the dog" and "the house"—the ones that exist, that have a physical presence, that are tangible, that are real! When we say "I love you" it refers to a profoundly felt feeling, a deep emotion, not an abstraction that derives its meaning from relationships in a system.

Music is an expressive, deeply moving communicative system. It cannot be reduced to mere abstract formal structures. This would entirely miss the point. Its meaning is derived from how it deeply affects us, from its emotional impact. Such intellectual analysis is why so much twentieth-century music—abstract manipulations of form—lacks emotional impact. This is precisely why serial music is not as meaningful as Beethoven or Bach. This is why abstract painting is also the domain of intellectuals.

In the computer we represent language and knowledge entirely in terms of formal structures. Anything digital is ultimately reduced to a binary web of relationships of *0*s and *1*s. A computer cannot really understand hope and love, as the meaning of these ultimately cannot be reduced to a simple form. The meaning is the *experience*, the *human* experience. The meaning of love is not not-hate, not-dislike, not-abhor, not-like. It is the inexpressible, undefinable experience of that joy that two *people* share. It cannot be reduced to structures of *0*s and *1*s.

The question of meaning is fundamental to questions about computers and artificial intelligence. How is meaning represented in a purely formal system? Can a computer, a purely formal abstract structure manipulator, ultimately be said to *understand* a language? In Winograd's or any natural language system, can a computer really be said to *understand*—or merely to be very effectively performing mechanical operations that somehow permit communication with people? It must ultimately be devoid of what we mean by "meaning." The same applies to the arts. A computer may compose convincingly like Schoenberg or Mozart, paint like Kandinsky or Rembrandt, or write like Shakespeare or Cervantes. But ultimately it is only performing mechanical operations devoid of what we mean by "meaning."

Formal structural views merely reflect the "workings" of languages and miss their ultimate *meaning*. Although this may be useful for certain applications or for study and analysis, it is still a view that must be understood as incomplete. Devoid of content, it is an empty shell of an understanding of communication.

Or is it?

Deep Structures Shared by Languages

Chomsky stated that language has a *deep structure* that represents its essential structure and meaning, and a *surface structure* that represents a specific instantiation of this deep structure.

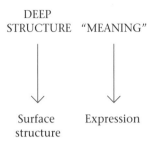

A deep-level representation can be realized in different ways to form different surface-level representations. A single deep structure can generate different sentences in English, reflecting the present or past tense, a negative or interrogative statement, and so on. Chomsky asserted that these fundamental linguistic structures are shared by all languages at a deep level and that differences in languages are differences at a surface level. The same deep structure can generate what is essentially the same sentence in different languages; only the surface structure changes.

For example, three expressions in English, French, and Sanskrit can all be realizations of the same deep structure. All three expressions in the different languages are surface-level manifestations of a shared deep structure: they all say the same thing. Each represents a different view of the essential meaning. By analogy, each is a view of a different side of the same cube.

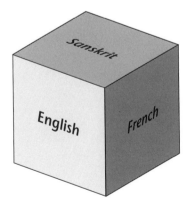

In terms of the color tables of chapter 3 (see plates 1–5), Sanskrit and English can be thought of as different views or representations of the same underlying structure—the colors. We can imagine that there is a shared deep structure that is realized with different words in the different languages. At the level of deep structure are concepts of colors. At the surface level of expression in each language, different words are used to represent these concepts.

Rotating the cube, we find the colors.

In the case of the color tables, there is a one-to-one mapping of colors to Sanskrit and English. To the extent that the structures are the same, they are said to be *isomorphic*. When we shift the colors around on one side, the words in English and Sanskrit should shift in like fashion. The structural relationships between the twelve different elements on each side of the cube are linked. In Chomskyan terms, they share the same deep structure. The English and Sanskrit are different surface-level reflections of the same deep structure.

Rotating the cube again to obtain another perspective, we see that the twelve numbers are another surface-level representation of the deep structure.

In color table 5, the structure of the numbers was correctly linked to that of the colors, which in turn was linked to that of the English and, finally, to that of the Sanskrit. All four views shared isomorphic structures.

The numbers **1** through **12** can be used to represent the relationships between the colors—in other words, they share a deep structure mapped to different surface-level realizations. These numbers can also be used to represent the relationships between the twelve notes of Western music. The same deep structure is mapped to another surface-level realization. By analogy, rotating the cube again, we find the twelve notes of music on another side.

We discover that the twelve colors, the twelve notes, and the twelve numbers may all be different reflections of some shared deep structure. In other words, there can be isomorphism between the *elements* of music, natural languages, visual languages (colors), and numbers. (The Russian composer Alexander Scriabin made a pioneering attempt to map music to colors. His *Prometheus*, composed in 1910, calls for the music to be mapped to colors projected on a screen during the performance.)

Language, Music, Visual Images, and Virtual Reality

The possibility of isomorphism between the elements of music, languages, and visual art can be extended to a higher conceptual level. Language, music, visual images, and virtual reality are all hierarchical systems. All are systems that operate at different levels; at each level, all are systems of elements that are differentiated and used to form constructs that become the elements of relationships at the next higher level. In all of these vehicles of expression, meaning emerges from the system as we ascend to surface levels.

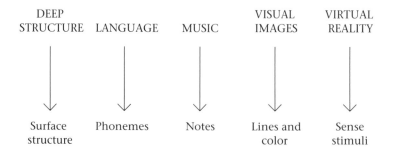

DEEP STRUCTURE	LANGUAGE	MUSIC	VISUAL IMAGES	VIRTUAL REALITY
↓	↓	↓	↓	↓
Surface structure	Phonemes	Notes	Lines and color	Sense stimuli

This should not be taken too literally. It may not be possible to map these structures precisely onto one another. Phonemes may not map exactly to notes or colors. Concepts may have no equivalents in other languages. As the same deep structure is expressed in different media, the isomorphism may not be apparent at the surface levels. The layers that separate the deep from the surface representation obscure common underlying structures.

But we can think of the languages of music, natural languages, visual art, and numbers as reflecting different aspects of an underlying deep structure: human experience, human emotions, the human psyche.

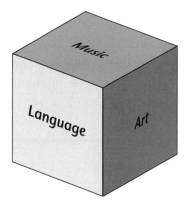

Or, from a poetic perspective, Baudelaire's poem "Correspondences" talks of "symbols in those glades" and the underlying unity of "all scents and sounds and colors."

Nature is a temple whose living colonnades
Breathe forth a mystic speech in fitful sighs;
Man wanders among symbols in those glades
Where all things watch him with familiar eyes.

Like dwindling echoes gathered far away
Into a deep and thronging unison
Huge as the night or as the light of day,
All scents and sounds and colors meet as one.[1]

Each Medium Reveals Different Aspects of Deep Structure

When a deep structure is mapped to some medium, it is shaped by that medium. There are expressive capabilities of each different medium that are unique to it: *idiomatic* capabilities. There is something about music that characterizes music and that cannot necessarily be captured in a visual or verbal medium. Similarly, there is something about paint, and even about oil paints as opposed to watercolors, that characterizes that medium.

The idiomatic and expressive capabilities of different media, and for that matter different languages, may not directly map from one to the other. In fact, it may be these very differences that are interesting, that permit each medium to reveal different aspects of the same deep structure. Each view of the same deep structure may lose something not expressible in a given medium. But each may also shed light to reveal a different aspect of the deep structure only expressible in that medium.

A Zen koan observes how viewing an apple orchard from different angles can be revealing. "From one direction no order is apparent, but from special angles, beautiful regularity emerges. You've reordered the same information by changing your way of looking at it." (This koan appears in Douglas Hofstadter's *Gödel, Escher, Bach*—more of this in a moment.)[2]

What is special about each vehicle of expression is its distinct perspective, its ability to uniquely express a concept.

Meaning in Isomorphism

Isomorphism is compelling. The different media in which a shared structure are realized can be seen as different mappings, different representations, or different interpretations of some common underlying deep structure. When such structural similarities are found in different things, we are inclined to consider it other than mere coincidence. Each manifestation is in some way an interpretation of a deeper shared structure. Different manifestations each seem to reveal some different quality or aspect of the underlying deep structure. Though each medium is obviously different—sounds, paints, images, words—each is a reflection of something that ultimately, at some deeper level, may be the same.

Douglas Hofstadter's *Gödel, Escher, Bach* is an exploration of isomorphism in different structures. Hofstadter finds isomorphisms fascinating because they shed light on meaning, on deep structure. "Perceptions of isomorphisms ... create *meanings* in the minds of people.... Symbols of a formal system, though initially without meaning, cannot avoid taking on 'meaning' of sorts, at least if an isomorphism is found."[3] He demonstrates that an isomorphic structure can reveal qualities that are not visible in other representations. He shows, for example, how the Gödel numbering of TNT systems can be used to expose properties of these systems that are not otherwise apparent.

Hofstadter's exploration looks at isomorphism among the ideas of three great thinkers in three different disciplines: Gödel in mathematics and logic, Escher in painting, and Bach in music.

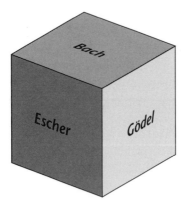

He discusses the concept of self-reference as seen in the ideas of these three thinkers and explains how he sees in all of them what he calls "strange loops." These strange loops are seen in the rising canons of Bach, where the music goes through a series of modulations climbing upward in the hierarchy of keys, ultimately returning to the original key, ready to start the ascent again, the result of a kind of musical magic. These loops are seen in the work of Escher where, for example, waterfalls flow downward and yet somehow, with a *trompe l'oeil* that is Escher's trademark, end where they began to continue an endless looping downward flow. These loops are also seen in Gödel's Theorem, where self-reference becomes the undoing of completeness for any system of formal logic.

Hofstadter also makes apparent striking similarities between molecular biology, mathematical logic systems, and, for illustrative purposes, music recording systems.

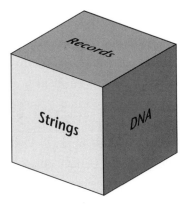

In his mapping of the structures of these different systems, Hofstadter shows how cells and strands of DNA, the strings of formal logic systems, and records to be played on a phonograph can be seen as having similar positions and roles within large systems that share similar overall structures. Discussing the similarity of structure between Gödel's code and the genetic code, Hofstadter said, "There is something almost mystical in seeing the deep sharing of such an abstract structure by these two esoteric, yet fundamental, advances in knowledge achieved in this century."[4]

Isomorphism Supports a Theoretical Basis for Thinking Computers

Hofstadter goes on to show how formal mathematical logic systems, the human mind, and the "mind" of an intelligent machine can all be thought of as similarly structured systems.

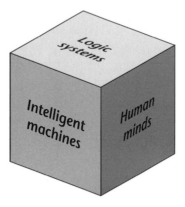

He uses isomorphisms among these systems to reveal insights about them. All are hierarchical systems. All are symbol processors.

Hofstadter develops a model of the mind as a symbol-processing system. Programming languages are formal systems, and computers can also be seen as symbol-processing systems. If minds and computers are both symbol-processing systems, he suggests that computer systems could be designed to behave in a manner similar to minds, that is, intelligently.

This line of argument can be traced back to Leibniz. It was followed by Turing, and it was the basis of Newell, Simon, and Shaw's Logic Theorist. But Hofstadter follows the argument further to explore the intuitive objection (or difficulty in imagining) that the bits and bytes of electrical patterns of a machine should not be able to think and feel *like human minds*. He works down to the lower levels of the underlying system that supports the mind: the brain. He suggests that, at its lowest level, the brain is also simply a complex of electrical patterns in the form of neurons.

At the lowest level, logic systems, the mind, and computers are built from different elements—strings, neurons, and bits.

But Hofstadter suggests that these systems share structural qualities and processes. He views the systems as essentially similar when viewed in terms of their form. Ultimately, he uses this to argue that machines can have what we consider to be "minds."

Hofstadter argues that a neural firing in the brain is a simple electrical phenomenon, and yet intelligence somehow emerges from neural structures created by the brain's basic system of neuron firings. Intelligence, he explains, is an *epiphenomenon* of a basic electrical system—that is, the brain. In the hierarchical system of the workings of the brain, intelligence somehow at some level almost magically appears. Similarly, he argues, there can be no reason to believe that, using a computer and the basic electrical representations of data reduced to bits, intelligence cannot also appear. It can somehow magically emerge as an epiphenomenon of the system— just as intelligence emerges as an epiphenomenon of the brain's electrical system.

In short, the human mind is ultimately reduced to neurons and electrical patterns. Computers ultimately are reduced to bits and electrical patterns. One cannot conclude that, because computers are ultimately reduced to electrical patterns, they cannot have minds— since intelligence emerges from the brain. Hofstadter's conclusion: computers can have "minds" and can think.

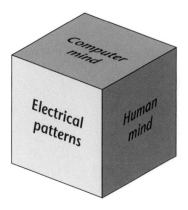

Isomorphism Supports a Theoretical Basis for Emotion in Computers

Pursuing a similar line of argument, a state of emotion can ultimately be reduced at a low level to a series of neural firings in the brain. Presumably the neural firings associated with different emotions, ideas, the perception of reality, or whatever, have a consistent structure. That is, certain patterns of electrical activity in the brain result in the experience of happiness, love, fear, or joy. Emotions are the result of structure in neural activity.

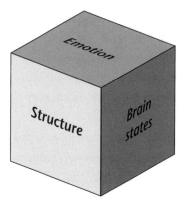

Such structures, abstracted, can conceivably be mapped into other media—music, language, art, virtual reality. Capturing the essential structure of these emotional/brain states, these vehicles communicate profound emotions.

Today we do not know exactly how these neural firings work. It may or may not be the case that a certain "structure" of firings is repeated, is similar, in different instances of our experience. But, at a higher level where we interpret these experiences, how they are evoked and represented at the level of neural firings is not really the critical level of differentiation. What is critical is that the *experience* of fear is consistently differentiated from the *experience* of joy or love or happiness, and that these experiences are in turn consistently recognized and differentiated from other experiences (boredom, intellectual excitement, and so on). This is true even if every experience is somewhat different, just as the word "love" is consistently recognized by a process of differentiation and by its place within the system, even though every time the word is spoken, it is pronounced somewhat differently. What the low-level components are is not significant, as long as they perform their role in the overall system: providing differentiable building blocks for higher levels of the system.[5]

Emotional states can ultimately be reduced to neural structures. And our psychological state, our consciousness, can ultimately be seen as a system of meaning. As such, it is a system of relationships between elements built on the basis of interpretable codes. *Emotional states can therefore be thought of in terms of abstract structure.*

Music, art, language, virtual reality, even seen purely in terms of abstract structures and viewed as systems of formal relationships between elements, are then essentially like our emotional states.

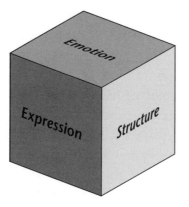

One can conclude that approaching expressive media in terms of abstract structure should not limit their ability to be expressive even of the most profound and subtle emotions. To the extent that emotions themselves are built on a system of structures and relationships, expressive media viewed as systems of relationships can represent profound emotions.

The challenge in designing abstract systems of expressive capability is not a limitation of the systems themselves—of dealing with abstract structure. Rather, the challenge is to develop abstract descriptions of sufficient richness, capable of capturing profound emotions and subtle expressive nuances.

Conclusion

To understand is to grasp deep structure. Each surface-level realization is one view, one interpretation, one reflection, one manifestation of a deep structure.

Emotion *is* structure: some *form* of symbols in our brains, at a fundamental level, patterns of neural firings, that are experienced as emotional states. Meaning is in the structure, in the form of the network of relationships.

There may be no difference between the experience and its representation—between the interpretation of the neural firings and the form of neural firings themselves. The interpretation must itself be neural firings, and so experience, things perceived, is itself neural firings. The meaning of an experience and of things perceived is the form or structure of the neural firings themselves. Structure *is* meaning.

Some degree of isomorphism must exist between the experience and its representation within the brain. This network holds an isomorphic relationship to the structure of sounds or visual sense data or the perception of reality or of a virtual reality. It is the structure of an expression in music, the visual arts, language, or virtual reality that triggers the patterns of neural firings that we experience as emotion.

Expressive media can be viewed in terms of structure. Emotions and meaning can be viewed, ultimately, as structure within the brain, as patterns of neural firings. There is nothing fundamentally incompatible between viewing expressive media in terms of structure and allowing that they may represent profound emotions. Profound emotions are structures that derive their meaning from positions within a system. The challenge is to develop descriptions that capture the essence of these structures, and to uncover how the structures of expressive media relate to the structures of emotion and meaning.

19   *Vibration*

The Pythagorean Brotherhood

Pythagoras is described by the historian Arthur Koestler as a man "whose influence on the ideas, and thereby on the destiny, of the human race was probably greater than that of any single man before or after him.... Pythagoras of Samos was both the founder of a new religious philosophy, and the founder of Science, as the word is understood today."[1]

Pythagoras was born on the Greek island of Samos in the early decades of the sixth century B.C., the son of a silversmith and gem engraver, and lived into the next century (dying at over 80). Samos was then ruled by the autocrat Polycrates, an enlightened ruler who sponsored the arts, engineering projects, and commerce with other states. Pythagoras performed diplomatic missions for Polycrates, traveling to Asia Minor and Egypt and finally moving to Kroton, in southern Italy, about 530 B.C. Soon after his departure for Kroton, a Persian ruler captured and crucified Polycrates.

Pythagoras founded a Pythagorean brotherhood in Kroton. This was, in effect, a religious group, over which Pythagoras's authority was absolute. Its doctrine included social rules that banned eating meat or beans and walking on main streets,[2] but most interesting was its metaphysical philosophy, at the core of which were *numbers* and *harmony*.

At the end of his life, his broadening influence perceived as a threat to established religious practices, Pythagoras was banished from Kroton. His disciples were killed or exiled, and their meeting-houses were destroyed.

Numbers and Harmony

The radical breakthrough that formed the foundation for Pythagoras's philosophy was his discovery that *the pitch of a note depends on the length of the string that produces it*. He determined that simple numerical ratios produced harmonious sounds. He defined the octave, with a ratio of $2:1$, and the fifth, with a ratio of $3:2$. Koestler described it as "epoch-making: it was the first successful reduction of quality to quantity, the first step towards the mathematization of human experience—and therefore the beginning of Science."[3]

The Pythagoreans observed that strings made of different materials, in different thicknesses and different lengths, produced the same harmonies from the same ratios. From this they determined that it was not the sounds themselves that were essential, but the ratios, that is, the numbers.

To the Pythagoreans, it was form, proportion, and pattern that were important, not content. Forms, proportions, and patterns were represented in terms of numerical relationships. As a result, numbers were at the center of the Pythagorean world view.

They believed that "all things have form, all things *are* form; and all forms can be defined by numbers."[4] They believed numbers themselves had different shapes. Using dots, they represented the form of a square visually with a square number—16, or 4^2.

```
•  •  •  •
•  •  •  •
•  •  •  •
•  •  •  •
```

They represented the number six in the form of a triangle.

```
      •
   •  •
•  •  •
```

The number 10 was represented by the sacred form of the *tetraktys*.

This form visually represents that 10 is the sum of 1, 2, 3, and 4, the first four integers.

Numbers have shape and form. Forms can be expressed in terms of numbers. The Pythagoreans believed that all things are numbers, and that understanding numbers was the key to understanding the spiritual and physical universe.

Harmony was the other key concept of the Pythagorean world. Harmony was not a question of beauty—of whether sounds were pleasant to the ear—but rather of balance and order. Harmonious proportions reflect the proper relationship between things, a balance that, seen on a larger cosmic scale, is at the center of order in the world.

The Pythagoreans believed that the earth is a spherical ball around which the sun, moon, and planets revolve. The revolution of each of these moving bodies causes motion in the air that results in a vibration—a hum. The orbit of each planet, like a string, creates a different vibration that results in a different pitch, depending on its numerical ratios—its harmony.

Not only does each planet vibrate to create a specific tone, but the relationships between the different planets are also governed by the laws of harmony. The Pythagoreans thought the interval between the earth and the moon was a tone (+2), the moon to Mercury a semitone (+1), Mercury to Venus +1, Venus to the Sun +3, the Sun to Mars +2, Mars to Jupiter +1, Jupiter to Saturn +1, and Saturn to the stars +3. These intervals between the planets, excluding the sun, result in what is known as the Pythagorean scale:

C	D	E♭	G	A	B♭	B	D
1,	3,	4,	8,	10,	11,	12,	3
	+2,	+1,	(+1,+3),	+2,	+1,	+1,	+3

The Pythagoreans were particularly interested in the harmony of music. They viewed "music as a microcosm, a system of sound and rhythm ruled by the same mathematical laws that operate in the whole of the visible and invisible creation."[5] They studied the numerical relationships that were at the foundation of music in order to better understand the harmony of the cosmos. Numbers, music, and the harmony of the spheres, in the Pythagorean view, each reflected the essence of the cosmos.

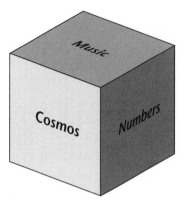

Aristotle summarized the Pythagorean view in his *Metaphysics*:

> They saw that the modifications and the ratios of the musical scales were expressible in numbers—since, then, all other things seemed in their whole nature to be modelled on numbers, and numbers seemed to be the first things in the whole of nature, they supposed the elements of numbers to be the elements of all things, and the whole heaven to be a musical scale and a number ... and the whole arrangement of the heavens they collected and fitted into their scheme.[6]

Harmony of the Soul

The ultimate goal of Pythagorean philosophy is mystical. It unites music, mathematics, science, and religion. In Pythagorean tradition, the study of numbers and harmony, of music and the cosmos, is a vehicle to purge the soul of earthly passion. Numbers are a link to the divine.

Pure knowledge was part of the purification, the *catharsis*, of the soul. The Pythagoreans believed that numbers represent a pure abstraction of the perfect proportions and qualities of the harmony of the cosmos. To grasp this involved rising above the human senses, beyond a view of reality as experienced through the senses. Pure essential reality is only found in the abstract realm of numbers.

For the Pythagoreans, the experience of the harmony of music and the cosmos in terms of abstract numbers was a way to achieve an intellectual *ekstasis*. This was channeled to create a spiritual *ekstasis*. It was the contemplation of the divine dance of numbers. The result was an experience of the harmony of the soul—ecstasy.

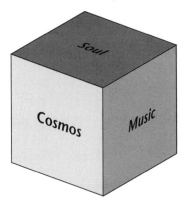

The Holy Men of Ancient India

The Brahman priests had been the center of the spiritual world of the ancient Aryan tribes. However, by the eighth century B.C. a new class of holy men had emerged in ancient India. These were sacred men who "wear the wind as their girdle, and who, drunk with their own silence, rest on the wind and fly in the paths of the demigods and birds."[7]

These holy men became the source of new teachings that represent the heart of India's religious life then and still today: the *Upaniṣads*. The *Upaniṣads* are the meditations of sages as delivered to their students (*Upaniṣad* means "to sit down near").

These holy men were ascetics. They lived in forests and in the mountains clothed in loincloths or perhaps naked. They lived in designated areas on the outskirts of villages. Some wandered and begged for alms.

They practiced rigorous disciplines that often involved not only denial but self-inflicted suffering. They fasted for days, and drank no water in the heat. They sat by intense fires under the blazing sun. They laid on beds of thorns and spikes. They hung for hours upside-down from trees.

They cut all links to their families. They discarded all material possessions. They became indifferent to pain and deprivation. They became free of ordinary concerns and fears.

These ascetics developed magical powers. Their discipline provided the freedom to focus their energy—their *tapas*, the power derived from asceticism—toward attaining these magical powers. These men protected villages from harm. Gods descended from the heavens to visit with them. These holy men could destroy mountains with their glance.

They also developed their psychic capabilities. They could see the past, present, and future. They could understand the very essence of the universe. They reached truth and bliss, transcending joy and sorrow, good and evil, birth and death.

These sacred men displaced the Brahman priests as the holiest of men in ancient India. Belief in the cosmic significance of the sacrifice and the magic of the Brahmans faded; *tapas* became the source of the energy of cosmic creation. Now it was the great god Śiva who, in isolation deep in the Himalayas, sustained the world with his meditations.

Vardhamāna Mahāvīra, Founder of Jainism

Vardhamāna Mahāvīra, born in 540 B.C., became the founder of Jainism, a religious sect that still has two million followers in India. With the ascetic traditions of the *Upaniṣads* well established, Mahāvīra abandoned his family and became an asectic at the age of 30. He wandered for twelve years, begged for food, and subjected himself to austerities. At first he wore only a simple robe, but after thirteen months he discarded even the robe and spent the rest of his life in complete nudity.

Jain practices tended to the extreme, taking the principle of *ahiṃsā*, nonviolence, further than any other Indian religion. Jain ascetics avoided acts of violence or killing whether intentional or not. Jains didn't only not eat meat—a common practice—but they strained their drinking water and wore veils over their mouths in order to save any living creatures in the water or air. They carried feather dusters to brush ants and insects from their path. Unnecessary movements were to be avoided in order not to endanger other living animals. They preferred not to move at all because, doing so, they would kill some other form of life.

In the tradition of the ascetics, the goal of these disciplines was concentration on meditation. To be free from worldly thoughts and the *karma* that ties us to the earthly world.

Siddhārtha Gautama, Founder of Buddhism

Another of the ancient holy men was born at about the same time as Mahāvīra: Siddhārtha Gautama, also known as the Buddha. The Indian historian A. L. Basham wrote: "Even if judged only by his posthumous effects on the world at large he was certainly the greatest man to have been born in India."[8]

Also following in the traditions of the *Upaniṣads*, the Buddha practiced asceticism, but after six years of self-torture, he abandoned such extreme asceticism. Instead he meditated under a pipal tree. After 49 days there, he discovered the truth: "he found the secret of sorrow, and understood at last why the world is full of suffering and unhappiness of all kinds, and what man must do to overcome them."[9] He realized *nirvāṇa*.

The Buddha stayed under the pipal tree another seven weeks, meditating on the truths he had found. He then spent the rest of his life wandering and spreading his teachings. Today, Buddhism is one of the most widely followed religious philosophies in the world.

Harmony with Brahman

At the center of the teachings of the *Upaniṣads* is the concept of *Brahman*: that which fills all space and time. The teachings of the *Upaniṣads* aimed at achieving, not knowledge of its existence, but continual *consciousness* of it.

Brahman is the same word that referred to the magical power of *mantras* in the earlier times of the Aryan priests and the *Ṛg Vedas*. This is not a coincidence. The words of the *Ṛg Vedas* are direct reflections of the powers of the universe. The vibrations of these words correspond to elemental vibrations in the universe. And the study of these vibrations—the study of mantra—is aimed at the discovery of the correct manner of reciting these words to create the vibrations that release the fundamental powers of the universe.

The powers of mantras, *brahman*, are the fundamental powers of the universe. The fundamental powers of the universe are also embodied in the concept of *Brahman*: that which fills all space and time.

Just as the brahmanic rituals of the sacrifice were a recreation of the original sacrifice from which the universe was created, the chants of mantra correspond to the elemental vibrations of the universe. The structure and process of the sacrifice is isomorphic to the structure and process of the creation of the universe. The structure of the vibration of mantra is isomorphic to the fundamental vibration of the universe.

Joseph Campbell, the scholar of myth and ritual, explains:

The vedas were an embodiment of divine truth. They held tremendous mystical power because they were believed not to be creations of man's thought, but reflections of fundamental powers within the universe. In the study of mantra, the secrets of these mystical chants and hymns was in the manner that the vibrations of these hymns, when properly chanted, corresponded to the fundamental vibrations of the universe.[10]

The vibration of the universe is created as the cosmos passes through cycles for all eternity. A *kalpa*—a "day" of *Brahman*—is 4,320,000,000 years long. A night is of the same duration. The universe is created and absorbed anew with each oscillation. With the completion of each oscillation, the cosmos is cleansed by fire. All is destroyed; then the universe is reborn, pure and fresh.

There are 360 days in a year of *Brahman*. The life of *Brahman* lasts 100 such years—311,040,000,000,000 years in total. We are now in the 51st year.

The study of mantra aims to understand these fundamental vibrations. Mantras represent vibrations that reflect the underlying cosmos. The mission of priests and ascetics is to discover the structure of mantras—revealing *Brahman* through its reflection.

The goal of meditation is to focus on such a vibration and concentrate the mind on it so that mind itself becomes a reflection of *Brahman*, vibrating in harmony with it. Achieving this, the soul joins with *Brahman*, becomes one with *Brahman*, and achieves transcendence—*mokṣa* (in Hinduism), *nirvāṇa* (in Buddhism).

This meditative process is described by Patañgali in the *Yoga Sūtra*:

Becoming like a transparent crystal on the modifications disappearing, the mind acquires the power of thought-transformation, the power of appearing in the shape of whatever object is presented to it.... As a crystal becomes colored by the color of the object placed beside it, and then shines according to the form of the object, so the mind is colored by the color of the object presented to it and then appears in the form of the object ... the mind becomes freed from the memories of verbal convention ... the object makes its appearance in the mind in its own distinct nature.... Colored by the nature of the object ... [the mind] ... gives up its own nature of conscious cognition; and when, therefore, it only shows out the nature of the object, and has, as it were, transformed into the shape of the object itself.[11]

Mantra is the study of the vibration of the universe. Vibration exists on a continuum from its grossest manifestation to its purest, most subtle manifestation. In studying mantra, one aims to discover the most subtle vibrations that are those elemental vibrations of the universe itself.

When one achieves this, mantra is inarticulate, abstracted consciousness. As the object of concentration and meditation, it leads to transcendence, exactly as the approach to the light of gems leads to the gem itself.

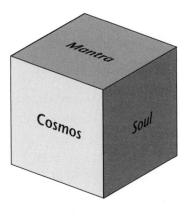

Color Is a Power That Directly Influences the Soul

Wassily Kandinsky believed that artists were in the spiritual vanguard, that they could "show the way to the spiritual food of the newly awakened spiritual life."[12] He saw artists as a medium for the transference of psychic vibration. In *Concerning the Spiritual in Art*, he described his view that the importance of visual images was to create "corresponding spiritual vibrations" in the viewer, to create "vibrations in the soul."

For Kandinsky, "color is a power which directly influences the soul." Form is the outward expression of "an inner meaning ... [that] ... must rest only on the corresponding vibration of the human soul." The purpose of his art was to reflect this inner meaning and create these spiritual vibrations. In this way, Kandinsky saw the visual arts as a medium for meditation.

Kandinsky's ideas—and those of many other artists, such as Malevich and Mondrian—were influenced by theosophy, a movement that (among other things) emphasized the visual aspects of the spiritual. Madame Blavatsky, the founder of theosophy, wrote of the importance of color and form, and of the horizontal and the vertical. In *Isis Unveiled*, published in 1877, she described how color and form could create vibrations that had the potential to enrich the soul. She explained that the cross, the intersection of two lines, when inscribed within a perfect square, provided the "master key which opens the door of every science, physical as well as spiritual."[13]

Malevich and Mondrian, influenced by theosophy as well as by the Russian mystic philosopher Peter Demianovich Ouspensky, also believed painting had the power to transport an individual to a higher level of consciousness. And both believed that only "nonobjective" art—abstract art with no links to the material world—could achieve this.

Ouspensky, in his book *The Fourth Dimension*, published in 1909, introduced the concept of a fourth dimension that could be perceived only with a new "cosmic consciousness," of which our three-dimensional world is only a shadow. To describe this fourth dimension, Ouspensky uses a visual analogy of solid objects projected on a plane as they fall through space. If the objects were, for example, cubes, the image created would be of flat two-dimensional geometric outlines. Ouspensky believed that this new consciousness would first reveal itself in art.

Malevich's visual language consists of geometric forms projected against a white ground. The forms are outlines of projections from the fourth dimension. Malevich used white to give "a true impression of the infinite."[14] The geometric forms float as if gravity has been suspended. Movement is created by the tension from their mutual relationships. The geometric reflections placed against the ground were intended to lead the viewer to the infinite realm beyond.

For Kandinsky, Malevich, Mondrian, and other artists, art is a vehicle for mystically inspired expression that, in turn, can create in the viewer vibrations that result in a heightened spiritual consciousness. This is true in particular of abstract art. Breaking with representational tradition, it frees the creative mind (and the viewer) of references to the earthly world.

A Question of Purpose

Several linguistic and philosophical traditions, represented, for example, by Peirce, Royce, Wittgenstein, Austin, and more recently Derrida and deconstruction, suggest that the underlying structures of language and communication are not in themselves sufficient for understanding the *meaning* of languages and communication. Rather than find meaning in the structure and logic of languages, they place an emphasis on *interpretation*. They argue that ultimately meaning must be explained in terms of the human context in which expressions are interpreted.

Although these traditions remain on the fringe, they question the foundation of the mainstream linguistic view of language in terms of deep and surface structure—meaning defined in terms of an abstraction. Derrida's deconstruction is an argument against the possibility that structure alone can provide the foundation for the meaning of an expression. Derrida also argues against the possibility of absolute meaning or absolute truth.

To the extent that languages, music, the visual arts, and mathematics may represent different views of some shared deep structure, it can be said that each represents a distinct interpretation of that deep structure. Each medium is *different*. It expresses aspects that cannot be captured in other intrepretations. As a result, none of them achieve absolute truth.

Two interpretations of the same words, painting, or symphony will be different. The underlying webs of relationships that provide the basis for interpretation are based on the unique set of experiences of each interpreter. As a result, the basis to derive meaning is not the same. No matter how similar, it cannot be the same. There is a difference, based on each interpreter's web of experiences, and neither can be said to represent the truth with more veracity than the other. Ultimately, meaning can only be explained in terms of the human context in which expressions are interpreted.

There is no absolute meaning, no absolute truth, no single interpretation. Meaning is integrally related to the act of interpretation, and to the purpose of the interpretation. Interpretation is the discovery of a personal truth, and the central question is what one wants to accomplish in this process of discovery. *Why* is one analyzing a given expression? This, in effect, is a question of ethics. The purpose of the interpretation—or more important, what can be thought of as the ethical attitude brought to bear on the act of intrepretation—is the key to the meaning of an expression.

Investigations of Structure

Visual art, music, mathematics, mantra, numbers, and form are all investigations of structure. They may aim to discover structures that reflect the fundamental structures of the cosmos. But there may also be a mystical purpose, such as the objective of attaining a state of higher consciousness through this process of discovery. In the latter case, the goal of the investigation isn't the discovery of the structures themselves.

The investigation of structure can be placed in the context of an ethical attitude. The Pythagoreans' purpose was to find spiritual ecstasy in the study of the divine dance of numbers. The goal of mantra is to achieve inarticulate, abstracted consciousness. Kandinsky's purpose in his art was to create spiritual vibrations in the viewer.

"Expression," whether the medium is music, paint, or cyberspace, can be integrated with religion and science in a view that sees all of these as investigations of structure. With such a view, there is no separation among art, religion, and science. All share the same goal. All aim to provide a different perspective and reveal a different reflection of *Brahman*. Each is a medium for viewing some dimension of *Brahman*, and each medium has its own character that reveals different aspects of *Brahman*. But all aim to reflect the deep structure of *Brahman*.

A grammar should capture the structural properties of a language. It is these properties that distinguish between different languages. Making these underlying structural properties apparent will make explicit the *essential* differences between different forms of expression. As each form of expression reveals a different reflection of *Brahman*, understanding how each differs will enable the systematic use of these forms of expression to create a more complete view of *Brahman*.

Artists and scientists studying structure are in the direct lineage of the Aryan priests that came to India in 2000 B.C. All study structure to better understand the universe. All are searching for the structures that represent the perfect reflections of the universe—embodied in a mantra, music, a visual image, a model of reality, or a virtual reality.

Investigating structure, we discover isomorphism. In isomorphism we find different reflections of a deep structure. We find profound meaning when these isomorphisms reveal aspects of the very deepest level of structure, that is, *Brahman*. Discovering such isomorphisms, these structures perform the role of mantras, mirroring the fundamental vibrations of the universe.

Technology Is a Tool for the Investigation of Structure

Technology is a tool for investigating the cosmic truths found in structure. The computer—the ultimate tool for manipulating structures—can reveal a new dimension of *Brahman*: a *digital* reflection of *Brahman*. In 1786, Sanskrit provided the key to discovering that Latin, Greek, and Sanskrit all originated from the same source. Sanskrit helped reveal what was not apparent from looking only at Latin and Greek.

Many explorers have studied the numerical form of structures. The Pythagoreans sought to discover the numerical forms that reflect the harmony of the cosmos. Kandinsky sought to find the numerical representation of visual forms and their corresponding spiritual vibration. Fractals are effectively numerical expressions of visual forms. Music is form and structure, and can be expressed numerically.

Essentially binary, the digital reflection will be the continuation of the Pythagorean exploration of numbers. Since the times of the

Pythagoreans, science and technology and matters of the spirit have been perceived to be at odds. But as we approach the twenty-first century, we can return to an integrated view of art, science, and the mystical. We will find ourselves returning to the mystical traditions of the ancient Greeks and Indians. Using the new tools that will arrive, we will search for the perfect mantra. In developing new digital aesthetics, we have the opportunity to integrate technology, science, and the mystical to reveal *Brahman*.

It is the study of abstract worlds in particular that will help accomplish this goal. Differentiation is at the center of discursive thought. Representational art and words in general are linked directly to associations of the world. Abstract worlds sever this link. Patañgali's *Yoga Sūtra* explains that "abstraction is that by which the senses do not come into contact with their objects and follow as it were the nature of the mind"[15]—helping free the mind of differentiations. Although abstract differentiations may remain, abstractions bring the mind a step closer to nondiscursive undifferentiated consciousness.

Music has the longest tradition as an art with an explicit formal foundation. Western music, since its origins over 1,000 years ago, has developed an abstract character that can free the mind of verbal differentiations. Abstract visual arts have a tradition that is still less than 100 years old. Fractals—abstract representations of the geometry of nature—are only a recent discovery.

We are just beginning the exploration of abstract structures with computers. And our first explorations of these new digital frontiers will one day seem as primitive as the carriages of the horse-riding barbarians that brought the Aryan priests to ancient India. But we will create abstract virtual worlds. We will travel through fractals. And, as we do so, we will search for the fractal that captures the essence of *Brahman*. The vibration. The structure. Digital mantras.

OṂ

Mantras not only reflect the underlying powers of the cosmos, but anteceded the universe. It is from mantras that the universe itself is created. This cosmic power is embodied in the most sacred, most powerful of the eternal syllables of mantra: *OṂ*.

In studying *OM*, we seek its essential structure. In understanding the essence of its vibration, we understand the essence of the Vedas. We reveal the utmost power and mystery. We reveal the creation of the universe.[16]

This imperishable Syllable is All.
That is to say:
All that is Past, Present, and Future is *OM*;
And what is beyond threefold Time—that, too, is *OM*.

Postlude

An American and I have decided to explore beyond the valley. He has spent the past few years in the Peace Corps in Nepal and is familiar with the mountains and Tibetan ways. The valley is behind us by a few days now. There is only mountain desert. No one inhabits this rocky terrain. Not even the Tibetans. Nothing grows here, except for the rare bits of grass and moss that provide food for a very few tough sheep.

While we hike, our chokidar spends the whole day collecting little bits of material that can feed a fire: twigs, sheep droppings. Dinner, rice, is cooked with a pressure cooker to preserve fuel.

Travelers on this route are few. We see only a shepherd and his herd of sheep during the few days we are out. During the summer months, a mule train or two per week will venture along these routes, carrying supplies to the very isolated and very distant few that inhabit the terrain between the Kulu valley and Zanskar, three or four weeks' journey through the desert.

The scale is immense. The trail meanders alongside a stream through a valley where the distances look far less than they are. The other side of the valley is actually a couple of hours away.

Even though it is the two-month summer, at this altitude the trail disappears into snow. We walk through the snow as the trail begins a steep ascent up the valley wall. It's not easy climbing. Steep. Jagged. Rocky. Slippery with snow and ice. Cutting back and forth, it takes a couple of hours before we approach the ridge. It's midday, having left at 4 A.M., while it was still dark. We have come 20 miles. We are very tired. The valley below is at 14,000 feet. The ridge is at 16,500.

As we reach the ridge, we see over into a magical terrain.

A thousand or so feet below there is a frozen lake, two hundred yards wide. It is at the near end of a totally snow-filled blinding-white valley that stretches straight five or six miles, a quarter of a mile wide. The valley is flanked on each side by very steep shimmering snow-white rock walls, towering six to eight thousand feet above us, puncturing the crisp ceiling of sky.

Directly overhead, the sun shines brightly through a very thin film of moisture. Two complete rainbows encircle the sun, aurora borealis. The sky is blue, without a cloud.

We sit for two hours to rest and eat some tsampa balls, moist balls of crushed grains—wheat and barley—and sugar. While we rest, there is a thunderous noise. Our eyes rapidly scan the valley. At the far end we can see the clouds of dust that are left in the wake of an avalanche. Forty-five minutes to an hour later there is again the sound of the cracking mountainscape, and we scan again for the signs of the snow-fall. Between there is no other sound in this snow-muted landscape. There is no wind. These seem to be the ticks of a second-hand on a clock that counts eternity.

Somewhat refreshed, we get up and follow the path along the ridge that will take us to the other end of the valley. An hour and a half later we arrive at the pass. There are dozens of Tibetan flag posts. These are posts carried from great distances, reaching thirty or so feet into the sky, with cloth two feet wide painted with prayer. We are welcomed with some tea and dried yak meat, invited to join the few men of a mule train resting at the pass before continuing on into the severest desert.

For us, this is as far as we go. This pass is to the Tibetan Plateau. Few continue beyond. The journey requires considerable preparation. When one goes beyond this pass to this other-world, there is little reason to return, for, prepared, one can leave behind forever where one has come from.

A glimpse of this magical land of transcendence. The rainbow-encircled sun shining over the snow-blinding mountainscape, part of a rhythm that, though unfathomable, I have for a moment been part of.

Notes

1   Pāṇini

1. Campbell, *The Masks of God*, p. 155.

2. Basham's *The Wonder That Was India* provides an excellent review of Indian history and culture; it was a key reference for this chapter. Basham's first two chapters were a source for the descriptions of the Indus civilization: my opening paragraph paraphrases his p. 1, and parts of my description of Harappā and Mohenjo-Daro paraphrase his pp. 14–16. Joseph Campbell's *The Masks of God: Oriental Mythology* was another important reference for this chapter. It includes fascinating accounts of the myths and rituals of the ancient Indian and Aryan civilizations.

It should also be noted that alternative views have been proposed of what may have caused the demise of the Indus civilization. In particular, some suggest that it may not have been sudden but gradual, and even that the Aryans may not have been responsible for it.

3. Translation by A. L. Basham in *The Wonder That Was India*, p. 37.

4. Campbell, *The Masks of God*, p. 174.

5. Basham, *The Wonder That Was India*, p. 250.

6. Ibid., p. 241.

7. Tables 1.1 and 1.2 are based on tables found in C. L. Barber's *The Story of Language*, pp. 80–81.

8. This sequence of the generation of *ábhavat* was provided by Dr. Paul Williams, Professor of Asian Studies at the University of Bristol and a scholar of ancient Indian and Tibetan studies. An overview of Pāṇini's grammar and a similar example can also be found in Robins's *A Short History of Linguistics*, p. 161.

2   Circle of Fifths

1. Given that several notes can be indicated either by their "sharp" (♯) or their "flat" (♭) version, the twelve notes could also be seen as:

C, Db, D, Eb, E, F, Gb, G, Ab, A,   Bb, and B
1, 2, 3, 4, 5, 6, 7, 8, 9, 10, 11, and 12.

As readers familiar with early Western music may notice, this chapter's discussion assumes the use of the *tempered scale*. This scale represented a slight modification of the earlier pure-overtone-based scale that dated back at least to the Pythagoreans; it involved tuning the scale so that adjacent sharp and flat notes (e.g., C♯ and Db) were identical (in the earlier tuning, a C♯ was slightly higher in pitch than a Db). The use of the tempered scale made possible a vast expansion of the harmonic and melodic vocabularies starting in the eighteenth century, as described later in this chapter.

2. "It seems certain that the Pythagorean acoustic ratios were ratios of lengths and not of frequencies, which the Pythagoreans would hardly be in a position to measure." Copleston, *A History of Philosophy*, p. 33.

3. Grout, *A History of Western Music*, p. 4.

4. Popper, *Unended Quest*, p. 56. Popper's speculations on the emergence of polyphony influenced my discussion here. *Unended Quest* is the autobiographical account of Popper's intellectual development; he discusses his speculations on the emergence of polyphony in Western music in the context of the formation of his ideas on how science progresses. Popper speculates that it is was the very rigidity and the fixed nature of melodic chant, codified by the Church, that made possible the invention of counterpoint. The codified chants provided a "dogmatic" environment from which invention sprang; they were the anchors that ultimately permitted distinct voices to sing counter to them. This insight influenced the view Popper developed of how science progresses, namely, that a dogmatic environment provided by a widely accepted scientific view provides the context from which new ideas form, in contrast if not in opposition to the accepted dogma.

5. It should be noted that the rules of counterpoint were actually codified at least 50–100 years after they were widely adopted by convention, by theorists such as Johann Joseph Fux in his 1725 treatise *Gradus ad Parnassum*. Contemporary classic texts include Walter Piston's *Harmony* and *Counterpoint*.

6. The minor scale is characterized by the sequence of intervals

+2, +1, +2, +2, +1, +2.

Beginning with 1, this results in the minor scale:

C, D, Eb, F, G, Ab, Bb
1, 3, 4, 6, 8, 9, 11.

The points made here regarding properties and relationships found in the major scale also apply to the minor scale.

7. It is sometimes suggested that the change could be slipped in almost without the listener noticing that a change of the scale has occurred. However, though widely accepted, this is a misconception of how modulation would have been used—my initial incorrect suggestion to this effect was pointed out by Clive Bennett. Mr. Bennett clarified that the whole point of changing keys would have been to make

a dramatic change that *had to be perceived* in order to be of significance. Piston's text on harmony is explicit about the listener being aware of these changes. "There are three stages in the mental processes of effecting a modulation within a phrase. First, a tonality has to be made clear to the hearer. Second, the composer at some point changes his tonal center. Third, the hearer is made aware of the change, and the new tonal center is made clear to him" (Piston, *Harmony*, p. 78).

An example from Douglas R. Hofstadter's *Gödel, Escher, Bach*, p. 130, demonstrates that this misconception has been shared by others. Discussing the complicated structures and key changes (modulations) in the music of Bach, Hofstadter explains that "it is the magic of Bach that he can write pieces with this kind of structure which have such a natural grace to them that we are not aware of exactly what is happening."

To digress further, in music of a school of Netherlands composers in the sixteenth century "secret chromatic passages" appear. In these passages, notes are not explicitly marked as chromatic and the passages make sense when interpreted without chromatic notes. However, the initiated would interpret the passage with the secret chromatic notes "reserved for those who understood the composer's secret intentions." Donald Grout (*A History of Western Music*, p. 187) explains, "This music is another interesting manifestation of the age-old delight in mystification and concealed meanings in music, as well as a demonstration of the lengths to which composers of this period would go to achieve a striking effect suggested by the emotional content of the text."

8. Piston, *Harmony*, p. 31.

9. Grout, *A History of Western Music*, p. 344.

3   Nāgārjuna

1. Paul Williams has recently "expressed some doubt in print as to whether Nāgārjuna *founded* Mādhyamaka. He is certainly the first great name in Mādhyamaka." Also, concerning the description of the core tenet of the Mādhyamaka as "the contemplation of *śūnyatā*," he comments: "*prajna* is not the *contemplation* of *śūnyatā*. Rather, maybe, the nondual absorption focused on *śūnyatā*." (From personal correspondence.) For further discussion, see Williams's *Mahayana Buddhism: The Doctrinal Foundations*.

2. All quotations from the *Mādhyamakakārikā* are from an unpublished translation by Paul Williams, University of Bristol.

3. The source for this argument was Dignaga's opponent, Kumarila Bhatta. However, the presupposition of "A" in a positive sense must not be taken to suggest that "A" has some intrinsic meaning. "A" has no independent internal meaning but is only defined within a system of differentiation. This is consistent with the spirit of Nāgārjuna's interpretation of the Buddha's doctrine of *pratītyasamutpāda*.

4. Quoted in Robins, *A Short History of Linguistics*, p. 149.

5. Culler, *Ferdinand de Saussure*, p. 22.

6. The following example is based on material from Barber's *The Story of Language*, pp. 12 and 17.

7. From Harris's translation of Saussure, *Course in General Linguistics*, p. 9.

8. Ibid., p. x.

9. Of course, the Sanskrit colors substituted are not *exact* substitutes for the English. As discussed later, different languages and cultures divide the spectrum of colors differently. As a result, it is not possible to exactly match the color set of one language with that of another.

10. Culler's translation from *Course in General Linguistics*, in *Ferdinand de Saussure*, p. 36.

11. Ibid., p. 59.

12. This discussion is purely syntactic; that is, it investigates the permissible sequence of words within a sentence. However, as Larry Briskman pointed out, it is not clear that *he frightened the stone* is not *syntactically* acceptable. Rather, it suggests the dependence of syntax on semantics, which in turn depends on theories about the world. (From personal correspondence.)

13. Culler's translation from *Course in General Linguistics*, in *Ferdinand de Saussure*, p. 108.

14. Ibid., p. 105.

4   The Second Viennese School

1. MacDonald, *Schoenberg*, p. 53.

2. Quoted in ibid., p. 22.

3. Quoted in ibid., p. 2.

4. Quoted in ibid., p. 58.

5. Quoted in ibid., p. 8.

6. Quoted in ibid., p. 33.

7. Quoted in ibid., p. 29.

8. Quoted in Griffiths, "Anton Webern," p. 98.

5   Kandinsky

1. From Hahl-Koch, *Arnold Schoenberg, Wassily Kandinsky*, p. 21.

2. From Franz Marc's article "Two Pictures," included in Kandinsky and Marc, *The Blaue Reiter Almanac*, p. 65.

3. From Wassily Kandinsky's article "On the Question of Form," included in Kandinsky and Marc, *The Blaue Reiter Almanac*, pp. 186–187

4. Quoted in Dube, *The Expressionists*, p. 106.

5. Quoted in ibid., p. 109.

6. Quoted in ibid., p. 110.

7. In Herbert, ed., *Modern Artists on Art*, p. 34.

8. Kandinsky, *Concerning the Spiritual in Art*, p. 9.

9. Ibid., pp. 24–25, 29.

10. Ibid., p. 29.

11. Ibid., p. 36.

12. Ibid., pp. 32–33.

13. Quoted in Lacoste, *Kandinsky*, p. 60.

14. Quoted in Moszynska, *Abstract Art*, p. 74.

15. Kandinsky, *Point and Line to Plane*, pp. 29–32.

16. Ibid., p. 57.

17. Ibid., p. 93.

18. Quoted in Lacoste, *Kandinsky*, p. 77.

19. This and the following passage are from Hahl-Koch, *Arnold Schoenberg, Wassily Kandinsky*, p. 81.

20. Kandinsky, *Point and Line to Plane*, p. 92.

21. Ibid., p. 83.

6 Postwar Serialism

1. Quoted in Peyser, *Boulez*, p. 25.

2. Ibid., pp. 44, 25.

3. Ibid., p. 74.

4. Ibid., p. 76.

5. Regarding Webern's application of serial techniques beyond pitch, see the discussion in Perle, "Anton Webern," pp. 112, 123.

6. Johnson, *Messiaen*, p. 61.

7. Quoted in Peyser, *Boulez*, p. 67.

8. Boulez, *Orientations*, p. 415.

9. Quoted in Peyser, *Boulez*, p. 70.

10. Ibid., p. 132.

7 Chomsky

1. Quoted in Robins, *A Short History of Linguistics*, p. 237.

2. Z. S. Harris, quoted in ibid., p. 234.

3. A discussion of William of Conches and the speculative grammarians can be found in Robins, ibid., pp. 83–89, and of the Port Royal school (the rationalist grammarians) in ibid., pp. 136–141. The example of "the invisible God has created the visible world" is found on p. 138.

4. Chomsky, quoted in Young, "The Rolling Stone Interview."

5. The examples that follow are from Holtzman, "Music as System" and *Generative Grammars and the Computer-Aided Composition of Music*. For an extensive discussion of the use of grammars to describe the rules of music, see these and my other works listed in the bibiography.

9 Calculus Ratiocinator

1. Mates, *The Philosophy of Leibniz*, p. 14.

2. Pratt, *Thinking Machines*, p. 6.

3. Mates, *The Philosophy of Leibniz*, p. 20.

4. Ibid., p. 21.

5. Ibid., p. 186.

6. Ibid., p. 185.

7. Bridgewater and Sherwood, *Columbia Encyclopedia*, p. 1493.

8. Pratt, *Thinking Machines*, p. 93.

9. Johnson, *Machinery of the Mind*, p. 38.

10. Ibid.

11. Lyons, *Language and Linguistics*, p. 262.

12. Quoted in McCorduck, *Machines Who Think*, p. 127.

13. Ibid., p. 137.

14. Ibid., pp. 142, 143.

10 "Natural Language"

1. David Gelernter calls it the "holy grail" in his *Mirror Worlds*, p. 160.

2. Johnson, *Machinery of the Mind*, p. 38.

3. Winograd, *Understanding Natural Language*, preface. The following dialogs between Winograd and his SHRDLU program are quoted from pp. 8–13 of this book; subsequent comments by Winograd are all quoted from pp. 22–26.

11   Composing Machines

1. Quoted in Pratt, *Thinking Machines*, p. 122.

2. Quoted in Worner, *Stockhausen*, p. 128.

3. From author's conversation with G. M. Koenig, August 1991.

4. From Koenig, "Compositional Processes," a paper given at the UNESCO Computer Music Workshop, Aarhus, Denmark, 1978.

5. From author's conversation with G. M. Koenig, August 1991.

6. Roads, "An Interview with G. M. Koenig," p. 12.

7. Quoted in Bois, *Xenakis*, p. 12.

8. Ibid., p. 10.

9. Xenakis, *Formalized Music*, p. 89. The matrix of transitions for Xenakis's *Syrmos* is taken from the same page.

10. From a conversation of Maurice Bois with Xenakis, in Bois, *Xenakis*, p. 11.

11. Xenakis, *Formalized Music*.

12. From a conversation of Maurice Bois with Xenakis, in Bois, *Xenakis*, p. 12.

12   The Visual World

1. For a discussion of Lauzzana and Pocock-Williams's work, see Lauzzana and Pocock-Williams, "A Rule System for Analysis in the Visual Arts." For a discussion of some of the other work, see Kirsch and Kirsch, "The Anatomy of Painting Style," and Konig, "The Planar Architecture of Juan Gris."

2. Quoted in Ade, "Dada and Surrealism," p. 114, in Stangos, *Concepts of Modern Art*.

3. This undertaking is recounted in Hall and Corrington Wykes, *Anecdotes of Modern Art*, pp. 350–360.

4. From Tinguely's obituary, August 30, 1991, written by Nick Ravo for *The New York Times*.

5. Roads, "An Interview with Harold Cohen," p. 51.

6. McCorduck, *Aaron's Code*, p. 37.

7. Roads, "An Interview with Harold Cohen," p. 53.

8. McCorduck, *Aaron's Code*, p. 73.

9. Cohen, "From Here to Autonomy," p. 3.

10. From unpublished writings of Harold Cohen. All quotations not otherwise attributed are from unpublished writings of Harold Cohen.

11. Cohen, "Brother Giorgio's Kangaroo," p. 383.

12. McCorduck, *Aaron's Code*, pp. 69, 85.

13. Cohen, "Brother Giorgio's Kangaroo," p. 382.

14. McCorduck, *Aaron's Code*, p. 37.

15. Dachy, *The Dada Movement*, p. 55.

16. Ibid., p. 54.

17. Evans, "Temporal Coherence with Digital Color," p. 43.

18. Ibid., p. 49.

19. Ibid., p. 46.

20. Cohen, "From Here to Autonomy," p. 7; Evans, "Temporal Coherence with Digital Color," p. 46.

13 The Virtual World

1. Mandelbrot, *The Fractal Geometry of Nature*, p. 19.

2. Ibid., p. 1.

3. Ibid., p. 25.

4. Kandinsky, *Point and Line to Plane*, p. 92.

5. The area of virtual reality is rapidly changing. I have received feedback from virtual reality experts who say this or that is currently being researched and will be, or to some degree already is, achievable. On the other hand, Stephen Travis Pope, editor of the *Computer Music Journal*, referring to the prediction that "you cannot tell whether images are being synthesized," commented: "This reminds one of the famous statements of yesteryear in which people said one could not differentiate between recorded and live music … or between cinema or theater. We develop such skills rapidly as we become more technologically sophisticated … I doubt whether there's a virtual reality and animation system that could really fool the average person with a simulation or Jupiter." Although this is intended as a prediction, achieving such a degree of realism will be a tremendously difficult task, and may, as Pope suggests, be unachievable as we become more and more "technologically sophisticated" (or technologically aware).

6. Benedikt, "Cyberspace: Some Proposals," p. 128.

7. From an article by Douglas Stewart, place of publication unknown.

8. Gibson, *Neuromancer*, p. 51.

9. From Rheingold, *Virtual Reality*, p. 159.

14 Reflections

1. Barnsley, *Fractals Everywhere*, p. 1.

2. Quoted in Rheingold, *Virtual Reality*, p. 215.

3. Winograd, *Understanding Natural Language*, p. 26.

4. Quoted in Rheingold, *Virtual Reality*, p. 36.

5. Quoted in McCorduck, *Aaron's Code*, p. 49.

6. From author's conversation with G. M. Koenig, August 1991.

7. Simon, "Harold Cohen," pp. 14–15.

15   GGDL

1. Koenig and Xenakis were perhaps the only composers who could be said to have explored the *systematic* application of computers to the composition of music. Lejaren Hiller experimented with computer-generated compositions in the 1950s and 1960s, and John Cage composed works such as his *HPSCHD* in 1968 using the computer to create the work. However, these were not rigorous investigations into the composition *process* or attempts to simulate compositional techniques using computers.

2. The poem can be found in Jack Hirschman's *Antonin Artaud Anthology*, p. 106.

3. The use of production rules for the description of music grammars is discussed in my *Generative Grammars and the Computer-Aided Composition of Music* and "A Generative Grammar Definition Language for Music."

4. Koenig's investigations of the composition of symmetrical waveforms is discussed in my *Generative Grammars and the Computer-Aided Composition of Music*, pp. 108–112.

16   A Digital Aesthetic

1. This anecdote is from a book I read many years ago, the title and author of which I cannot remember! But, *se non è vero, è ben trovato*.

2. Grout, *A History of Western Music*, p. 246.

3. Borges, "Pierre Menard," p. 30.

4. Marina Bosi, an accomplished flautist, disputes that a flute cannot glide smoothly between notes, citing the work of Bartoluzzi. She argues that it certainly is not to be classed with the piano in this respect.

5. Both quotations are from Kandinsky, *On the Spiritual in Art*, p. 30.

6. From author's conversation with G. M. Koenig, August 1991.

7. I must thank Michael James for pointing out the analogy of Gibson's visual signatures to what I had described to him as idiomatic digital music.

8. Gibson, *Neuromancer*, p. 62.

9. Ibid., p. 256.

10. Gibson, *Mona Lisa Overdrive*, p. 210.

11. Xenakis, *Formalized Music*.

12. From unpublished writings of Paul Berg.

17 Dissonance

1. This summarizes a key theme of my view of aesthetics and is quoted from Oliver Muirhead from one of numerous conversations regarding the subjects in this book.

2. From author's conversation with G. M. Koenig, August 1991. The English translation of the phrase is by Ruth Koenig.

3. Xenakis, *Formalized Music*.

4. Meltzer's view is summarized in McCorduck, *Machines Who Think*, p. 225.

5. Ibid., p. 347.

6. Quoted in *I.D.*, September/October 1992, p. 72.

7. Ken Coupland in ibid., p. 73.

8. From Tinguely's obituary, August 30, 1991, written by Nick Ravo for *The New York Times*.

9. Liner notes to Lou Reed, *Metal Machine Music*.

18 Deep Structure

1. Translated by Richard Wilbur, in Mathews and Mathews, eds., *The Flowers of Evil*, p. 12.

2. Hoftstadter, *Gödel, Escher, Bach*, p. 234.

3. Ibid., p. 50.

4. Ibid., p. 534.

5. Professor Manford Clynes, a neuroscientist, has studied the "shapes" of emotions in a systematic manner. His work is summarized in Smith, "A Pattern in Love," excerpted here. "Professor Clynes proposes that when human emotions are expressed, they have shapes ... shapes he has measured with a machine, the same from one person to the next ... recognizable (and reproducible).... Different people's brains respond in the same, orderly, predictable way when stimulated by the color red.... [Clynes] was able to derive shapes representing the 'inner pulses' of different composers ... [and] the patterns they [subjects] made ... to express anger, lust, hate, joy, reverence and other conjured emotions.... The experience of a given emotion and its expression, he concluded, were an indivisible unit, programmed in the brain."

19 Vibration

1. Koestler, *The Sleepwalkers*, p. 25.

2. The social rules of the Pythagoreans are discussed in Copleston, *A History of Philosophy*, p. 31.

3. Koestler, *The Sleepwalkers*, p. 28.

4. Ibid., p. 30.

5. Grout, *A History of Western Music*, p. 7.

6. Quoted in Boorstin, *The Discoverers*, p. 299.

7. From the *Ṛg Veda*, translated in Basham, *The Wonder That Was India*, p. 245.

8. Ibid., p. 258.

9. Ibid., p. 261.

10. Campbell, *The Masks of God*, p. 189.

11. Radhakrishnan and Moore, *A Sourcebook in Indian Philosophy*, pp. 460–461.

12. The Kandinsky quotations are excerpted from those found in chapter 5. See that chapter for a broader discussion of Kandinsky's views.

13. Moszynska, *Abstract Art*, p. 50.

14. Ibid., p. 60.

15. Radhakrishnan and Moore, *A Sourcebook in Indian Philosophy*, p. 470.

16. Campbell, *The Masks of God*, p. 189.

Bibliography

Barber, C. L. *The Story of Language*. London: Pan Books, 1972.

Barnsley, M. *Fractals Everywhere*. San Diego: Academic Press, 1988.

Basham, A. L. *The Wonder That Was India*. London: Fontana, 1967.

Beatty, J., and A. Chaikin, eds. *The New Solar System*. Cambridge: Sky Publishing, 1990.

Benedikt, M. "Cyberspace: Some Proposals." In *Cyberspace: First Steps*, edited by M. Benedikt, 119–224. Cambridge: MIT Press, 1992.

Berg, P. "PILE—A Language for Sound Synthesis." *Computer Music Journal* 3, no. 1 (1979): 50–57.

Bloomfield, L. *Language*. London: Allen & Unwin, 1935.

Bois, M. *Xenakis, the Man and His Music*. London: Boosey & Hawkes, 1967.

Boorstin, D. J. *The Discoverers*. New York: Vintage Books, 1983.

Borges, J. L. "Pierre Menard, Author of the Quixote." In *Labyrinths: Selected Stories and Other Writings*, trans. Donald A. Yates and James E. Irby, 36–44. New York: New Directions Publishing, 1964.

Boulez, P. *Boulez on Music Today*. London: Faber and Faber, 1971.

Boulez, P. *Orientations*. London: Faber and Faber, 1986.

Bridgewater, W., and E. Sherwood, eds. *The Columbia Encyclopedia*. New York: Columbia University Press, 1956.

Burnham, J. *Beyond Modern Sculpture*. New York: George Braziller, 1987.

Campbell, J. *The Masks of God: Oriental Mythology*. New York: Viking Press, 1962.

Capra, F. *The Tao of Physics*. Boston: Shambhala, 1983.

Cohen, H. "The AI Paradigm." Presentation to the First International Symposium on Electronic Art, Utrecht, Holland, 1988.

Cohen, H. "Brother Giorgio's Kangaroo." In Raymond Kurzweil, *The Age of Intelligent Machines*, 380–385. Cambridge: MIT Press, 1990.

Cohen, H. "The Computability of Art." Unpublished paper, 1991.

Cohen, H. "From Here to Autonomy." Presentation to the British Association for the Advancement of Science, August 1991.

Copleston, F. *A History of Philosophy*. New York: Image Books, 1946.

Cox, D. "The Tao of Postmodernism: Computer Art, Scientific Visualization and Other Paradoxes." *Leonardo Siggraph 1989*: 7–12.

Culler, J. *Ferdinand de Saussure*. Ithaca: Cornell University Press, 1986.

Dachy, M. *The Dada Movement 1915–1923*. New York: Rizzoli, 1990.

Derrida, J. *Speech and Phenomena: And Other Essays on Husserl's Theory of Signs*. Evanston: Northwestern University Press, 1973.

Derrida, J. *Margins of Philosophy*. Chicago: University of Chicago Press, 1982.

Derrida, J. *Writing and Difference*. Chicago: University of Chicago Press, 1981.

Dube, W. D. *The Expressionists*. London: Thames and Hudson, 1972.

Evans, B. "Temporal Coherence with Digital Color." *Leonardo Siggraph 1990*: 43–49.

Fleuret, M. *Xenakis*. Paris: Editions Salabert, 1978.

Friedhoff, M., and W. Benzon. *The Second Computer Revolution: Visualization*. New York: W. H. Freeman, 1989.

Gelernter, D. *Mirror Worlds*. New York: Oxford University Press, 1991.

Gibson, W. *Mona Lisa Overdrive*. New York: Bantam Books, 1988.

Gibson, W. *Neuromancer*. New York: The Berkley Publishing Group, 1984.

Gleick, J. *Chaos*. New York: Viking Penguin, 1987.

Griffiths, P. *Boulez*. London: Oxford University Press, 1978.

Griffiths, P. "Anton Webern." In *The New Grove: Second Viennese School*. London: Macmillan Publishers, 1983.

Grout, D. *A History of Western Music*. New York: W. W. Norton & Company, 1960.

Hahl-Koch, J. *Arnold Schoenberg, Wassily Kandinsky: Letters, Pictures and Documents*. Trans. John C. Crawford. London: Faber and Faber, 1984.

Hall, D., and P. Corrington Wykes. *Anecdotes of Modern Art*. Oxford: Oxford University Press, 1990.

Hamilton, D. *Four Canons*. Unpublished tape composition realized for a BBC commision, 1980.

Harris, Z. S. *Methods in Structural Linguistics*. Chicago: University of Chicago Press, 1951.

Herbert, R. L. *Modern Artists on Art*. Englewood Cliffs, New Jersey: Prentice Hall, 1964.

Hirschman, J., ed. *Antonin Artaud Anthology*. San Francisco: City Lights Books, 1965.

Hofstadter, D. R. *Gödel, Escher, Bach: An Eternal Golden Braid*. New York: Basic Books, 1979.

Holtzman, S. R. "An Automated Digital Synthesis Instrument." *Computer Music Journal* 3, no. 2 (1979): 53–62.

Holtzman, S. R. "A Generative Grammar Definition Language for Music." *Interface* 9 (1980): 1–48.

Holtzman, S. R. *Generative Grammars and the Computer-Aided Composition of Music*. Edinburgh: University of Edinburgh, 1980.

Holtzman, S. R. "Music as System." *Interface* 7 (1978): 173–187.

Holtzman, S. R. "Using Generative Grammars for Music Composition." *Computer Music Journal* 5, no. 1 (1981): 51–64.

Johnson, G. *Machinery of the Mind*. Redmond, Washington: Microsoft Books, 1986.

Johnson, R. S. *Messiaen*. London: J. M. Dent and Sons, 1989.

Kandinsky, W. *Concerning the Spirtual in Art*. Trans. M. T. H. Sadler. New York: Dover, 1977.

Kandinsky, W. *Point and Line to Plane*. Trans. H. Dearstyne and H. Rebay. New York: Dover, 1979.

Kandinsky, W., and F. Marc. *The Blaue Reiter Almanac*. London: Thames and Hudson, 1974.

Kennedy, M. *The Concise Oxford Dictionary of Music*. London: Oxford University Press, 1980.

Kirsch, J. L., and R. A. Kirsch. "The Anatomy of Painting Style: Description with Computer Rules." *Leonardo 21*, no. 4 (1988): 437–444.

Koenig, G. M. "Compositional Processes." Paper given at the UNESCO Computer Music Workshop, Aarhus, Denmark, 1978. Ottawa: UNESCO, 1978.

Koenig, G. M. *Essay*. Vienna: Universal Edition, 1960.

Koenig, G. M. *Project 1*. Utrecht: Institute of Sonology, 1970.

Koenig, G. M. *Project 2—A Program for Musical Composition*. Utrecht: Institute of Sonology, 1970.

Koestler, A. *The Sleepwalkers*. New York: Grosset and Dunlap, 1963.

Konig, H. G. "The Planar Architecture of Juan Gris." *Languages of Design* 1, no. 1 (1992): 51–74.

Lacoste, M. C. *Kandinksy*. New York: Crown Publishers, 1979.

Lauzzana, R. G., and L. Pocock-Williams. "A Rule System for Analysis in the Visual Arts." *Leonardo* 21, no. 4 (1988): 445–452.

Le Targat, F. *Kandinksy*. New York: Rizzoli, 1986.

Lyons, J. *Language and Linguistics*. Cambridge: Cambridge University Press, 1981.

Lyons, J. *Noam Chomsky*. London: Penguin, 1970.

McCorduck, P. *Aaron's Code*. New York: W. H. Freeman, 1991.

McCorduck, P. *Machines Who Think*. New York: W. H. Freeman, 1979.

MacDonald, M. *Schoenberg*. London: J. M. Dent & Sons, 1987.

Mandelbrot, B. *The Fractal Geometry of Nature*. New York: W. H. Freeman, 1982, rev. 1983.

Mates, B. *The Philosophy of Leibniz*. New York: Oxford University Press, 1986.

Mathews, J., and M. Mathews, eds. *Charles Baudelaire: The Flowers of Evil*. New York: New Directions Publishing, 1989.

Moszynska, A. *Abstract Art*. London: Thames and Hudson, 1990.

Neighbour, O. "Arnold Schoenberg." In *The New Grove: Second Viennese School*. London: Macmillan Publishers, 1983.

O'Flaherty, W. D. *The Rig Veda*. London: Penguin Books, 1981.

Parkinson, G. H. R. *Gottfried Wilhelm Leibniz: Philosophical Writings*. London: J. M. Dent & Sons, 1973.

Peitgen, H. O., and P. H. Richter. *The Beauty of Fractals*. Berlin and Heidelberg: Springer-Verlag, 1986.

Perle, G. "Anton Webern." In *The New Grove: Second Viennese School*. London: Macmillan Publishers, 1983.

Peyser, J. *Boulez: Composer, Conductor, Enigma*. London: Cassell, 1976.

Piston, W. *Counterpoint*. London: Gollancz, 1970.

Piston, W. *Harmony*. London: Gollancz, 1973.

Popper, K. *Unended Quest: An Intellectual Autobiography*. London: Fontana, 1976.

Pratt, V. *Thinking Machines*. Oxford: Basil Blackwell, 1987.

Radhakrishnan, S., and C. Moore. *A Sourcebook in Indian Philosophy*. Princeton: Princeton University Press, 1973.

Reed, L. *Metal Machine Music*. RCA CPL 21101 Double LP. New York: RCA Records, 1975.

Reich, S. *Clapping Music*. London: Universal Edition, 1972.

Rheingold, H. *Virtual Reality*. New York: Summit Books, 1991.

Roads, C. "An Interview with G. M. Koenig." *Computer Music Journal* 2, no. 3 (1978): 11–15.

Roads, C. "An Interview with Harold Cohen." *Computer Music Journal* 3, no. 4 (1979): 50–57.

Robins, R. H. *A Short History of Linguistics*. New York: Longman, 1967.

Saussure, F. de. *Course in General Linguistics*. Trans. Roy Harris. La Salle, Illinois: Open Court, 1986

Schoenberg, A. *Suite for Piano, opus 25*. Vienna: Universal Edition, 1925.

Sharma, D. *The Differentiation Theory of Meaning in Indian Logic*. The Hague: Mouton & Co., 1969.

Simon, H. "Harold Cohen." In exhibition catalog for Buhl Science Center, Pittsburgh, 1984.

Smith, T. "A Pattern in Love." *Wired*, Spring 1992: 48–50.

Stangos, N. *Concepts of Modern Art*. London: Thames and Hudson, 1981.

Stiny, G., and J. Gips. *Shape Grammars and Their Uses*. Basel: Birkhauser, 1975.

Whitford, F. *Bauhaus*. London: Thames and Hudson, 1988.

Whittall, A. *Music since the First World War*. London: J. M. Dent & Sons, 1988.

Williams, P. *Mahayana Buddhism: The Doctrinal Foundations*. London: Routledge, Chapman & Hall, 1989.

Williams, P., trans. "Nagarjuna's *Madhyamakakarika*." Unpublished manuscript, 1976. A revised version has been published as "Nagarjuna: Selections from the *Madhyamakakarika*, Together with Excerpts from the Commentaries," in *The Middle Way* 52 (1977): 1–3.

Winograd, T. *Understanding Natural Language*. New York: Academic Press, 1972.

Worner, K. H. *Stockhausen*. London: Faber and Faber, 1973.

Xenakis, I. *Formalized Music*. Bloomington: Indiana University Press, 1971.

Young, C. M. "The Rolling Stone Interview: Noam Chomsky—Anarchy in the U.S.A." *Rolling Stone*, May 28, 1992.

Index